Islam

ISLAM

A Thousand Years of Faith and Power

Jonathan Bloom
and
Sheila Blair

NEW YORK

LIBRARY OF CONGRESS CATALOGING-IN-PUBLICATION DATA
Blair, Sheila.
Islam : a thousand years of faith and power /
Sheila Blair and Jonathan Bloom.
p. cm.
Includes Bibliographical references and index.
ISBN 1-57500-092-X
1. Islam—History. 2. Islamic Empire—History.
I. Bloom, Jonathan (Jonathan M.). II. Title.
BP55.B57 2000
297'.09—dc21
00-023449

Art credits can be found on page 258.

The publisher has made every effort to secure permission
to reproduce copyrighted material and would like to
apologize should there have been any errors or omissions.

TV Books, L.L.C.
1619 Broadway
New York, NY 10019
www.tvbooks.com

Interior design by Rachel Reiss
Manufactured in the United States of America

Contents

A Note on Terminology	7
INTRODUCTION	9
I MUHAMMAD AND THE ORIGINS OF ISLAM, 600–750	17
1. The World at the Rise of Islam	19
2. Muhammad and the Revelation of Islam	27
3. The Sources of Faith	35
4. Muhammad's Successors	49
5. The Spread of Islamic Power	65
II. THE GOLDEN AGE, 750–1250	77
6. The Crucible	79
7. City and Country	103
8. The Flowering of Intellectual Life	119
III. THE AGE OF EMPIRES, 1250–1700	157
9. Regional Powers	159
10. Consolidation	181
11. Expansion	221
EPILOGUE	233
Glossary	241
Notes for Further Reading	245
References	251
Art Credits	258
Index	259
About the Authors	269

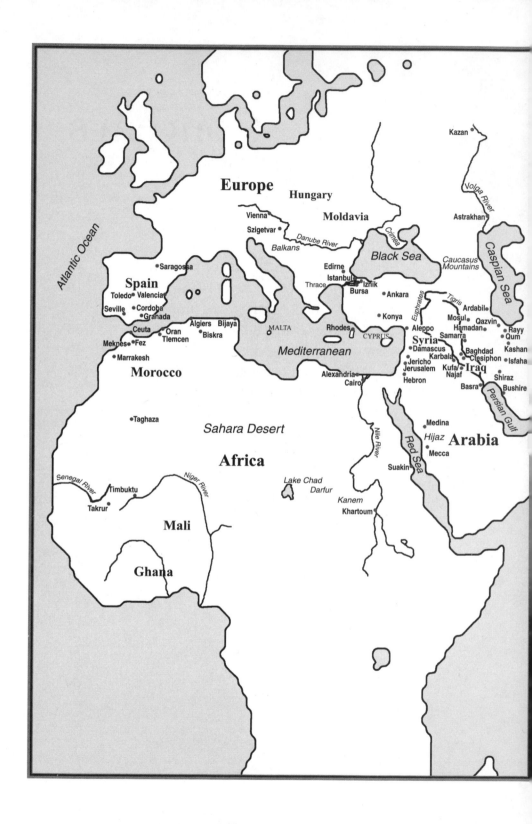

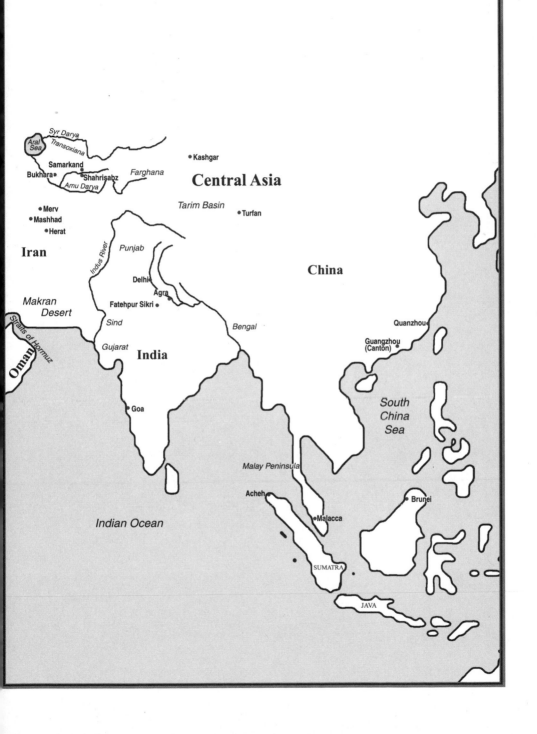

Syr Darya

Aral Sea

Transoxiana

Samarkand

Bukhara

Shahrisabz

Amu Darya

Farghana

• Kashgar

Central Asia

• Merv

• Mashhad

• Herat

Iran

Tarim Basin

• Turfan

Indus River

Punjab

Delhi

Agra

China

Makran Desert

Straits of Hormuz

Fatehpur Sikri •

Sind

Bengal

Quanzhou

Guangzhou (Canton)

Oman

Gujarat

India

• Goa

South China Sea

Malay Peninsula

Acheh •

• Brunei

Indian Ocean

• Malacca

SUMATRA

JAVA

a Note on Terminology

WE RECOGNIZE THAT MANY READERS ARE UNFAMIL-
iar with the geography, religion, history, and
culture with which we are dealing. We have tried to
introduce all of these facets without burdening the
reader with too many technical terms. A glossary at
the back of the book gives definitions for some of
the unfamiliar terms we use repeatedly.

We have also simplified our spelling as much as
possible, trying to be user-friendly rather than ab-
solutely consistent. Many of the unfamiliar names
and terms in this book come from Arabic, the language of religion in all the Islamic lands. As Arabic is
an alphabetic language, specialists transcribe Arabic
into other languages with one-for-one equivalents,
using special signs to indicate the letters that have
no exact equivalents in English. Thus the Prophet's
name can be rendered as Muhammad (with or without a little dot under the h to show that it is the em-
phatic, rather than the regular, h), or Mohamed, or
even (in Turkish) Mehmed or Mehmet. This complex
system can be extremely confusing (and off-putting)
to nonspecialists, and so we have tried to use common English spellings for unfamiliar terms and

place-names. For example, specialists now transcribe the name of the Muslim holy book as *Qur'an,* to show that the first letter is an "occlusive uvulovelar surd," not an "occlusive post-palatal surd," and that the second vowel, a long "a," follows an "unvoiced glottal occlusive," not a "voiced pharyngeal fricative." We have preferred the standard English "Koran."

Arabic is now spoken from Morocco to Oman, and many Arabic words have entered the languages spoken in other Muslim lands, such as Turkish, Persian, Tajik, Swahili, and Urdu. Inevitably, many Arabic words have come to be pronounced differently in different places. For example, a theological college, known as a madrasa (MAD-ra-sa) in classical Arabic, is known as a medersa (me-DER-sa) in Morocco, a medrese (MED-re-se) in Turkey, and a madrassa (ma-DRA-sa) in other lands. While all are correct, we have arbitrarily chosen to use the classical form of this and other terms.

We have given dates strictly according to the Common Era calendar, where events are given as B.C.E. (before the common era) and C.E. (common era). We have used C.E. rather than A.D., which comes from the Latin *anno domini,* "in the year of our Lord," so as not to offend non-Christians. Whereas the Common Era calendar is based on a solar year, Muslims use a strictly lunar calendar, reckoning events from the year 622. Specialists normally give dates in both Muslim and Common Era equivalents, often separated by a slash. When most of the Western world celebrated the beginning of the third millennium on January 1, 2000, Muslims recognized the date as 24 Ramadan 1420 and Jews as 23 Tevet 5760.

Introduction

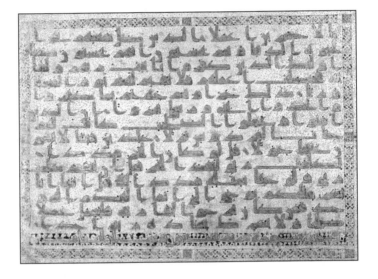

T O MOST AMERICANS AT THE END OF THE SECOND MIL-
lennium, the word "Islam" evokes a range of
negative images, from turbaned terrorists to stern-
faced mullahs exhorting the faithful to shun the temp-
tations of Western civilization. News reports from
Jerusalem and Grozny hint that the Muslims there are
somehow essentially different from "us." The constant
barrage of inflammatory news reports, designed to
make news even when there isn't any, has colored
Western perceptions of a faith followed by over a billion
people, approximately one fifth of the earth's population. Even in the United States, Islam is the fastest-
growing religion, and there are now more American
Muslims (over four million) than Episcopalians.

In reality, Islam, which is only a half dozen centuries
younger than Christianity, created a long and brilliant
civilization which is responsible for much of the way
we are today. For example, you are reading this book
on sheets of paper, and its pages are numbered with
Arabic numerals; both of these inventions were
brought to the West thanks to the efforts of Muslims in
the Islamic lands of the Near East during the Middle
Ages. When a few medieval monks were desperately
trying to preserve what little they knew of Greco-
Roman civilization, academies and universities flourished in the splendid cities of the Muslim lands.

Newspaper and magazine articles reinforce contemporary stereotypes and unwittingly depict differences between what Muslims believe and what other monotheists believe. Articles often state that Muslims worship Allah. *Allah* is simply the Arabic name for the one God worshiped by all monotheists, just as Germans worship *Gott* and the French worship *Dieu*. By using the Arabic name, rather than the common English one, Western writers unwittingly create a difference between what Muslims believe and what other monotheists believe, rather than underscore the similarities and relationships between the great monotheistic religions. As we will show, however, Islam stands firmly in the Judeo-Christian tradition of monotheistic world religions, and the similarities among these three religions are much greater than their differences.

Furthermore, our modern stereotypes, to judge from political cartoons and current jokes, suggest that Islam is a religion of desert nomads, but it has always been a religion of cities. It is not too much of an overstatement to say that at a time when unwashed Europeans in northern forests wore leather jerkins and ate roast game and gruel when they weren't beating each other over the head with clubs to solve disputes, bathed and perfumed Muslims inhabited splendid palaces with running water and sanitation systems, dressed in silken robes, and ate haute cuisine off fine porcelain, while sitting on plush carpets discussing the subtleties of ancient Greek philosophy. Most people also think of Islam as a Near Eastern religion. Although it was revealed in Arabia, Islam is no longer an exclusively Arab or even Near Eastern religion, and the largest Muslim populations are now found in Indonesia, Bangladesh, Pakistan, and India. The number of Muslims in Indonesia alone (175 million) is more than the combined total in Egypt, Syria, Saudi Arabia, Iraq, and Iran—the traditional heartlands of Islam.

Given Islam's importance in the world today, we must try to approach it with more than our old stereotypes, and we wrote this book to show some of the positive aspects of Islamic civilization in its first thousand years. This millennium was one in which the essential features of Islamic civilization were elaborated and disseminated throughout Eurasia. During this period, Islamic civilization was preeminent, as the unities of religion, language, and culture allowed people to travel with ease between the shores of the Atlantic and the Pacific, between the steppes of Central Asia and the deserts of Africa, spreading not only the tenets of their faith but also the glories of their civilization.

This book is designed to accompany Gardner Films' three-hour television documentary made for PBS, *Islam: Empire of Faith.* Like the documentary, we concentrated our coverage on the period between 600 and 1600. The former date is about when Muhammad, the Prophet of Islam, began to receive God's revelation. The latter date marks the apogee of the great Islamic empires: the Ottomans in eastern Europe and the Mediterranean, the Safavids in Iran, and the Mughals in the Indian subcontinent. Over the course of this millennium, Islam spread from the Near East halfway around the globe.

Despite their similarities, the book and the documentary are not the same. Some of the subjects covered in the documentary are only mentioned in this book, and many others not found at all in the documentary are covered here at length. Some subjects naturally lend themselves to dramatic rather than written presentation, while others can only be explained with the more detailed treatment possible on a page of text. The book and the documentary are therefore meant to be complementary works, and while each stands alone, they are best understood and used together.

We have divided our book into three main sections, corresponding to the three parts in the documentary. Like the first part of the documentary, our first section covers the revelation of Islam and the extraordinary spread of this new religion within a century of the Prophet's death as far as the shores of the Atlantic, the Sahara, the Indian Ocean, and the steppes of Central Asia. The second deals with the Golden Age of Arab–Islamic civilization, when the fabled city of Baghdad was an international capital whose fame was celebrated in the stories of the *Arabian Nights*. In this crucible, ideas from the ancient civilizations of Greece, Rome, Byzantium, India, and China were forged into a brilliant new culture under the aegis of a tolerant and inclusive Islam.

The third section continues the story after the cataclysmic invasions by the Mongols in the early thirteenth century. Although these invaders, who traced their descent from Genghis Khan, assassinated the caliph of Baghdad by wrapping him up in a carpet and trampling him to death (because they did not want to be held responsible for spilling his blood), the Mongols too were eventually incorporated into the Islamic fold. New empires, combining traditional Islamic ideas with many new ones introduced by the Mongols, arose in their wake, and Islam was brought to new areas, from tropical Africa to the islands of southeast Asia.

Our main story stops here. Some readers may be disappointed that we have chosen to avoid current political debates surrounding Islam, be they the Arab-Israeli conflict or idle speculations that Islam poses a mortal threat to contemporary Western civilization, but we believe that in order to make an informed decision about these questions, it is essential to understand the historical background of Islam.

This book, like the film it is designed to accompany, was made by outsiders looking in. Although Muslims were involved in the evolution of these projects, our primary purpose was not to explain the religion and history of Islam to Muslims, but, as writers with our feet firmly planted in late twentieth-century (or twenty-first-century!) America, to help Americans—of whatever (or even no) religion—understand the religion and culture of another place and time. Nevertheless, we hope that American Muslims will find that they can learn about the history of their religion and its civilization from our book.

We have tried to be clear, comprehensive, and evenhanded, taking our examples from a wide range of situations over many centuries of Islamic civilization. Thus, a Moroccan Muslim may find many of the situations we describe different from his or her own experience, while an Iranian Muslim may find exactly the same case. Despite what we read in the newspapers—and in many books—there never really has been any single Islam.

As historians specializing in the art of the Muslim lands, we have emphasized the cultural aspects of Islamic civilization. As a husband-and-wife (or wife-and-husband) team, we see things from differing but complementary perspectives, and we know that our book has benefited from our constant give-and-take. Our own specialized research interests lie in somewhat different parts and eras of the Islamic world—the medieval Mediterranean on the one hand and Mongol Iran on the other—and we hope that our different interests have brought a broader perspective to this book.

Our broad sweep has necessitated generalizations and omissions. Many books on some aspects of Islam and the Middle East proclaim that they are intended for a general audience, but in reality few are, because they overwhelm the uninitiated reader with too much specialized information. We have tried to keep this book simple and clear, without compromising the accuracy of our statements. While we have benefited from the work of many great scholars, and we have written many scholarly books and articles, this is not intended to be a scholarly work. There are, for example, no footnotes to sources, but we trust that the *Notes for Further Reading* at the end of the book will identify the sources from which we took our quotations and point the reader in other directions.

We are most grateful to Rob and Char Gardner for suggesting that we write this book in the first place, as well as for their constant support and encouragement along the way. Professor Donald Little generously agreed to read the manuscript on a moment's notice and provided incisive comments which saved us from our own ignorance. Our editor, Albert DePetrillo, smoothed many infelicitous phrases and offered constructive advice to make this book more accessible to the readers to whom it is addressed. We thank them all.

We dedicate this book to the memory of William S. Blair (1917–2000), whose way with words and ideas inspired all who knew and loved him.

PART I

Muhammad
and the Origins of Islam
600-750

In 630 the Prophet Muhammad returned triumphantly from Medina to his native town of Mecca, where three hundred and sixty idols stood in a wide circle around the Kaaba [the square stone shrine in the center of the city]. The Prophet rode around the Kaaba, repeating the words "The truth has come and falsehood vanished away; surely falsehood is certain to vanish [Koran 17:83]." As Muhammad pointed at the idols with his rod, each one fell forward on its face to the ground. Muhammad then entered the Kaaba, where he found the walls inside covered with pictures of pagan deities, along with an icon of the Virgin Mary and the child Jesus, as well as a painting of an old man, said to represent Abraham. Placing his hands over the icon, the Prophet told his companion Uthman to see that all the other paintings, except that of Abraham, were effaced.

—from the biography of the Prophet by al-Waqidi (d. 822)

1

The World at the Rise of Islam

I N THE LATE SIXTH AND EARLY SEVENTH CENTURIES, TWO great powers—the Byzantines and the Sasanians—ruled the Near East. The Byzantines were the inheritors of the Roman Empire and rulers of the lands around the Mediterranean Sea. In 324, some two and a half centuries before Muhammad was born, the emperor Constantine had moved the capital from Rome to the city of Byzantium, on the shores of the Bosphorus in modern-day Turkey, where Europe and Asia are separated by only a narrow strait. The city was renamed New Rome and later Constantinople, the city of Constantine, in recognition of the emperor's initiative. Constantine had proclaimed toleration for Christians with the Edict of Milan in 313, and now embellished the new capital and other major cities with magnificent churches for the newly respectable faith. Although their capital stood in the land of ancient Greece and the people spoke and wrote Greek, the Byzantines (as the eastern Romans are known) always considered themselves to be the only true Romans, which got them into endless trouble with the popes. Arab authors later acknowledged the Byzantines' claim by designating them the "Rum," meaning "Romans, " and calling the Europeans, including the pope in Rome, the "Franks."

Christianity, which had begun as a religion of the poor and dispossessed in the pagan Roman Empire, became the religion of the establishment under the Byzantines. The emperor was the head of the Church and God's vice-regent on earth. The Church developed a complex administrative hierarchy of archbishops, bishops, and priests, who not only mediated between man and God but also became powerful presences in the political and economic spheres, so that the Church permeated all aspects of life. Doctrinal differences were rife. People argued vehemently and even took up arms over such questions as the nature of the Godhead and whether it was possible to represent God or use images in worship. Some pious individuals went off alone into the wilderness to come closer to God, while others joined together in monasteries to worship communally.

Over the course of the fifth and sixth centuries, it became increasingly difficult for the Byzantine emperors to control their far-flung lands from Constantinople, and barbarians repeatedly breached the empire's defenses. The Vandals entered Gaul and Spain between 406 and 409, the Goths under Alaric's command sacked Rome in 410, and the Burgundians settled in the Rhône valley in the mid-fifth century. By 451 the Visigoths were persuaded to join the Roman army to defend Rome against the avalanche of Attila and his Huns, who had moved across the Eurasian steppes, the great grasslands stretching between China and Hungary, to invade the settled lands to the south.

This incessant pressure against the Byzantine empire was temporarily alleviated in the mid-sixth century during the brilliant reign of the emperor Justinian (r. 527–65). Justinian and his able general Belisarius temporarily reconquered many of the further reaches of the empire, including such regions as North

Africa, Sicily, and the Italian peninsula. To celebrate the central ceremonial role of the emperor in Byzantine society as head of the church and the state, in the 550s Justinian decided to re-build Hagia Sophia, Constantine's great church of the Holy Wis-dom, which had been destroyed in a riot. Justinian's vast, domed church, the largest interior space in premodern times, remained for centuries the symbol of Constantinople and the Byzantine empire.

Yet despite his successes in the west, Justinian—like his pred-ecessors—faced a constant threat from the second great power of the day: the Sasanian empire, which lay to the east. Persian-speakers who had come from the Iranian plateau to make their capital at Ctesiphon in present-day Iraq, the Sasanians (r. 224–651) ruled territory corresponding roughly to modern Iraq and Iran. For centuries the Byzantines and the Sasanians had waged continuous war against each other, broken only by periodic truces. In 540 the Sasanian emperor of Persia, Khus-raw I, broke his truce with Byzantium and sacked the city of Antioch in northern Syria, the second most important city in the Byzantine empire. Justinian quickly responded by fortifying and securing his eastern frontier against the Sasanians.

Although what was once the Sasanian empire is now divided among several countries, the empire had natural boundaries. On the west, the Euphrates River marked the uneasy border with Byzantium. On the north, the Caucasus Mountains pro-vided a natural border and refuge to many petty chiefs, who, as in modern times, created small principalities there. On the northeast, the Amu Darya River, known in antiquity as the Oxus, marked the border with various nomadic and princely states on the Central Asian steppes. This border was commemorated in later times when the northern region became known as "the lands beyond the river," in Arabic *ma wara' al-nahr,* or Transox-iana. On the southeast, the inhospitable Makran Desert cut Iran off from India, and on the south the mountainous region along the coast of the Persian Gulf provided few harbors.

The Sasanian capital, Ctesiphon, was located on the east bank of the Tigris River, about twenty-two miles south of modern Baghdad and opposite the capital built by the Sasanians' predecessors, which was called Seleucia. Although the Sasanians derived much of their power and wealth from the Iranian plateau, the city in lowland Iraq remained their administrative and cultural center, as well as the site of their coronations and of the royal mint. The city was dominated by the royal palace, of which today only the majestic Taq-i Kisra, the "arch of Khusraw" remains. Standing over one hundred feet high, the parabolic brick vault was the centerpiece of an elaborate multi-storied building, "the most magnificent palace ever built," according to the early Arab geographer Ibn Khurradadhbih (ca. 864). An enormously heavy bejeweled crown hung on a golden chain from the top of the vault, and the Sasanian emperor would seat himself under it on an immense and beautiful carpet studded with gems and pearls known as the "Spring of Khusraw." Like Hagia Sophia, the arch of Khusraw was considered one of the architectural wonders of the world and, even in a ruined state, its memory provided an inspiration to generations of later builders for nearly a millennium.

In contrast to the Byzantines, whose state religion was Christianity, the state religion of Sasanian Iran was Zoroastrianism, based on the teachings of Zarathustra, also known in the West as Zoroaster, who lived in eastern Iran, probably around 1400 B.C.E. Zoroaster developed a doctrine of cosmic scope centering on Ahura Mazda, lord of wisdom, the one, eternal, uncreated, good, wise, and munificent god. Opposed to him is Ahriman, the evil spirit, who struggles with the forces of good but is doomed to perish at the end of time. Zoroaster appointed fire as the life-giving force in whose presence his followers should pray, and so Zoroastrians are sometimes, but incorrectly, known as "fire worshipers."

Zoroastrianism had been adopted as the official religion of the Achaemenid dynasty (r. 538–331 B.C.E.), rulers of the first Persian empire, but under the Sasanians, Zoroastrianism developed a centralized hierarchical structure, somewhat comparable to the Christian church as it developed under the Byzantines. Magi, renowned in Christianity for attending Christ's nativity, were Zoroastrian priests *(majus)* whose principal job was tending the sacred fire and mediating between the believers and the complex Zoroastrian array of forces of darkness, mighty powers, and divine beings.

In the fifth century the Sasanians suffered a series of devastating political, social, and economic disasters. Like the Romans to the west, they were invaded by the Huns who lived in the steppes to the north. Drought and famine led to internal chaos. In the late sixth and early seventh centuries, however, economic and social reform, coupled with aggressive military tactics, brought a recovery and expansion of the Sasanian empire. In 614, Persian armies invaded Syria and sacked Jerusalem, the holiest city of Christianity, returning home with one of the most sacred of all Christian relics, fragments of the True Cross on which, it was believed, Christ had been crucified.

BY THE EARLY SEVENTH CENTURY THE STRUGGLE BETWEEN THE BYZANtines and Sasanians had been going on for so long that neither side was able to see that the greatest political challenge they faced came not from their traditional arch-rival but from a totally unexpected quarter, the deserts of Arabia. A broad boot-shaped peninsula covering 1.25 million square miles between Africa and Asia, Arabia contains the largest uninterrupted sand desert in the world, the Rub al-Khali, or Empty Quarter, which covers more than 150,000 square miles and dominates the southern part of the peninsula. Much of the northern region, which blends imperceptibly into Palestine, Syria, and Mesopotamia, is also desert.

Despite all this desert, the Arabian peninsula is not entirely desolate. On the east, there is a broad coastal plain, which in antiquity was dotted with fishing and trading settlements. Along the west or Red Sea coast, there is a mountain escarpment known as the Hijaz ("barrier"), home to such important oases as Mecca and Medina. South Arabia, or Yemen, flourished from the first millennium B.C.E., when a lucrative trade in frankincense and myrrh developed there. These two precious substances, collected from the sap of local tree, were used for incense, particularly in the Mediterranean lands, by the Romans and then later by the Byzantines for ceremonies in Christian churches. The incense trade gave rise to the great south Arabian kingdoms of Saba (whose Queen of Sheba is known from the Bible), Hadramawt, and Himyar. Thousands of rock-cut inscriptions have come to light there from the centuries before the rise of Islam, showing that it must have been the most literate—and culturally developed—part of the Arabian peninsula.

The inhabitants of Arabia, known as Arabs, comprised both nomads and settled townsfolk. The desert nomads, known as Bedouins, eked out a living by herding sheep, goats, and camels, whose domestication in the third millennium B.C.E. had made life and trade in the desert possible. Horses, which were highly prized for sport and war, were not suitable as beasts of burden in this region. Neither were wheeled carts useful for transporting goods across sandy deserts, so the camel became supreme. The nomads lived in tents, portable structures of goat-hair cloth held up on wooden poles, which could be disassembled and packed on camels when the pasturage was exhausted. Nomads subsisted on milk and meat from their herds,

and traded with the settled peopie of the oases for such commodities as grain and dates.

The townspeople in Arabia were richer than the Bedouins
and lived in settlements built of mudbrick and stone. Structures
in Yemen were particularly striking, towers often rising to one
hundred feet or more, whereas buildings in the oases were
more often modest structures of mud and palm thatch. In com-
parison to the townsfolk, who were thought to have lost their
authentic roots, the Bedouins were believed to be the keepers
of true Arabian culture. Everywhere, Arabian society was organized into tribes and clans, in which a group of people traced
their descent from a common ancestor through the male line
and remained under the authority of the eldest male. The pre-
cariousness of existence made competition for supplies inevitable. The fierce rivalries that developed between clans for
scarce resources often escalated into blood feuds.

The culture of pre-Islamic Arabia was largely aural and oral.
Many dialects of Arabic were spoken, but every tribe throughout the region used and understood the same poetic language,
which had an extremely complex grammar and a rich vocabulary. Poetry was regarded as the highest form of art, and the
poet was considered like a prophet or king when people gathered for markets. The *qasida,* or ode, was the supreme verse
form. In general poems were short and were composed to be
recited in public, either by the poet or by a professional reciter,
who would add his own details and background. The professional reciter relied on his prodigious memory, and the great
pre-Islamic poems were not written down until several centuries after their composition.

Arabia was a land of mixed religions and cultures. In the
fourth and fifth centuries both Byzantium and Sasanian Iran
had extended their influence over the northern part of the
peninsula through the medium of competing chieftains—the

Ghassanids, based in the northwest, and the Lakhmids of Hira in the northeast. In the early sixth century, one of the Himyarite kings of south Arabia converted to Judaism, an act that provoked the Christian king of Axum in Ethiopia, distantly abetted by the Byzantine emperor Justinian I, to launch an invasion of south Arabia.

By the late sixth century a power vacuum had developed. The Persians had conquered Yemen in the south; meanwhile the Ghassanid and Lakhmid buffer states in the north had begun to decline, as the endless wars between the Persians and Byzantines disrupted the trade on which these states depended. The collapse of the kingdoms in the north and south allowed the Quraysh, the Arab tribe which had been settled in the Hijaz oasis of Mecca since about 500 C.E., to emerge from obscurity and begin to dominate the scene.

From their base at Mecca, the Quraysh controlled trade along the west coast of Arabia and sent annual caravans north to Syria and south to Yemen. In addition to its central position commanding the north–south trade route, Mecca had the advantage of being home to two pagan cults. One was centered on the Black Stone, a meteorite built into the wall of the cubic structure known as the Kaaba (from the Arabic word for cube, on account of its shape) in the town itself. The other cult was centered on the hill of Arafat, just outside town. Both of the Meccan cults under the guardianship of the Quraysh were polytheistic, and the deities were regarded as patrons and guarantors of the caravan trade. Delegations arriving from all over the peninsula had to put down their arms in the sanctuary, or *haram,* around the Black Stone. This laying-down of arms facilitated the conduct of trade because one was forbidden to carry on a feud while buying and selling. This was the world in which the third of the world's great monotheistic religions arose.

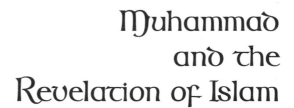

2

Muhammad and the Revelation of Islam

Little is known about the early life of Muhammad, the prophet of Islam, and most of it has been embellished by later retellings. Muhammad, whose Arabic name means "praised," was born around the year 570 into the Banu Hashim, one of the less prosperous clans of the Quraysh tribe. Before he was six he was orphaned, but in a tribal society where clan and family relationships were everything, he was quickly adopted by his grandfather and uncle, Abu Talib, chief of the Hashim clan.

The importance of family and lineage in Arabian society is clear from the way people were named. Last names were unknown, and people were called, in addition to their given names, *ibn* (son) or *bint* (daughter) of someone else. Thus Umar ibn Ali was Umar son of Ali, and Layla bint Ali was Ali's daughter, Layla. Parents were often known after their firstborn offspring, as *abu* (father) or *umm* (mother) of the child. Thus Umar Abu Ali was Umar, the father of Ali, and Layla Umm Ali was Layla, Ali's mother.

These genealogical names could be combined with names indicating where someone came from or what they did for a living. Thus Ali al-Hijazi was Ali from the Hijaz, while Ali al-Tajir was Ali the Merchant. Many of these names were combined in long strings with honorific titles. The full name of the noted Egyptian historian al-Maqrizi, for example, was Taqi al-Din (preserver of religion) Abu'l-Abbas (father of Abbas) Ahmad (the historian's given name) ibn Ali (his father) ibn Abd al-Qadir (his grandfather, servant of the Powerful [God]) al-Maqrizi (from a district in the Syrian town of Baalbek where his family had originated).

Being an orphan in a society obsessed with lineage made a deep impression on the young Muhammad, who very early developed a passionate sense of concern for those who were left out. At about age twenty, he began working as a merchant and is said to have made trading journeys into Syria, where he supposedly met the Christian monk Bahira, who prophesied Muhammad's future greatness. He became known for his trustworthiness, and when he was about twenty-five years old, he married Khadija, an older widow whose wealth and status elevated his position in Meccan society.

At this time, the Quraysh decided to rebuild the Kaaba, the shrine in the center of Mecca, because its walls were too low and the roof had fallen in. When construction was nearly finished, the leaders of the various clans began to argue over who would have the honor of lifting the precious Black Stone into place. They were about to defame the sanctuary of Mecca by taking up arms against each other when one of the elders presciently suggested that they accept the advice of the next person to walk through the gate. Muhammad appeared and devised an ingenious solution: he ordered a cloak to be brought which he then spread on the ground. Taking up the Black Stone, he laid it in the middle of the garment. Then he had a member of each of the four major clans take hold of a corner of the cloak, and together they lifted the stone to where Muhammad himself could put it in place. The story of Muhammad's cloak was often retold and embellished in later times, and the cloak became an important symbol for poets and writers.

Muhammad and Khadija had four daughters, each of whom played a role in the early history of Islam, and two sons, both of whom died in infancy. Other than the names of his children, the sources have little to say about Muhammad's life between his marriage and the time, some fifteen to twenty years later, when he began to have visionary dreams and hear voices. Like other visionaries before him, he attempted to understand the visions and voices by seeking solitude. He chose a cave on Mount Hira, which lies on the outskirts of Mecca. Taking provisions with him, he would spend a month on the mountain, and then return to his family. One night during Ramadan, the traditional month of spiritual retreat, when Muhammad was about forty years old, an angel appeared to him in the form of a man and ordered him to

> Recite in the name of your lord who created—
> Created the human from an embryo
> Recite your lord is all-giving
> who taught by the pen
> Taught the human what he did not know before.

Muhammad, fearing that he was being attacked by an evil spirit, or *jinn* (whence our English word "genie"), fled down the mountain in terror. The voice called after him, "O Muhammad, you are the messenger of God, and I am the angel Gabriel." Muhammad ran home, where he was comforted by his wife. This revelation was soon followed by others about the one true

God, who is known in Arabic as *Allah* (distinct from *ilah,* which could refer to any of the gods worshiped in Arabia).

Eventually, the angel told Muhammad to begin proclaiming God's message, and the record of Muhammad's public ministry in Mecca reveals his passionate inspiration. The revelations of this period have a strong moral and religious appeal, with the key themes of God's creation of man, man's moral responsibility, and the Last Judgment on the Day of Resurrection. They contain vivid descriptions of the damned in Hell and of the pleasures promised to believers in Paradise. The signs of God in nature are evident to those who will take the time to look for them. God's power is greater than man's, and the wise will acknowledge it and cease their greed and suppression of the poor. The truly pious person is a "believer." The believer has few specific religious duties, but should lead a chaste life, refrain from cheating, and not expose female infants to die in the desert, a barbarous custom practiced in Arabia at that time and probably brought on by widespread poverty.

Muhammad slowly began to attract some followers, most of them young and of modest social standing, including his cousin Ali, the son of his uncle Abu Talib. Muhammad began to impugn the traditional polytheism of his native town, and some of the rich and powerful merchants of Mecca began to view the religious revolution taking place under their noses as disastrous for businesses protected by the Meccan pantheon of gods and goddesses. Members of the ruling elite ganged up against Muhammad and his followers, and began to persecute them. A few Meccans of higher status, including Umar ibn al-Khattab and Muhammad's uncle Hamza, began to accept Muhammad's message, while other members of his clan, the Banu Hashim, came to support their kinsman out of family loyalty, even if they did not yet believe in his cause.

Muhammad's position in Mecca became hopeless, however,

when his wife, Khadija, and uncle, Abu Talib, died in quick succession. In 622 the Quraysh forced Muhammad and his small band of followers to leave Mecca. He accepted an invitation to settle in the oasis of Yathrib, some eleven days (280 miles) north by camel, for the oasis had been nearly torn apart by wars between the clans, many of which were Jewish.

Muhammad's emigration from Mecca, called the *hijra* in Arabic and "hegira" in English, marks the beginning of a new polity. For the first time in Arabia members of a community were bound together not by the traditional ties of clan and tribe but by their shared belief in the one true God. Later believers, looking back on this event, recognized its seminal importance by designating it as the first year of their new era. It was decided that the new era had begun on the first day of the first lunar month (1 Muharram) of the year in which Muhammad arrived in his new home. (This date corresponds to July 16, 622 C.E.) In the eyes of believers, all later events can be dated from this year, and the time before is known as the "period of ignorance," or *jahiliyya,* because God's true religion had not yet been revealed. In further recognition of this great event, the oasis of Yathrib came to be called Medina, from the phrase *madinat al-nabi,* "the city of the Prophet."

Muhammad, surrounded by his followers, lived in Medina for ten years. At first, he slowly won over converts, principally from among the pagans of the oasis. He hoped to convert the local Christians and Jews, who also believed in the one true God, but the Christians clung to their belief that the Incarnation was the pivotal event in time and the Jews clung to theirs that they were God's chosen people. Muhammad made repeated attempts to attract the Jews to his cause. For example, he directed that believers worship like the Jews in the direction of Jerusalem. These conciliatory attempts, however, failed, and henceforth the direction of worship (known in Arabic as the *qibla*) was toward Mecca. Muhammad's native town, which had long been a center of paganism, thereby became the center of the true religion, the focal point of the believers' daily prayer, and eventually the object of their annual pilgrimage.

Raiding and warfare were the primary economic activities of the new community in Medina, and the rich caravans organized by the Quraysh of Mecca were particularly attractive targets. In 624 at the Battle of Badr, Muhammad and his small band of followers successfully attacked an important Meccan caravan. Muhammad's victory was seen as confirmation of the righteousness of their belief in the one God. It also demonstrated that the powerful commercial city of Mecca was not invulnerable. In retaliation, the Quraysh sent an expedition against Muhammad and his followers, and the inconclusive outcome following the Battle of Uhud in 625 temporarily weakened Muhammad's authority. An army of ten thousand Meccans then besieged Medina in 627, but they were deterred by a protective trench dug around the city, leading the Medinans to call their victory the Battle of the Trench. Finally in 628 a truce was negotiated between Muhammad and the Meccans at a place called Hudaybiya on the edge of the sacred territory around Mecca.

Muhammad returned to Mecca in 629 as a pilgrim to its holy sites, but he considered the murder of one of his followers an infraction of the treaty and used it as a justification to attack the city. On the 8th day of the month of Ramadan in the 8th year since the hegira (December 30, 629), Muhammad set out at the head of a huge army. The Meccans were so afraid that they came out of town to surrender, obtaining amnesty for all the Quraysh who had abandoned armed resistance. Muhammad entered his native city without a struggle, and almost all the inhabitants rallied to his cause. In marked contrast to other conquerors, Muhammad acted generously to the Meccans, giving some of them gifts. His only immediate demand was that the pagan idols around the Kaaba be destroyed.

Muhammad's prestige among the Arabs rose after the surrender of the Meccans, and over the course of the following year embassies from all over Arabia came to Medina to submit to him. In the spring of 632, Muhammad returned once again to Mecca to perform rites of pilgrimage, at which time God revealed this verse to him: "Today I have perfected your religion for you; I have completed My blessing upon you; I have approved Islam as your religion." The term *al-islam,* meaning "the submission (to God)," appears infrequently in the revelations, but it has come, particularly in modern times, to designate the religion revealed to Muhammad. *Islam* is derived from the Arabic root *s-l-m,* conveying the notion of submission and peace, as in *salam alaykum* ("Peace be upon you," the traditional Arabic greeting and cognate to the Hebrew *shalom aleichem*). It is generally used to refer to the religion and *Muslim* to the person who follows its tenets.

Muhammad's extraordinary life and career were cut short by his sudden death on June 8, 632, aged about sixty. He was buried under the floor of a room in his house in Medina. Less than a decade had passed since he had set off from Mecca with his small band of followers. Muhammad's death created several problems for the nascent community of believers. One was to define the nature and practice of the religion God had revealed to Muhammad through the angel Gabriel. Another was to determine the nature of the succession to Muhammad and how such successors should be chosen in the future. These key problems persist to this day.

3
The Sources of Faith

I N CONTRAST TO OTHER RELIGIONS OF THE TIME, THE practice of Islam as revealed to Muhammad is simplicity itself. A believer worships God directly without the intercession of priests or clergy or saints. The believer's duties are summed up in five simple rules, the so-called Five Pillars of Islam. The first rule is to testify in Arabic that "There is no god but God and Muhammad is His messenger." This phrase, known as the Profession of Faith, is central to Islam. It is used in many ways, being inscribed on all kinds of settings from flags to coins. In contrast to the Judeo-Christian tradition, which exhorts believers not to take the Lord's name in vain, Muslims constantly call on God by name in all sorts of situations. A believer, for example, might begin any number of activities with the invocation to God known as the *basmala,* from the Arabic words *bi'smi llahi al-rahman al-rahim,* "in the name of God, the Compassionate, the Caring." Other common expressions invoking God include *al-hamdu li'llah,* "Praise God!," said in congratulation, and *insha'llah,* "God willing!," said when talking of events to come.

God is also invoked in personal names, as in *Abdullah*, "God's servant," or *Abdurrahman*, "Servant of the Merciful [God]."

The second Pillar of Islam is to worship God five times a day—at dawn, noon, midafternoon, sunset, and nightfall. To do so, the believer washes according to a particular ritual and prostrates himself or herself in the direction of Mecca, while reciting certain phrases. This rite takes only a few minutes to perform and can be done anywhere. Worshipers are summoned to prayer by a person known as a muezzin, who calls the faithful together with the following lines:

> God is most great
> God is most great
> God is most great
> God is most great
> I testify that there is no god but God
> I testify that there is no god but God
> I testify that Muhammad is the messenger of God
> I testify that Muhammad is the messenger of God
> Come (alive) to the prayer
> Come (alive) to the prayer
> Come (alive) to flourishing
> Come (alive) to flourishing
> God is most great
> God is most great
> There is no god but God.

For the dawn prayer, the muezzin adds, after the second "Come to flourishing," the phrase "Prayer is better than sleep" twice. Muslims believe that the call to prayer by the human voice distinguishes Islam from Judaism, where the *shofar*, or ram's horn, is used, and Christianity, where a bell is used. The first muezzin was Bilal, a black Abyssinian slave who was one of the first converts to Islam. Because of his status, he was tortured severely by Muhammad's enemies, but was rescued and freed by the Prophet's uncle Abu Bakr. Bilal then emigrated to Medina where he became one of the Prophet's close companions. Bilal's important position shows that from the beginning Islam accepted people of all races.

On Fridays, in addition, all male believers are required to gather together for the noon prayer and listen to a sermon, called a *khutba* in Arabic. The rules for women's attendance at Friday worship have varied over time. In many places today, women also attend Friday worship although they are segregated from the men and pray in a group behind, next to, or above the men. As the preacher traditionally invokes the name of the ruler in his sermon, the *khutba* became an important sign of authority.

The third rule is to abstain from food and drink (as well as smoking and sex) between sunrise and sunset during the month of Ramadan, the ninth month in the Muslim calendar. Abstinence during Ramadan brings Muslims to greater awareness of God's presence and helps them acknowledge their gratitude for God's provisions in their lives. It heightens the sense of community among believers, as Muslims around the world join together in the performance of this ritual.

Although the root of the Arabic word *ramadan* means "to be hot" and suggests that the month originally fell in the summer, the month of fasting can come at any time during the year. To distinguish themselves from the pagan Arabs and Christians, Muslims measure their year by the cycles of the moon rather than the sun, so the Muslim lunar year is eleven days shorter than the Christian solar year. Muslims are also forbidden to adjust their year by adding an extra month, as the Jews do to keep their lunar calendar in synch with the seasons. Hence, the months of the Muslim year do not relate to the seasons. Ramadan, like all the other months, therefore progresses around the solar or seasonal year. It may be easier or more difficult to fast, depending on the season in which Ramadan falls. The end of the month of Ramadan is always marked by a feast, known as the Id al-Fitr, or break-fast feast.

The fourth rule is give alms to the poor. Muslims are supposed to donate a fixed amount of their property to charity every year. Many pious individuals, from the mightiest rulers to modest merchants, give money to help out the less fortunate by establishing soup kitchens, hospitals, schools, libraries, and mosques. One of the most common forms of charity in Islamic cities in medieval times was to establish a public drinking fountain, where fresh sweet water was distributed freely to all passers-by. Such a drinking fountain was commonly known as a *sabil,* from the common Arabic expression *fi sabil allah,* literally meaning "in the path of God" and referring to doing something for God charitably or disinterestedly.

The fifth rule is to go on a pilgrimage to Mecca at least once in one's lifetime, if one is able, during the first days of Dhu'l-Hijja, the twelfth month of the Muslim calendar. People who have performed this pilgrimage, called in Arabic *hajj,* earn the epithet "hajji," which is a title of great respect. The ceremonies of the pilgrimage are associated with the prophet Ibrahim (the biblical Abraham) and center on the Kaaba, which Muslims believe to be the house that Ibrahim erected for God. The pilgrimage then moves to Arafat, a plain some twelve miles east of the city, where the ceremonies culminate on the tenth day of the month in the Feast of the Sacrifices. Livestock is sacrificed in commemoration of Ibrahim's readiness to sacrifice his son Ismail, and the meat is distributed to the poor.[1] This event is also known as the Great Feast, and it usually lasts three or four days. In contrast to the spontaneous cheer with which people celebrate the end of Ramadan, the celebration of the Great Feast is a more solemn holiday. Many of the pilgrimage rites commemorate the Prophet's activities during the "farewell" pilgrimage he undertook just before he died.

THE CENTRAL MIRACLE OF ISLAM IS GOD'S REVELATION TO MUHAMMAD. These revelations, known collectively as the Koran, from the Arabic word *qur'an,* "recitation," are considered God's literal words revealed in the Arabic language and form the basis of faith for all Muslims. (In contrast, the Gospels are the reports of Jesus's associates about his life and works.) Muslims believe that in the same way God had revealed Himself to earlier prophets of the Judeo-Christian tradition, such as Abraham, Moses, and Jesus, and therefore accept many of the teachings of both the Jewish Torah and the Christian Gospels. Muslims believe that Islam is the perfection of the religion revealed first to Ibrahim (who is therefore the first Muslim) and later to other prophets. Muslims consider Jews and Christians to have strayed from God's true faith but hold them in higher esteem than pagans and unbelievers. They call Jews and Christians the "People of the Book" and have allowed them to practice their own religions in the Islamic lands. In contrast, because Muslims believe that Muhammad is the "seal of the prophecy," by which they mean that he is the last in the series of prophets

---

1. According to Muslims, Ibrahim prepared to sacrifice his older son Ismail, while Jews believe that Abraham prepared to sacrifice his younger son Isaac, who is known to Muslims as Ishaq.

God sent to mankind, Muslims abhor the followers of later prophets. This attitude serves to explain the extreme Muslim animosity toward Bahais, followers of a nineteenth-century—and to the Muslim mind false—prophet.

Since they were revealed over a period of more than two decades in two places, the revelations that constitute the Koran are not all alike. The first revelations from the period of Muhammad's residence in Mecca, for example, are short and incantatory verses of extraordinary poetic beauty. The later revelations from the period after Muhammad emigrated to Medina are longer, legalistic texts more appropriate to a developing community of believers in need of rules and regulations. Muhammad and his followers initially committed God's revelations to memory, but as the number and complexity of the revelations grew, some were written down on whatever materials were at hand. At the simplest the verses were written on flat bones or potsherds; at best they were copied onto separate sheets of papyrus or parchment, which were later gathered together in bundles.

After the Prophet died, his followers were pressed to preserve the purity of the revelations and began to write them down more methodically. There was apparently no great variety in the wording of the texts preserved by one transmitter or another, but the order in which they were kept was not yet fixed, and slight variations in readings and interpretations were undoubtedly generated by the peculiarities of the Arabic script, in which several different letters share the same shape and short vowels are not written at all. According to the traditional view (sometimes disputed by revisionist Western historians), a uniform written text of the revelations to Muhammad was collected and collated within twenty years after his death.

The Koran as a book contains 114 *suras* or chapters of varying length. It opens with the *Fatiha,* a beautiful short prayer which serves as an invocation in many situations and is used by Muslims somewhat as Christians use the Lord's Prayer:

> In the name of God
>> the Compassionate the Caring
>
> Praise be to God
>> Lord sustainer of the worlds
>
> the Compassionate the Caring
>
> master of the day of reckoning
>
> To you we turn to worship
>> and to you we turn in time of need
>
> Guide us along the straight road
>
> the road of those to whom you are giving
>
> not those with anger upon them
>
> not those who have lost the way.

The following chapters are arranged in descending order of length, from the 286 verses of Chapter 2, known as "The Cow," to the final two chapters, which are short prayers of a few lines. The chapters are thus arranged neither in the order in which the verses were revealed nor in a narrative sequence. Muslims know the chapters by name, whereas Western Orientalists usually refer to them by number.

Muslims believe that the Koran, as God's literal word, can only be read and truly understood in the majestic and glorious Arabic in which it was revealed. The necessity of reading the Koran in Arabic has meant that all believers should learn the language. This requirement has had important ramifications on the development of Islamic civilization. It has created a linguistic bond among believers, particularly as Islam spread beyond the boundaries of Arabia to regions inhabited by speakers of other languages. Having learned to use Arabic as the language of religion, the new converts also used it as a language of literature, science, commerce, and social intercourse. The primacy of Arabic as the language of God's revelation has also helped to preserve the purity of Arabic, and although the language has evolved over the fourteen centuries since, it has not changed as much as English has changed in the six centuries since Chaucer. This primacy of the Arabic language has also encouraged the spread and use of the Arabic script, which has been used to render a variety of languages, including Arabic, Persian, Kurdish, Pashto, Kashmiri, Urdu, Sindhi, Ottoman Turkish, Chaghatay, and Malay.

Yet as the influence of Islam proliferated, there have been many attempts to render the text of the Koran into other languages. Some medieval manuscripts of the Koran have Persian or Turkish translations written between the lines, often in a script of a different color. The first person to render the Koran in a Western language was Robert of Ketton, a monk who translated the text into medieval Latin in 1143. Robert made his translation for Peter the Venerable, abbot of the monastery of Cluny, who wanted to understand the Koran the better to counter it. The first translation into a modern European language was the Italian version made by Andrea Arrivabene in 1547. His translation was based not on the Arabic original but on Robert of Ketton's Latin text, which had finally been printed at Basel in 1543, exactly four centuries after its composition. There are many versions of the Koran in English, the first of which, by George Sale in 1734, was made directly from the Arabic and renders the text in an English familiar from the King James translation of the Bible.

The Koran contains various types of material, including prayers, oaths, "sign" passages (in which certain aspects of nature and human life are "signs" [Arabic *ayat*] of God's omnipotence and benevolence toward man), "say" passages (in which believers are told to say something), narratives, and regulations. Among the sign passages, the great Throne Verse (2:255) is one of the most lyrical evocations of God's majesty:

> God! There is no god but He, the Living, the Everlasting.
> Neither slumber nor sleep seizes Him.
> To Him belongs all that is in heaven and on earth.
> Who is there that can intercede with Him except by His
>   leave?
> He knows what lies before them and what is after them,
> And they comprehend nothing of His knowledge except as
>   He wills.
> His Throne comprises the heavens and the earth;
> The preserving of them oppresses Him not.
> He is the All-High, the All-Glorious.

Along with the concept of divine omnipotence, the Koran maintains the concept of man's responsibility for his actions. On the Day of Judgment, those who have acted rightly will gain Paradise and its pleasures, but those who have acted wrongly will earn eternal fire and its chastisements. Paradise is described in the Koran as a verdant garden through which rivers flow and in which the residents, adorned with jewels and rich clothing, recline on silken couches beneath God's throne and are attended by winsome *houris*. By contrast, the damned endure a variety of torments in Hell's burning furnaces, where they must eat fruits shaped like devils' heads. Subsequent generations of Muslims elaborated these episodes as well as Muhammad's famous night journey *(miraj)* from the Sacred Mosque to the Furthest Mosque (mentioned in Koran 17.1).

Much of the Koran's message can be summed up in the beautiful Chapter 112, called *Ikhlas* or "Sincerity." This "say"

passage was one of the first verses to be revealed in the early
Meccan period:

> In the name of God, the Compassionate the Caring
> Say he is God, one
> God forever
> Not begetting, unbegotten
>   and having as an equal none

Needless to say, the English translation conveys little of the poetry in the Arabic original, where rhythm and rhyme combine
to emphasize the subtle majesty of the thought.

Narrative elements in the Koran are the easiest to remember,
but—in contrast to the Bible—they actually form a very small
part of the whole. Most of the narratives are versions of traditional stories found in other Near Eastern cultures. (For example, God's creation of the world in six days and His throne from
which He controls the universe are both mentioned several
times.) The largest category of Koranic narratives comprise stories concerning the prophets. Special importance is given to
Nuh (Noah), Lut (Lot), Musa (Moses), and Harun (Aaron), the
prophets who, like Muhammad, were sent by God but rejected
by their contemporaries. Abraham, known in the Koran as
Ibrahim, occupies a particularly prominent position with his
two sons Ismail (Ishmael), with whom Ibrahim founded the
Kaaba, and Ishaq (Isaac). Similarly, Yusuf (Joseph) appears several times, particularly in a long story in Chapter 12, in which
Potiphar's wife, who is unnamed in the Bible, gets the name
Zulaykha. The Koran also contains episodes paralleled in the
New Testament and apocryphal gospels, such as those about
the birth of Yahya (John the Baptist), the childhood of Maryam
(the Virgin Mary), and the Annunciation, the Nativity, and the
life of Isa (Jesus). There are also narratives concerning histori-

cal and legendary characters, such as Alexander the Great (known as *dhu'l-qarnayn,* "the two-horned"), who is said to have built a wall of bronze to contain the evil forces of Gog and Magog, and the Seven Sleepers.

Many passages in the Koran contain specific injunctions: Muslims are forbidden from drinking wine or eating pork; a man must divide his estate, bequeathing specific portions to his widow, children, and other members of his family. Nevertheless, the Koran does not cover all situations Muslims may encounter, and so the second basis of Muslim faith is the example of the Prophet: the perfect Muslim, Muhammad served—and still serves—as the model for all believers. His sayings and deeds were remembered by his associates and preserved in the Traditions, known in Arabic as *hadith.* These Traditions normally take the form of a chain ("So-and-so heard from so-and-so, who heard from so-and-so"), followed by a report of what the Prophet had said or done. The Traditions also help explain and elaborate the circumstances under which obscure passages in the Koran were revealed. The Traditions were transmitted orally for several generations before being written down. By the ninth century the jurist al-Shafii (d. 820) came to consider the *sunna,* or custom of the Prophet, the second most important root of Islamic jurisprudence after the Koran. Together, the Koran and the Traditions, along with consensus and analogy, provide the basis for the *sharia,* the rules and regulations that govern the day-to-day lives of Muslims.

The *sharia* as it evolved transformed the nature of society and the family. Several kinds of social units had been known in pre-Islamic Arabia, but the most common was the patriarchal agnatic clan, descendants through the male line from a common ancestor who lived under the authority of the eldest male. In this male-dominated society, women and girls were of inferior status, and men might have several wives (although in some Arabian tribes, women might have several husbands!). Marriage brought wealth and honor to the clan—and dishonor when the clan's women were violated by outsiders. Property was regulated by the clan, and crimes against the clan were avenged by its other members.

Although the Koran's teachings strengthened the patriarchal agnatic clan, they prohibited many barbarous pre-Islamic practices, such as incest and the killing of female children by leaving them outside to die. Ease of divorce was mitigated by urging delay, reconciliation, and mediation. To ensure both knowledge of paternity as well as support for a child if a woman was pregnant, she could not remarry until three menstrual periods had passed. Women were given some possibility of initiating divorce, although men could initiate it more easily. To reduce the devastating effect of blood feuds, the Koran encouraged compensation in money rather than blood; if the aggrieved party insisted on blood, only the culprit himself could be slain—not any male relative. The Koran enhanced the status of women and children by considering them individuals with rights of their own. Marriage was a relationship sanctioned by God's will and had, therefore, important spiritual and religious values. The Koran urged men to respect women's modesty and privacy, and granted women specific rights they had not held before, such as the right to retain the bridal gift in case of divorce, and the right to inherit at least part of their dead husband's estate. Women, however, only got half the share that men did. The Koran said that the testimony of four men can convict a woman of prostitution.

The Koran and Muhammad's example were more favorable to the security and status of women than history and later practice might suggest. The Koran permits Muslim men to have as many as four wives, but only on the condition that the husband treats them all equitably, a difficult requirement that has in practice limited polygamy to relatively few—and usually wealthy—men. Muhammad permitted himself eleven lawful wives, partly to cement alliances with various tribal groups. Wives must obey their husbands, and husbands must treat their wives well.

Like many other Koranic injunctions, the passages on women have been interpreted in many different ways over the centuries. For example, a woman's legal testimony in court was reckoned to carry only half the weight of a male witness, but the Koran itself says nothing explicit on the subject. It is also said that the Koran insists that women must wear veils. The Koran (24.31 and 33.59) actually says that women should "guard their private parts," "cast their veils over their bosoms" or "draw their veils close to them," and not reveal "their ornaments" to men other than close family members. Although one of the Prophet's wives, Aysha, wore a veil from the time of her marriage, not all women in Medina did. With the expansion of Islam, however, the custom spread rapidly among townswomen, especially those belonging to the leisured class who had servants to do their work. A veiled woman silently announced that her husband was rich enough to keep her idle. In contrast, it was impractical for working women, Bedouins, and peasants to carry on their daily activities wearing a veil, so they didn't.

The Koran also tried to improve the lot of the downtrodden. It did not preach the abolition of slavery—which was widely practiced in pre-Islamic Arabia—but, like Judaism and Christianity before it, endeavored to moderate the institution and mitigate its legal and moral aspects. Slaves in early Islamic Arabia were often African blacks from across the Red Sea, but as the Islamic empire expanded in later times, slaves might just as easily be Berbers from North Africa, Slavs from Europe (who have given us our word "slave"), Turks from Central Asia, or

Circassians from the Caucasus. If he accepted Islam, a slave, although his status in life was inferior, had the same spiritual value and the same eternity in store for him as that of a free man. Muslims considered the basic condition of man to be liberty, and so slavery was an exceptional condition. The emancipation of slaves was deemed a meritorious act, and the unemancipated slave was to be treated with kindness.

Female slaves could not be prostituted, and none but their master or husband could lawfully enjoy their favors. Muslims could not be enslaved, although slaves could convert to Islam. Children born to a free man and a slave woman were regarded as freeborn, for otherwise they would be their father's slave, a condition that was a legal impossibility. It was forbidden to separate a slave mother and her young child. A concubine who had a child by her master enjoyed improved status in life and automatically became free on her master's death. Slaves could marry and own property, lead Friday prayers, and even hold some offices. Often in Islamic history, slaves were even able to occupy positions of great power. For example, India and Egypt were governed for centuries in the medieval period by two sequences of sultans who were manumitted slaves, known in Arabic as *mamluks*.

4

Muhammad's Successors

MUHAMMAD'S DEATH IN 632 DEPRIVED THE MUS-lim community of both its religious and po-litical leader. It was clear in Muhammad's lifetime that the Koran was the basis of faith and that Muhammad derived his authority from his position as God's messenger, but the possibility and nature of any succession to Muhammad was completely open, for he left no legal successor. All his sons had predeceased him, and he had only one surviving daughter, Fatima, who was married to his nephew Ali, son of Abu Talib. Many of the Bedouin tribes felt that they had sworn loyalty only to Muhammad, not to the community of believers, so Muhammad's death rendered any pact between Muhammad and the tribes null and void. Abu Bakr and Umar, the Prophet's uncles and two of the early converts to Islam, put forth a more ambitious concept, arguing that Islam was not merely a matter of each individ-ual's obeying God but, despite Muhammad's death, a continuing pact in which all Muslims were bound to each other.

This view prevailed, and Abu Bakr was elected the first "successor," *khalifa* in Arabic (whence the English word "caliph"). Some of the Arab tribes tried to withdraw, but a bitter two-year war put an end to this attempt. At the same time, during the caliphate of Abu Bakr (r. 632–34), Muslim forces conquered all of Arabia and penetrated into Palestine and lower Iraq. These conquests dramatically expanded under his successor, the second caliph, Umar (r. 634–44), when Muslim armies began to conquer the Fertile Crescent, Egypt, and the highlands of western Iran. These stunning conquests upset the traditional balance of power in the region, forcing the Byzantines to retreat north of the Taurus Mountains and totally destroying the Sasanian empire.

After this initial spurt, the pace of conquest slowed during the 650s but continued nonetheless. By the early eighth century, the Islamic empire stretched from North Africa on the west to Transoxiana and Sind (in modern-day Pakistan) on the east, nearly one quarter the way around the globe, an area that made the empires of the Persians, Alexander the Great, and the Romans seem puny. Although Islam later expanded south (into sub-Saharan Africa), northwest (into Anatolia and the Balkans), northeast (into China), and southeast (into India, Southeast Asia, and the Chinese coast), the frontiers established by the early eighth century demarcate the zone within which the fundamental characteristics of Islamic society and culture would be elaborated. The Muslims, no longer Arab merchants from the heartland of Arabia, became masters of the economic and cultural heartland of the Near East, and their faith, Islam, was no longer an obscure Arabian cult but the religion of an imperial elite.

Despite the unparalleled territorial expansion and the extraordinary wealth it brought, the new community of Muslims was far from unified, and old habits of behavior died hard.

Conflicting visions emerged about how to create the just society mandated by the Koran. Those who felt wronged accused their opponents not merely of tyranny but also of apostasy. Disaffected believers murdered the third caliph, Uthman (r. 644–56), forever tainting the legitimacy of the caliphate and opening the gates to centuries of intermittent civil war. Uthman was succeeded by Ali, the Prophet's cousin, son-in-law, and one of the first converts to Islam, who had waited in the wings while he was repeatedly passed over for the succession. Having been elected caliph, Ali was himself assassinated after five years in office.

Within this tumultuous period, three main positions developed about the nature of authority over the Islamic community. The first was represented by the small group known as the Kharijites, literally "seceders." They believed that sinners, including sinful rulers, had renounced their faith. Consequently the head of the community must be replaced if he was shown to have committed any injustice or sin. They rejected not only Uthman's claim to the caliphate but also Ali's because of wrongs they had committed. Stressing the equality of all believers, irrespective of race, the Kharijites initially attracted large numbers of non-Arab converts to Islam, who had begun to feel excluded from the largely Arab community of believers. Over time, the Kharijites' doctrine became more extreme, and they were eventually doomed to the margins of Islamic political life.

A second position about the nature of authority was represented by the partisans of Ali, who are collectively known as Shiites, from the Arabic word *shia* meaning "party" or "faction." The Shiites initially pointed to Ali's justice, religious knowledge, and closeness to the Prophet, arguing that any head of the community should be a direct descendant of Muhammad through his daughter Fatima and her husband Ali.

Their doctrine evolved so that by the eighth century most Shiites also held that the caliph, or Prophet's successor, would also be a divinely guided, infallible religious teacher, or *imam*. They believed that only such a leader could guide the Muslim community to achieve the justice and salvation promised by the Koran.

All Shiite groups accept that in 661, after Ali was assassinated by a Kharijite, the imamate passed first to his son Hasan. Hasan immediately put himself out of the running and retired as a wealthy man to Medina, where he earned the epithet of "the Divorcer" by marrying as many as ninety times and having three or four hundred concubines. For the next twenty years, however, Hasan's brother Husayn attempted to gain support over a deeply divided community. Husayn was martyred at Kerbala in Iraq on 10 Muharram (October 10, 680), a day solemnly commemorated by Shiites as Ashura (the tenth). The imamate then passed to Husayn's son Ali Zayn al-Abidin ("Ornament of [God's] Servants").

From this point the succession became more complicated. Some Shiites believe that the fifth imam was this Ali's younger son, Zayd, and they are consequently known as Zaydis, or Fiver Shiites. Zaydis, who did not recognize any hereditary line of imams but were prepared to support any member of the Prophet's family who might claim the imamate, became politically prominent in medieval times along the Caspian coast of northern Iran and in the highlands of Yemen.

The majority of Shiites, however, believe that the succession passed not to Zayd but to Ali's older son Muhammad al-Baqir, who had died before Zayd but left a son named Jafar al-Sadiq (d. 765). All Shiite groups other than Zaydis recognize Jafar as the sixth imam, but there was a major split over which of Jafar's sons became the seventh. One group believes that the succession passed to Jafar's son Ismail, who had, however, also died before his father, and through Ismail to his descendants. This group came to be known as the Ismailis, or Sevener Shiites. They became politically prominent in medieval North Africa and Egypt as the Fatimid dynasty, as well as in medieval Iran, where their followers became known to their opponents as the Assassins. Eventually the center of Ismailism shifted to Central Asia and India, where the most prominent group of Ismailis in modern times comprise the followers of the Aga Khan and the Bohoras. As many Ismaili Shiites have emigrated from India and Pakistan, there are now large communities in East Africa, the United States, and Canada.

Another group of Shiites believes that the imamate passed after Jafar al-Sadiq's death to his son Musa al-Kazim, and from him to his lineal descendants, culminating in the twelfth imam. The twelfth imam went into hiding in 940, and until he reappears on the Day of Judgment, it is believed that he is represented on earth by a viceroy, who reinterprets the *sharia* for every age. Twelvers constitute the largest group of Shiites in modern times, making up most of the population of modern Iran and sizeable minorities in neighboring countries. Although Iran is now a Shiite country, Twelver Shiism only became the state religion in the sixteenth century, when it was adapted by the Safavid dynasty, partly to differentiate Iran from its neighbors. Iranian Shiites developed a particularly elaborate hierarchy of interpreters of the *sharia* unknown elsewhere in the Muslim world. In the late eighteenth century, this viceroy was termed a *mujtahid.* In the twentieth century, the pinnacle of this hierarchy became the *ayatollah* (from the Arabic *ayat allah,* literally "sign of God"), the title given to Ruhollah Khomeini, leader of the 1979 Iranian Revolution. Following the revolution, however, the number of individuals calling themselves *ayatollah* proliferated to such an extent that it was necessary to create the title *ayatollah al-uzma* ("the greatest sign of God").

Despite their varying and conflicting claims and genealogies, all Shiite groups trace the legitimacy of their rulers through their descent from the Prophet. Apart from the Zaydis, all Shiites believe that the imam is hidden from the world and will reappear only on Judgment Day. Although Shiite dynasties were in power in much of the Muslim world in the tenth and eleventh centuries, internecine rivalries and sometimes extremist doctrines prevented the entire Muslim community from ever accepting a descendant of Ali as its leader.

The third position vis-à-vis the nature of authority in the Islamic community, and the one ultimately accepted by the majority of believers, was that of the caliphal loyalists. By the middle of the eighth century, they came to call themselves the "people of tradition and unity," in Arabic *ahl al-sunna wa'l-jamaa,* or more simply *sunni*s. Sunni Muslims constitute the overwhelming majority of the more than one billion Muslims in the world today.

The caliphal loyalists believed that the most important thing was to keep the Islamic community together, and—within reason and unlike the Kharijites—they were willing to accept any ruler who could do so. Like Shiites, they venerate the Prophet Muhammad and accept Ali as the fourth caliph. They differ from Shiites in believing that Ali's nomination to the caliphate was through public acclamation, just like that of the first three caliphs, and not because the Prophet designated Ali as a member of his family to be the leader of the community. After Ali's defeat in the first civil war, the caliphal loyalists recognized his rival and successor, Muawiya, and when Muawiya bequeathed the caliphate to members of his own family, the loyalists went along, albeit reluctantly. Sunnis respected the caliphs as Muhammad's political successors but rejected their claims to be his spiritual heirs. They believed that the caliphs should submit to and enforce the legal and theological doctrines articulated by the community's learned men, called the *ulema,* from the Arabic word *ulama,* or "learned men" (plural of *alim,* a learned man). Sunni Islam differs dramatically from most organized religions in that the status of the learned men is validated neither by the state nor by any formal religious institution, but simply by the reputation the individuals held among each other.

Despite its predominance, Sunni Islam itself was not monolithic. During the eighth and ninth centuries, Sunni religious scholars developed various ways of interpreting the Koran and the Traditions, the two sacred sources of faith. In the early years of Islam, the Traditions, like the Koran, had been passed orally from generation to generation of Muslims, but in the ninth century they were collected in large, multi-volume compendia. Scholars devoted themselves to judging the authenticity of the initial reports and the accompanying chains of transmission, for both could be manipulated or even falsified to justify specific ideological positions or actions.

Perhaps the most famous collection of Traditions is al-Bukhari's *Sahih* ("true," "valid"), widely accepted by Sunni Muslims as their most important book after the Koran. Al-Bukhari (d. 870), who was prized in his lifetime for his minute knowledge of detail and his perspicacity, is said to have spent over sixteen years traveling from his hometown of Bukhara in Central Asia across Iran to Egypt. Along the way, he heard six hundred thousand Traditions from over one thousand shaykhs, and from this mass he culled 7,397 Traditions, with full chains of transmissions, arranged by subject. Even if we omit repetitions, the total is still an impressive 2,762 reports, covering subjects from prayer and ablution to Creation, Paradise, and Hell. Not all Traditions dealt specifically with the Prophet, but all treated matters of utmost concern to all Muslims.

By the mid-ninth century, religious scholars had begun to

cluster into "schools" of law, which are known in Arabic as *madhhabs*. These "schools" traced their doctrines about the religious and legal obligations incumbent on all Muslims back to the teachings of a particular learned scholar. Although initially there were many different schools, by the eleventh century four had come to prevail. The Hanafi school, which developed in Kufa in southern Iraq, traced its concepts and doctrines back to Abu Hanifa (d. 767). Free in its interpretation, it became the most widespread school, reaching prominence under the Abbasid caliphs who ruled from Iraq between 749 and 1258. It eventually became the official school of the Ottoman dynasty, which ruled over Anatolia, the Balkans, Arabia, North Africa, and the Levant from the thirteenth century.

The Maliki school traces its origins to Malik ibn Anas, who died at Medina in 795. It developed in the Arabian peninsula from where it spread to the lands bordering the Persian Gulf, the Sudan, and North Africa. Rigidly conservative, particularly with regard to women, the Maliki school, unlike the other Sunni schools of law, refused to accept the traditions of Ali and was intolerant toward schismatics. The school gives much weight to consensus among Muslims to the extent that consensus sometimes prevails over Tradition.

The Shafii school, which traces its origins to al-Shafii, synthesized the teachings of Hanafis and Malikis. It was first formulated in Iraq, but then spread to Palestine and particularly Egypt, where al-Shafii died in 820. It grew deep roots as Cairo increasingly became a religious and cultural center in medieval times, and al-Shafii's monumental tomb in the southern cemetery there became a focus of popular piety and religious education. Shafii's methods, if not his interpretations, were accepted by all the other schools of Islamic jurisprudence.

The Hanbali school, which traces its origins to Ibn Hanbal (d. 855), is noted for its rigorous reliance on the sources of faith and the rejection of later interpretations. It was adopted in the fourteenth century by the Mamluk theologian Ibn Taymiyya and in the eighteenth century by the conservative Wahhabi movement in Arabia, and with the rise to power of the Saudi family, it was established as the official school there. The Hanbalis' use of Koranic punishments, including hand-chopping, flogging, and public stoning, for such crimes as theft and adultery are often reported in Western news media.

Sunnis consider all four schools authentic and acceptable in God's sight, although their doctrines differ significantly, and members of one school have often quarreled fiercely with those of another. Adherence to a particular school of law created strong ties within districts and cities. These affiliations also extended among regions, as scholars traveled from one city to another in search of knowledge, and important works written in Iraq, for example, were quickly debated in Iran and Syria. As there was no official religious hierarchy, these loose-knit and far-flung communities maintained cohesion through their search for consensus on significant problems. Consensus emerged through decades and even centuries of debate and teaching among hundreds of scholars all over the Islamic world.

Alongside the development of these outward-oriented affiliations based on the legalistic interpretation of the Koran and the Traditions, Muslims from the earliest times developed another, more inward oriented approach toward their belief. This attitude has come to be called Sufism, from the Arabic word *suf* (wool), referring to the coarse woolen garments some early ascetics wore. Like the word "Islam," "Sufism" is a relatively new word, introduced to European languages by Orientalist scholars in modern times. It is usually translated as "mysticism," but more properly it reflects a wide range of inward-directed beliefs and practices. Just as believers have held many different views about the nature of authority and the ways to interpret the

Koran and the Traditions, they also have followed different inward approaches to achieving ethical and spiritual goals.

Modern fundamentalists, in an attempt to return to some imagined "pure" form of early Islam, have tended to view Sufism as a corruption of "true" Islam, whatever they imagine that to have been. They see Sufi practices as survivals of pre-Islamic and extra-Islamic superstition and idolatry and have tried to make Sufism something distinct from, and even hostile to, Islam. Nevertheless, inward-directed forms of piety have existed since the time of Muhammad, and throughout the history of Islam many of the most important thinkers have been intimately engaged in practices that would today be encompassed by the term "Sufism."

Like the legalists, Sufis looked to the same two sources—the Koranic revelation and the model of the Prophet Muhammad—but viewed them differently. Rather than devoting themselves to scrupulously obeying the letter of the laws laid down in the Koran, Sufis hoped in some way to re-create the ecstatic experiences that Muhammad must have had when he received God's message. Sufis believed that instead of learning about God, they could directly and intuitively experience Him. Hence they celebrated Muhammad's birthday and other events of his life. For example, at both the popular and elite levels Sufis transformed Muhammad's *miraj,* or mystical journey to heaven, into an elaborate poetic and pictorial tradition.

In his short treatise *The Cosmic Tree of Existence,* the great Andalusian mystic Ibn Arabi (1165–1240) described Muhammad's passage through four stations. Muhammad first entered into existence and responded to God's command to arise and warn humankind. In the second, "praised" station, he received the office of intercessor for humankind at Judgment Day. The third station was Muhammad's eternal dwelling in Paradise and his visit to each abode therein. Finally the Prophet came but "two bows' length" from God. Then Ibn Arabi described the Night Journey itself. Muhammad was carried on five "steeds": the human-headed Buraq took him to Jerusalem, the ladder *(miraj)* took him to the lowest heaven. Angels' wings then took him to the seventh heaven. Gabriel's wing took Muhammad to the tree beyond which even Gabriel could not pass, and finally Muhammad floated on a flying carpet to God's throne. There God summed up the Prophet's mission:

> Now what is demanded of a witness is truthfulness about that to which he bears witness, and it is not permissible for him to bear witness to something he has not seen, so I shall show you my Paradise that you may see what I have prepared for my friends, and I shall show you my Hell that you may see what I have prepared for my enemies. Thus shall I have you witness my majesty and uncover for you my beauty, that you may know that I in my perfection am far removed from anything in ordinary existence.

Popular Arabic stories of Muhammad's mystical ascent were translated first into Castilian and then into Latin as *The Book of Muhammad's Ladder.* It gave rise to a furious polemic in late medieval Europe and ultimately inspired the great Italian poet Dante to write his *Divine Comedy.*[2]

Another central feature of the Sufis' inward approach to belief is the importance they give to saints and sainthood. While all Muslims believe that God hears the prayers of all believers, Sufis believe that particularly pious individuals, whom they call

---

2. Ascension literature is still popular in the Islamic world today. There are, for example, two prose and several verse versions in Swahili, and in Java, Muhammad's ascension is celebrated with an elaborate festival with fireworks.

God's "friends," developed an unusually close and personal relationship with God. Such relationships are marked on the divine side by protection and responsibility, and on the human
side by worship and obedience. (Westerners often liken these
individuals to the saints of the Christian tradition, noting these
individuals' shared holiness or sanctity.) Sufis' veneration of
God's "friends" has many parallels to Shiites' veneration of the
imams. For Shiites, Ali is God's friend, and many of the qualities Sufis ascribe to their saints are also ascribed by Shiites to
their imams.

Saints, as exemplary Muslims, represent the highest virtues
and religious commitment worthy of emulation. Although
sharia-centered Islam does not allow for such mediating presences as saints to close the gap between the divine and the
human, in practice millions of Muslims believe that God has
endowed these moral exemplars with extraordinary powers.
Hagiographical accounts describe many such people renowned for their sanctity, and often embellish their lives with
many miraculous details. Saints could be male or female. For
example, Rabia, the eighth-century mystic of Basra, was born
into a poor home, stolen as a child and sold into slavery, but
secured her freedom because of her sanctity. She retired to a
life of seclusion and celibacy, at first in the desert and then in
Basra, where many disciples and associates gathered around
her. She was supposedly so ascetic that later writers attributed
miracles to her and even said that her food was supplied by
miraculous means. The renowned thirteenth-century mystic
Attar wrote that

> On one occasion Rabia's servant was going to prepare wild
> onions, because for some days they had not prepared any
> food, and she needed an onion, so the servant said, "I will go
> and ask for one from a neighbor," but Rabia said, "Forty years

ago I made an oath with God that I would not ask for anything except from Him. I can do without the onion." Immediately after she had spoken, a bird flying in the air dropped an onion—already peeled—into Rabia's frying pan. But she was still doubtful and said, "I am not safe from a trick" (i.e. perhaps Satan had sent the onion), so she left the fried onion alone and ate bread without any seasoning.

Her tomb was venerated at least from the twelfth century, and her semi-legendary personality continues to inspire: she is the subject of romantic biographies as well as two Egyptian films.

Like other branches of Islamic learning, Sufism is passed directly from master to pupil, for an individual can more easily develop a close relationship to God in proximity to a person who already has one. The saint's closeness to God is demonstrated by extraordinary power (known in Arabic as *baraka*), which permits him to perform miracles, such as healing the sick, reviving the dead, or even flying. The power does not necessarily diminish after death, so Sufis venerate not only living saints but also their tombs in the hope of sharing some of the saints' power.

The inward approach to belief was, at first, a fairly private movement of like-minded individuals, but it soon grew into a major social force. In the ninth and tenth centuries, just after the legalists had begun codifying their positions, Sufis also began to write theoretical treatises about their approaches to belief. Perhaps the culmination of classical Sufism is found in the figure of Abu Hamid Muhammad al-Ghazali (1058–1111). Originally a theologian and therefore an adherent of the legalistic approach to belief, he adopted more mystical beliefs after a personal crisis. His four-volume masterpiece, the *Ihya ulum al-din* ("Revivification of the Religious Sciences"), synthesized theological science with mystical inner knowledge in a comprehensive guide for the devout Muslim to every aspect of religious life, including worship and devotional practice, conduct in daily life, purification of the heart, and advance along the mystical path.

This period in which individual Sufis articulated their beliefs was followed in the twelfth and thirteenth centuries by the growth of many circles of teaching. In Arabic they are known as a *silsila* (chain) or *tariqa* (path), as distinct from the "order" or "brotherhood" of Christian monasticism. Each of these chains traces its lineage to a particular master, who codified and institutionalized the order's distinctive teachings and practices. Each order is known for a particular approach to mystical practice, whether repeating a formula such as the Ninety-Nine Names of God (a practice known in Arabic as *dhikr*) or ecstatic dancing, singing, or whirling.

Of all the Sufi orders, the Mevlevi—often called the Whirling Dervishes because they practice an individual but synchronized whirling dance that emulates the movement of planets on their journey of spiritual fulfillment—has become the most famous in the West. The Mevlevis trace their lineage to Jalal al-Din Rumi (d. 1207–73), who is known in Persian as *maulavi* or in Turkish as *mevlana,* from the Arabic *mawlana,* "our master." Son of an eminent theologian and mystic, Jalal al-Din was born in Balkh, which is now in Afghanistan, where he is known as *al-Balkhi.* Fleeing the Mongol invasions of Central Asia, his father found work at the Seljuk court at Konya in Anatolia (then called Rum and now in Turkey). Jalal al-Din started his career as a preacher and theologian, but after meeting a dervish, he became a mystic. He wrote the largest corpus of lyric poetry in the Persian literature, amounting to 40,000 couplets, as well as a 25,000-couplet mystical epic, the *Mathnavi,* which one later poet called "the Koran in the Persian tongue." It opens with an unforgettable evocation of the reed cut from the reed-bed to make a flute. Rumi uses it as a metaphor for the soul, emptied of self and filled with the divine spirit:

> Hearken to this Reed forlorn,
> Breathing, even since 'twas torn
> From its rushy bed, a strain
> Of impassioned love and pain.
>
> "The secret of my song, though near,
> None can see and none can hear.
> Oh, for a friend to know the sign
> And mingle all his soul with mine!
>
> 'Tis the flame of Love that fired me,
> 'Tis the wine of Love inspired me,
> Wouldst thou learn how lovers bleed,
> Hearken, hearken to the Reed!"

The reed flute has, therefore, become a hallmark of Mevlevi devotions, and its haunting songs accompany the devotees as they whirl.

At first Sufis principally operated in the central areas of Islamic power in Iraq and Iran, but with time they became active on the Islamic frontiers in such distant regions as North and East Africa, Central Asia, India, and southeast Asia. Sufis preached their message of the love of God and the Prophet not in theological Arabic but in vernacular idioms, and Sufis became, therefore, responsible for converting to Islam many of the non-Muslims living on the Islamic borderlands.

5
The Spread of Islamic Power

THE FIRST FOUR CALIPHS—ABU BAKR, UMAR, UTH-
man, and Ali—are known to Sunni Muslims
as the *rashidun* or "rightly guided" caliphs. They
were elected because of their close association
with the Prophet and the esteem in which they
were held by large segments of the community. In
contrast, succeeding caliphs held power because
they belonged to a certain family. The first of these
families was the Umayyads (r. 661–750), who were
descendants of the Meccan clan of Umayya, the
same clan to which Uthman, the third caliph, belonged. The founder of the dynasty, Muawiya
(r. 661–80), was a close kinsman of Uthman and
served as governor of Syria for two decades before
he proclaimed himself caliph.

The Umayyads' rise to power brought many significant changes. The capital of the Islamic empire
was moved from Medina, an Arabian oasis, to Damascus, an ancient Syrian metropolis in a rich hinterland which was able to provide the surplus capable
of sustaining a large court, government, and army.
Damascus was strategically situated, having access

to both the Mediterranean and the Fertile Crescent. Much more than the remote Arabian oasis town, Damascus was an ideal site for the capital of a rapidly expanding world power, which soon stretched from the shores of the Atlantic to the steppes of Central Asia. Although Damascus was far from the Arabian religious centers of Mecca and Medina, it was close to another Islamic religious center—Jerusalem. Not only had Jerusalem been the original direction toward which Muslims had prayed but it was also believed to be the place from which Muhammad made his mystical journey to heaven. Jerusalem came therefore to be considered the third holiest city in Islam, a position that has only strengthened over the centuries.

The new Islamic empire demanded a new style of government. As the caliphs were transformed from Arab chieftains to imperial rulers, the consensus politics of the early period gave way to an autocratic form of government, modeled on old Byzantine and Persian notions of kingship and ceremonial. The Arab armies that had been paid with the spoils of war were replaced by regularly paid troops, and the old families of Mecca and Medina were supplanted by a new elite of army leaders and tribal chiefs. These new rulers were townspeople committed to a settled urban life.

The new style of government also demanded a new language of administration. At first, Muslim rulers were content to adapt to existing systems of government and tax collection by using local languages, such as Greek and Middle Persian. From the 690s, however, Arabic, which had been the language of the ruling elite and the religious establishment, became the language of administration and finance. Umar had established the first government offices to organize payments, register the army, and regulate the treasury, but under the Umayyad caliph Abd al-Malik (r. 685–705) these documents were recorded in Arabic for the first time. During his reign Abd al-Malik also began to issue a new type of coin that was struck to a new weight standard and decorated only with Arabic writing. On the front of the coin, the center bears the statement that "There is no god but God alone without partner" surrounded by the legend "Muhammad is the messenger of God who was sent with the religion of Truth to proclaim it over all other religions." On the back of the coin is an adaptation of Koran 112, stating God's oneness and refuting the Trinity, surrounded by the invocation, the name of the mint, and the date. All of this writing appears on a coin smaller than an American quarter. This change was so important that virtually all coins minted in the Islamic lands still have only writing and no pictures.

At the same time that Abd al-Malik introduced the new style of coins in Syria, he also improved the roads leading to Jerusalem and Damascus, his capital. To advertise his public works program, he ordered milestones written in Arabic and showing the distance to the cities or describing the work done, such as the leveling of a difficult pass. The texts contain the same statement of faith found on the front of the coins as well as the caliph's name and titles, all done in a bold, clear script.

Abd al-Malik's public works program also included great buildings. The early caliphs had spent neither money nor effort on building, perhaps in accordance with the Tradition of the Prophet that nothing was so wasteful as to spend money on buildings. Nor had the first Umayyad caliphs been interested in building, as they had been preoccupied with consolidating their power and suppressing dissent. Once these problems were taken care of, however, Abd al-Malik and his son and successor al-Walid (r. 705–15) could embark on an ambitious program of public construction, just as Byzantine and Sasanian emperors had celebrated their triumphs by erecting beautiful buildings.

The first Islamic work of architecture was the Dome of the

Rock in Jerusalem. Ordered by Abd al-Malik in 692, it stands in splendid isolation in the center of a huge platform in the southeast corner of the Old City of Jerusalem, where Solomon's Temple had once stood until it was destroyed by the Romans in 70 C.E. The Dome of the Rock stands over a rocky outcrop, giving the structure its name. The rock, one of the most sacred places on earth, has been variously identified as the place of Adam's burial; the site where God tested Ibrahim by demanding he sacrifice Ismail; the location of the Holy of Holies of the ancient Jewish temple; and the spot where Muhammad began his night journey. The exact purpose of the Dome of the Rock is still unclear, but of one thing we can be sure: it was meant to announce to the Jews and Christians who held Jerusalem holy that Islam was here to stay.

The glory of the building is its mosaic decoration, a technique typical of Byzantine architecture in which millions of tiny cubes of colored and gilded glass are placed side by side to form pictures and designs. The interior preserves the most lavish program of mosaics to survive from ancient or medieval times anywhere. Mosaics envelop the upper walls with designs of crowns, jewels, flowers, and plants, while the lower walls are covered in plaques of veined marbles, cut and fitted in patterns. Many if not all of these features might also be found on a Byzantine building, but what makes this building specifically Islamic is a narrow band of Arabic writing running around the top of the arcade. Written in gold cubes on a blue ground, the text quotes passages from the Koran that refute the Trinity and attest to the majesty of Islam. It ends with the patron's name, his title, and the date. The harsh Jerusalem climate eventually cracked and disintegrated the exterior's mosaics, and in the sixteenth century, they were replaced with tiles, which were replaced again in the twentieth century, but the interior remains, in all its glory.

Many of the other buildings the Umayyad caliphs erected at this time were large mosques meant for congregational prayer on Friday. It is generally believed that the origins of the mosque lie in Muhammad's house in Medina, which had also served as a kind of community center and prayer hall. Like all buildings in an Arabian oasis, Muhammad's house was probably a simple structure of sun-dried bricks with palm-thatch verandas around an open courtyard. These covered spaces provided the faithful with shelter and shade from the blazing Arabian sun as they worked, prayed, or rested. Muhammad's house had three features that later became requirements for all buildings used for communal prayer: a praying space, a way of showing the direction of Mecca so that the worshipers would know which way to face for prayer, and some sort of covering to protect worshipers from the weather.

WITH THE RAPID SPREAD OF ISLAM, MUSLIMS OUTSIDE MEDINA ALSO required places for their Friday congregational prayer. Since Muhammad had not specified the form these buildings should take, Muslims used whatever was at hand, either reusing older buildings or erecting simple structures from scratch. Under Abd al-Malik's son al-Walid, however, money was available to build grand new mosques in major cities like Medina, Jerusalem, and Damascus. The scale and magnificence of these buildings showed that Muslim patrons wanted to make their religious buildings the equals of the great temples and churches of the past.

The mosque of Damascus gives us the best idea of what an Umayyad congregational mosque must have looked like. Although damaged, especially in a great fire in 1893, and somewhat garishly restored, the building retains much of its original appearance and is a tangible example of how Muslims grafted their new religion onto the earlier religious traditions of the region. The mosque began as a Roman temple, which the Byzantines had turned into a church. Like their counterparts in Jerusalem, the original Muslim settlers in Damascus had first contented themselves with using part of this church for their communal prayers, but by the time of al-Walid, the Muslim community had grown so large that a new, bigger structure was needed. Both the Roman temple and the Byzantine church had stood inside an enormous enclosure with massive walls.

The builders of the Damascus mosque bought the church and tore it down, keeping the walls of the Roman temple enclosure for the walls of the mosque. The mosque has a broad courtyard surrounded by arcades and a huge prayer hall constructed against the southern—or qibla—wall. In a move that would become one of the hallmarks of later Islamic architecture, builders at Damascus turned the major façade of the building to face the interior court rather than the street outside. This practice would have great ramifications in later times: as the courtyard was considered the core of the mosque, builders could expand the building in any direction to accommodate an increased number of worshipers.

Like the Dome of the Rock in Jerusalem, the Umayyad mosque in Damascus was lavishly decorated with marble plaques and glass mosaics, including a large wall panel showing an idyllic landscape of a river flowing beneath fantastic houses and pavilions separated by trees. This and other now-vanished mosaics illustrated the beautiful landscape of Paradise described in the Koran, where true believers go after death, just as the mosaics in Byzantine churches showed the company of saints the Christian believer would keep in Heaven. Bands of inscriptions from the Koran drove home the message. This pictorial program was apparently an unsuccessful experiment, for later mosques were not decorated with such specific pictures on their walls. Rather, the decorators of later mosques used Koranic inscriptions and abstract geometric and vegetal designs because these subjects allowed believers to focus their attention on God's word alone.

The official public face of Islam promulgated by the Umayyads used words, specifically the revealed text of the Koran, to proclaim the triumph of Islam. It did not use images of people or animals. It has often been said that from the start Islam banned figures from its art, but this is false. The Koran itself has very little to say on the subject. As Muslims believe that God is unique and without associate, He cannot be represented. As He is worshiped directly without intercessors, images of saints have no place in the religion. As the Koran is not a narrative like the Torah or the Gospels, which begin with the Creation and the Nativity, respectively, there was little reason for Muslims to make their religious art pictorial. Hence the absence of figures was a characteristic feature of Islamic religious art. Instead, it focused on God's word, accompanied by geometric and floral designs. Figures were quite acceptable, however, in private secular art.

The Umayyads' official attitude toward religious art did not necessarily hold in private. Along with their public role as leaders of the faith, the Umayyad caliphs also had private lives, which they lived in palaces in the major cities and the countryside. Although all of the urban palaces have long since been destroyed, several Umayyad country estates have been discovered by archaeologists working in the Syrian steppe. The most remarkable is Khirbat al-Mafjar ("the ruins of Mafjar"), which was probably built by the libertine prince al-Walid II (r. 743–44), who partied for twenty years while waiting to succeed his uncle as caliph. Al-Walid's amorous exploits and tastes for wine, women, and song were extolled by contemporary poets, whom he supported liberally. The prince himself

was a poet, and he often had professional singers recite his
works. Among the tamest is:

> Another cup! Another drop! Of the wine of Isfahan!
> Of the wine of the Old Man Kisra, or the wine of Qayrawan!
> There's a fragrance in the cup, or on the hands of him who pours;
> Or is it just a lingering trace of musk from filling the jars?
> A wreath, a garland for my head! And take my poem for your song!
> Here's my rope to let me loose, and here to bind me take my thong!
> Springtime's only in the cup that's handed with the fingertips.
> And now the ardor of the cup has crept between my feet and lips!

Al-Walid's estate, near Jericho at the north end of the Dead
Sea, was leveled in an earthquake in 747, but in its heyday the
complex included a residence, a mosque, and a huge music
hall with attached steam bath and communal toilets that could
accommodate forty people at once. The music hall was the
most lavishly decorated part of the complex, with a splendid
mosaic pavement overseen by statues of voluptuous half-
naked women. There al-Walid entertained his guests with poetry and song. According to reports preserved by later poets,
the prince filled his swimming pool with rose-water mixed
with musk and turmeric. A curtain was hung across the pool,
and a famous musician was commanded to sing. At the end of
his song, slave girls appeared and lifted the curtain, revealing
the prince. Instantly throwing off his scented robe, he then
dived back into the water. When he climbed out, slave girls
were waiting to dress him with a fresh robe which they had
censed and perfumed. Al-Walid took a sip of wine, offered one
to the musician, after which the whole process was repeated
again and again.

Ultimately the autocratic rule of the Umayyad family engen-
dered widespread opposition. Although the Koran carries a

message of equality among believers, principle and practice increasingly diverged as the Islamic empire grew and power and wealth became concentrated in the hands of a few. Although the Umayyads projected an image of strength, their empire was held together with spit and glue. Syria, the heartland of their power, was weakened economically when the closing of the frontier with Byzantium disrupted the trade on which its wealth had depended. In contrast, the eastern provinces of Iraq and Iran were growing stronger, as trade with Central Asia, India, and China increased with the coming of Islam. Furthermore, agriculture flourished in southern Iraq and northeastern Iran because networks of irrigation systems made these lands extremely rich and productive. By contrast, the dry-farming practiced along the Mediterranean coast in Syria made this region more dependent on seasonal rainfall.

The conquest of a region did not mean that it suddenly became a Muslim country, and everywhere social tensions developed between the Arab Muslim rulers and the indigenous populations. These tensions were especially apparent in eastern Iran, where the wealth and promise of the eastern frontier had attracted many Arab settlers. As elsewhere, Muslim immigrants enjoyed certain privileges over non-Muslim natives. Non-Muslims, for example had to pay special taxes. Some non-Muslims were willing to pay this price in order to continue practicing their religion and maintaining their identity, but others did not and began to convert to Islam.

There were many reasons for conversion. Some people accepted the truth of the new religion. Others were attracted to its elegant simplicity and absence of ritual, particularly in the face of the elaborate hierarchy that marked contemporary Christianity and Zoroastrianism. Still others saw conversion to Islam as a means of financial or social advancement. Some converts even attached themselves to Arab tribal leaders as their "clients." Nevertheless, the line between Arabs and non-Arabs was not erased in the Umayyad period, and Iranian converts felt that they were being treated as second-class members in the supposedly classless fellowship of believers.

Opposition to Umayyad family rule crystallized in the 740s with revolts breaking out in many regions of the empire. In the west, the rebels included Kharijites who challenged the legitimacy of all the caliphs. In the east, the rebels included many Shiites, who believed that Muawiya and his family had usurped power from Ali and his descendants. The rebels, under the command of an Iranian convert known only by the nom de guerre of Abu Muslim ("father of a Muslim"), cleverly refrained from naming any specific member of the Prophet's family as their leader in order to attract the widest possible support. From northeastern Iran the rebels moved westward to Syria, eventually defeating the Umayyads in a series of battles in 749–50. The last caliph of the Umayyad family, Marwan II (r. 744–50), fled to Egypt, where he was killed. Only one member of the family, Abd al-Rahman, escaped the slaughter by fleeing to Morocco, the homeland of his Berber mother. He then crossed the straits of Gibraltar to the Iberian Peninsula, where he established a new branch of the line in 756. With Córdoba as their capital, the Umayyads of Spain flourished there until 1031.

In 749, the rebels appointed Abu'l-Abbas, a descendant of the Prophet's uncle Abbas, to be the new caliph, and hence they are known to history as the Abbasid dynasty. The Abbasids had been brought to power by an uneasy coalition of people who had been united only in their opposition to the Umayyads. Once in power, the Abbasids faced the problem of how to transform their loose movement into a permanent government. They began by getting rid of all the supporters who had helped them come to power. They killed Abu Muslim and eliminated many others, including members of the ruling family. This massacre earned the dynasty's founder the nickname of "the bloody." Although the Abbasids had come to power on the back of the Shiites, promising to give precedence to the family of Ali, this did not materialize and many of the Shiite imams met their deaths under the Abbasids.

The Abbasids replaced the Arabian aristocracy of the Umayyads with a new governing elite. Some members were new converts drawn from old Iranian families which had traditionally served the state. Others belonged to the ruler's household and included freed slaves. Power was therefore concentrated in the hands of a small group, which was orchestrated by the Abbasid caliph. In many ways early Abbasid rule turned out to be not very different from that of the later Umayyads.

Abbasid rule did differ from that of the Umayyads in one significant way, however: its eastward orientation. In addition to including many Persians in the administration and Turkish slaves in the army, the Abbasids moved the capital from Syria to Iraq. At first they chose a site near Kufa, one of the garrison towns founded during the conquest of Iraq a century earlier. After a few years the second Abbasid caliph, al-Mansur (r. 754–75), decided on a new site located at the point where the Tigris and Euphrates Rivers flowed closest to each other and were connected by canals. The new capital, built over the village of Baghdad, which stood near the ruins of Ctesiphon, former capital of the Sasanian dynasty, was officially called *Madinat al-Salam,* or "The City of Peace." Commonly known simply as Baghdad, al-Mansur's new capital would come to symbolize a long period of peace, prosperity, learning, and culture often called the Golden Age of Islam.

PART II

The Golden Age

750-1250

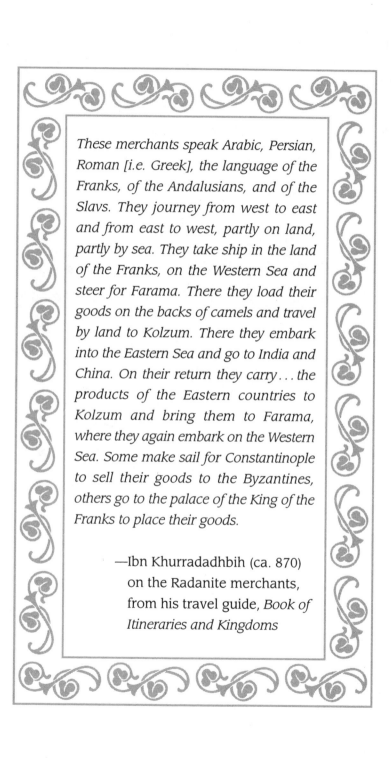

These merchants speak Arabic, Persian, Roman [i.e. Greek], the language of the Franks, of the Andalusians, and of the Slavs. They journey from west to east and from east to west, partly on land, partly by sea. They take ship in the land of the Franks, on the Western Sea and steer for Farama. There they load their goods on the backs of camels and travel by land to Kolzum. There they embark into the Eastern Sea and go to India and China. On their return they carry . . . the products of the Eastern countries to Kolzum and bring them to Farama, where they again embark on the Western Sea. Some make sail for Constantinople to sell their goods to the Byzantines, others go to the palace of the King of the Franks to place their goods.

—Ibn Khurradadhbih (ca. 870)
on the Radanite merchants,
from his travel guide, *Book of Itineraries and Kingdoms*

6

The Crucible

ONE THOUSAND YEARS BEFORE THE RISE OF ISLAM, in the fourth century B.C.E., Alexander of Macedon had created an empire that spread east from Greece to Central Asia and northern India. After his death, however, it evaporated, and only with the Islamic conquests in the seventh century C.E. were the Mediterranean and Iranian worlds permanently integrated into a huge empire and vast common market. The empire stretched from the shores of the Atlantic to the steppes of Central Asia and the plains of northern India, drawing in supplies from the jungles and savannahs of tropical Africa, the river valleys of the Far East, and the forests of northern Europe. As trade within the empire and with its neighbors brought merchants and their rulers great riches, old cities were expanded and new ones constructed. Regional and imperial capitals, such as Córdoba, Fez, Cairo, Baghdad, Isfahan, and Samarkand, burgeoned and flourished at a time when, after the fall of the Roman Empire, European urban civilization had withered.

In the Islamic lands, not only Muslims but also Christians and Jews enjoyed the good life. They dressed in fine clothing, had fine houses in splendid cities serviced by paved streets, running water, and sewers, and dined on spiced delicacies served on Chinese porcelains. Seated on luxurious carpets, these sophisticated city dwellers debated such subjects as the nature of God, the intricacies of Greek philosophy, or the latest Indian mathematics. Muslims considered this Golden Age God's reward to mankind for spreading His faith and His speech over the world.

Whereas the initial revelation and spread of Islam in the first century of Islamic history had been initiated and directed largely by Arabs, the Golden Age of the following centuries was one in which Arabs were joined by large numbers of people from other ethnic and religious backgrounds, including African blacks, Armenians, Berbers, Circassians, Georgians, Mongols, Persians, and Turks who professed various forms of Christianity, Judaism, Zoroastrianism, Buddhism, Shamanism, and animism. At first many of them had been either individual converts to Islam or hirelings of the dominant Arab elite, but within a few centuries many of these "outsiders" became not only significant minorities (or even majorities) but often important rulers. In this way, Islam was transformed from the religion of a relatively small number of Arabs to a universal faith.

This Golden Age was not only a time of great prosperity but also one of continuous struggle, as Muslims attempted to elaborate their faith and expand its applicability to the new situations they encountered. In addition to the Koran and the Prophetic Traditions, Muslims looked to the wisdom of ancient Greeks, Persians, and Indians and attempted to reconcile these teachings with the demands of their faith. The intellectual and artistic ferment that characterized life in the capital at Baghdad has led some to liken this Golden Age to a crucible in which ideas from all times and places were blended and refined to produce one of the great periods of world civilization.

THE INITIAL TRANSFORMATION OF ISLAMIC SOCIETY INTO A UNIVERSAL religion and the evolution of a true Islamic culture took place during the epoch—from 749 to 1258—when the Abbasid caliphs ruled from Baghdad. Abbasid rule fell into two periods. The first began with the foundation of the dynasty and lasted until 945, when the once powerful caliphs were reduced to puppets by the arrival in Baghdad of a band of Persian adventurers known as the Buyids. The second period, which lasted until the fall of Baghdad to the Mongols, was one in which Persian and Turkish warlords wielded real power while a series of nominal Abbasid caliphs continued to preside over the palace and not much else.

In the wake of the bloody revolution that had brought the Abbasids to power, the family was blessed by a series of powerful and able caliphs. Al-Mansur (754–75) established the new capital of Baghdad, which not only became the political center of the empire but also assumed a preeminence in science, literature, and the arts that it would maintain long after its political power had dwindled. (Destroyed and rebuilt many times over, al-Mansur's Baghdad is known only from the descriptions by medieval authors of its days of glory.) The site was chosen for its easy communication upriver with Mesopotamia and northern Syria and downriver with the Persian Gulf and the Indian Ocean, as well as by land routes with the Iranian plateau, southern Syria, and the Hijaz (western Arabia). Measuring about one and a half miles in diameter, the circular city probably copied an older Persian town plan, perhaps that of the city of Firuzabad. Baghdad was protected by a double set of sturdy mud-brick walls and a broad moat fed by the Tigris. The walls were pierced with four great gates named for the four quarters of the empire they faced. Within the gates four major streets lined with shopping arcades and other buildings crossed the city, passing through an outer ring of residences just inside the wall for the caliph's family, his staff, and his servants, and an inner ring housing the arsenal, the treasury, and the government offices. The innermost zone was an immense plaza in which stood the police station, the congregational mosque, and the caliph's palace, set in the exact center.

The caliph's palace, which was four times the size of the mosque, had two reception halls crowned with high domes. The highest dome stood twelve stories above the ground and supported a weathervane in the shape of a horseman carrying a lance. Contemporaries considered the horseman the "crown" of Baghdad, a sign of the region, and it was said that if the figure's lance pointed to a given direction, the caliph knew that rebels would appear from there. Like a political weathervane, the horseman was supposed to predict trouble before it blew in. Consequently, when the dome and the weathervane on it collapsed during a storm in 941, people accounted it an ill omen, and indeed, within a few years the Buyids muscled their way into Baghdad and established themselves as the caliph's "protectors."

The early Abbasid caliphs had initially been assisted by members of the Barmakid family, descendants of the Buddhist abbots (parmaks) in the city of Balkh in Afghanistan. Not long before the Muslim conquest, the Barmakids had converted to Zoroastrianism, and by the eighth century they converted to Islam and moved to Iraq, where they entered government service. They played an enormous role in the development of new administrative systems to unite the far-flung Abbasid empire. For example, they were probably responsible for introducing the use of paper—which had been known for some time in Central Asia—to government offices. Before then, records had been kept on papyrus (which was made only in Egypt) or parchment (which was made from animal skins). Paper could be made virtually anywhere from rags and waste fiber, and although it was not cheap it did have the great advantage of being difficult to erase—an important consideration when documents and records had to be secure from forgery. The use of paper soon spread from government offices to all segments of society, and by the middle of the ninth century the Papersellers' Street in Baghdad had over one hundred shops in which paper and books were sold.

The Barmakids, however, were apparently too ambitious, and al-Mansur's grandson, Harun al-Rashid (r. 786–809) suddenly imprisoned and executed these once powerful ministers.[3] Harun ably defended the empire's northwestern frontier against Byzantine incursions and was also said to have entered into diplomatic relations with Charlemagne, the king of the Franks, who proclaimed himself emperor in Rome on Christmas day 800. Harun unwisely left the empire in the hands of his three sons. On Harun's death, al-Amin, who was the son of an Abbasid mother, got Baghdad and the caliphate. Al-Mamun, the son of a concubine from northern Afghanistan, got the governorship of the immensely rich and powerful province of Khurasan as well as the right to succeed his brother, while a third brother got the lands along the Byzantine frontier. When al-Amin tried to dispossess his brothers in favor of his own son, four years of bitter civil war (809–813) ensued before al-Mamun emerged triumphant. In winning,

---

3. Their fame lived on, however. A story in the *Thousand and One Nights* recounts that one of the Barmakids put a succession of empty dishes before a beggar, pretending that they contained a sumptuous repast. The beggar humorously accepted this fiction, and the word *Barmecide* has thereby come to mean "providing only the illusion of plenty or abundance." Harun is himself famed for his appearance as the just ruler in the *Thousand and One Nights*, where dressed in disguise he wanders through the streets of Baghdad inquiring about the state of affairs.

however, he alienated the population of Iraq and the defeated Abbasid armies, whose support he and his successors desperately needed.

Al-Mamun (r. 813–33) was the most intellectual of the Abbasid caliphs. He transformed the caliphal library, which his father Harun had founded as the "Treasury of Knowledge," into the great "House of Knowledge" in Baghdad. This remarkable institution, which was modeled on the Sasanian academy at Jundishapur in southwestern Iran, maintained a staff of translators, as well as copyists and bookbinders. At first they translated from Syriac and Greek, but by the end of the ninth century they and their successors had translated all the important books of Persian and Indian geography and science into Arabic. The caliph al-Mamun even sent a delegation of scholars to purchase philosophical and scientific manuscripts in Constantinople. He repeatedly tried to lure the brilliant Byzantine philosopher and mathematician Leo to Baghdad. The caliph's repeated requests, however, only led the Byzantine emperor Theophilos to finally offer his mathematician a position in Constantinople.

Although the Abbasids based their claims to the caliphate on their descent from the Prophet's uncle, they did not return to the "first among equals" principle of the early caliphs and began instead to adopt pre-Islamic Persian models for government and the court. The caliph stood at the pinnacle of an enormous court characterized by elaborate ceremonial and luxurious display. In the army, Arabs were replaced by Turkish slave and mercenary troops imported from the steppes of Central Asia. The rulers became increasingly remote from the ruled, withdrawing into immense palaces built outside Baghdad, where they were guarded by their Turkish troops. As the troops evolved into a dominant military caste, the native population became restive, and in 836, the caliph al-Mutasim

(r. 833–42) was forced to move the capital—and his guard—seventy-five miles upriver to Samarra, where he built a new city. He and his successors remained there for more than half a century.

Unlike the planned circular city of Baghdad, Samarra was an immense and sprawling complex of palaces, mosques, barracks, and playgrounds spread along the banks of the Tigris. Whereas medieval Baghdad was rebuilt again and again, Samarra was largely abandoned after the caliphs left, and its ruins stretch for miles. Archaeologists have found the remains of houses, palaces, and mosques there, along with many of the accouterments of daily life. The Dar al-Khilafa, or "House of the Caliphate," was a complex of courts and gardens built by al-Mutasim. It covered over four hundred acres and measured well over a mile from the entrance stairway along the riverbank to the viewing stand that overlooked an enormous racetrack in the shape of a cloverleaf. Within the immense and extremely intricate palaces, row upon row of courtyards and chambers led to special halls. Sunken apartments arranged around pools provided relief from the torrid climate.

Medieval historians give some idea of how big these palaces were when describing how the Abbasid caliph al-Muqtadir received an embassy from the Byzantine emperor in 917. Although the incident took place in Baghdad, the description fits Samarra perfectly. The caliph impressed the ambassador by having him led through an endless succession of palaces, courtyards, corridors, and rooms to a palace where he was told to wait. The ambassador cooled his heels for two months waiting for the caliph to receive him. Finally, the envoy was conducted to another palace, passing by 160,000 cavalry and infantry before reaching a vaulted underground passage. He was then taken about the palace in which 7,000 eunuchs, 700 chamberlains, and 4,000 black pages were stationed along the rooftops and in upper chambers. Later, he was led to a third palace, and from there through corridors and passageways which led to a zoological garden. The entourage was then brought to one courtyard with four elephants and to another with a hundred lions. The group proceeded to a building set between two gardens, from which it was conducted to the Tree Room and then to the Paradise Palace. Next the group was taken along a passageway nearly five hundred feet long. After touring twenty-three palaces, it was conducted to a large court known as the Court of the Ninety. Because it was such a long tour, the author of the account adds, the ambassador's retinue sat down and rested at seven places, and was given water whenever they desired.

On the military front, the Abbasids were too absorbed with consolidating their own power to successfully extend the empire beyond the borders achieved by the Umayyads. The only active frontier was the one between Syria and Anatolia, where the caliphs continued to wage an inconclusive campaign against the Byzantines. In hope of turning the tide, the Abbasids even granted large outlying portions of their empire to local governors in return for tribute. By passing rule to their children, these governors established local dynasties. In the west, for example, the Aghlabid family controlled Tunisia and Sicily between 800 and 909, although they professed nominal allegiance to the caliph in Baghdad and sent him annual gifts and slaves. In Egypt, Ahmad ibn Tulun, the son of a Turkish slave who had served the caliph at Samarra, became governor and established his own dynasty, which ruled Egypt and Syria from 868 to 905. A similar process took place in the east, where the Samanid family established a semi-independent principality (819–1005) in Transoxiana and Khurasan, and the Saffarids (861–1003) founded a similar one in Sistan (southeast Iran and southwest Afghanistan).

Malcontents of all stripes found refuge on the fringes of the Abbasid empire, a safe distance away from the capital. The Rustamids (778–909), for example, Kharijites who challenged all unjust rulers, set up a dynasty in what is now western Algeria, while Abd al-Rahman, the only Umayyad to escape the Abbasid massacre of his family, founded an independent Umayyad principality in Spain. Both principalities were too far away from the Abbasid heartland to do the caliphs much harm, and in Córdoba, the Umayyad capital, the latest fashions from Baghdad were eagerly copied.

IN THE TENTH CENTURY, ISMAILI SHIITES MOUNTED A MORE SERIOUS challenge to the authority of the Abbasid caliph. The Fatimids (909–1171), who claimed descent from the Prophet himself, established their own rival caliphate, based first in North Africa and, after 969, in Egypt, where they founded the city of Cairo. They claimed that they would bring about a world of peace and harmony and dreamt of reuniting the entire Muslim world under their white banners. Their initial success in winning territory, if not necessarily converts, caused the Abbasids considerable consternation. By the end of the tenth century, for example, the Fatimids controlled Mecca, Medina, and Jerusalem, the three holiest cities of Islam, and appeared well on their way to realizing their dreams of world domination.

Not to be outdone by the Fatimid caliphs, the Umayyad princes of Spain, who had been content with modest titles until 929, also assumed caliphal honorifics. The new Umayyad caliphs of Spain transformed Córdoba, a somewhat sleepy provincial outpost, into a splendid Mediterranean capital. Córdoba traced its origins to a provincial commercial center in the Roman empire. Under the Umayyads in the ninth and tenth centuries it grew to become the most civilized city in Europe. By the year 1000 its population had swelled to almost 100,000, although medieval chroniclers regularly exaggerated the number tenfold. For Arab chroniclers, Córdoba was the "bride of al-Andalus." The Saxon nun Hrotsvitha called it the "ornament of the world." The Moroccan historian and chronicler al-Maqqari wrote that Córdoba surpassed the capitals of the world in four ways: the bridge over the Guadalquivir River, the mosque, the palace at Madinat al-Zahra, and knowledge. He wrote that the city had 1,600 mosques, 900 public baths, 213,077 homes for ordinary people, 60,300 mansions for notables, officials, and military commanders, and 80,455 shops. His numbers are probably exaggerated, but they give some idea of the city's prosperity. It was clean, well-paved, well-lit, and abundantly supplied with running water at a time when all other European cities were dirty, dark, and rank with disease. The Umayyad caliph exchanged ambassadors with Byzantium, Baghdad, Cairo, Aachen, and Saxony. The city's power and wealth stretched far and wide. Merchants brought gold and ivory across the Sahara from tropical Africa, and skilled craftsmen transformed these precious materials into coins, jewelry, and luxury goods for the caliph and his courtiers.

The Great Mosque of Córdoba (now the city's cathedral) exemplified the city's prosperity and international connections. It was begun in 784–85 by the Umayyad prince Abd al-Rahman I as a typical congregational mosque with an open courtyard leading to a prayer hall supported on many columns. It differed, however, from other mosques in the way the roof was held up. As only short and stubby columns were available in the ruined Visigothic buildings left over from earlier times, the builders ingeniously invented a double-tiered system of columns and arches supporting the wooden roof. By stacking two short columns on top of one another, the designers of the mosque achieved the necessary height, transforming a utilitarian space into one of the most memorable architectural creations of medieval Europe.

In the following centuries, as the population of Córdoba grew, the mosque was repeatedly enlarged and embellished. These renovations culminated when the Umayyad caliph al-Hakam II (r. 961–76) expanded the prayer hall and added fancy ribbed domes in front and on either side of the new mihrab. The walls and ceiling were covered with gold mosaic, meant to recall the glories of such earlier Umayyad buildings as the Mosque of Damascus and the Dome of the Rock. As no local workmen in Córdoba knew how to make such mosaics, the Umayyad caliph sent a letter to the Byzantine emperor in Constantinople asking him to send an artisan as well as gold mosaic cubes. While workmen toiled in Córdoba and its mosque, the Umayyad caliphs themselves—like their rivals in Baghdad—retired to splendid garden palaces in the city's suburbs.

By the middle of the tenth century, then, the Abbasid caliph had two rivals who also claimed universal authority over the Islamic lands, although none of these rulers was more than a regional power. The Abbasid caliph controlled only a much-reduced empire in Iraq, and his power diminished even further with the arrival of the Buyids in Baghdad in 945. The Buyids, a Shiite clan of adventurers from the mountains of northern Iran, became "protectors" of the Abbasid caliphs, who retained only their religious authority as spiritual heads of Sunni Islam. In the eleventh century the Buyids were followed by the Seljuqs, a family of Oghuzz Turks from Central Asia who had converted to Islam and adopted strong Sunni beliefs. Under their leader, Tughril, the Seljuqs muscled their way into Baghdad to replace the heterodox Buyids.

On December 15, 1055, Tughril's name was included in the Friday khutba pronounced in the main mosque of Baghdad, lending him authority as a leader; three days later he and his entourage paraded into the capital. Fighting then broke out between the city's inhabitants and the Turkish soldiers, who subsequently pillaged the city. The caliph, who was in no position to object to anything, granted Tughril the title of *sultan,* an Arabic word literally meaning "power," in return for restoring the name, if not the authority, of the orthodox Abbasid caliph whose family had ruled for over three hundred years.

The Seljuqs established a new quasi-feudal social and economic order and renewed the campaign against Shiism. The most effective weapon in their arsenal was the madrasa, a state-sponsored theological college, and Seljuq rulers and their ministers established such colleges in all the major cities of their empire. The Shiites fought back as best they could: a group of Ismailis established themselves in the mountains of northern Iran from where they harassed the Turks by stealthily murdering their leaders. Said by their detractors to have been led to their murderous frenzy by the use of hashish, these medieval insurgents were known to their enemies as the *hashhishiyyun,* a word that eventually surfaced in European languages as "assassin."

For centuries individual Turks had been important soldiers in Abbasid society, but the establishment of the Seljuq sultanate marked a major change in Islamic society. In contrast to the individual Turks who had served in Abbasid armies as mercenaries or slaves, large numbers of nomadic Turks began to migrate westward during this period, ethnically transforming the Middle East. While this happened in most places, the change was most notable in Anatolia, or Asia Minor. This mountainous peninsula with a central plateau, bounded by the Mediterranean and Black Seas and the straits separating Europe and Asia, had been an important province of the Byzantine empire and was largely inhabited by Greek-speaking

Christians. On the east and south, high mountains and deserts generally kept the Muslims of Syria and Iraq at bay. Following the battle of Manzikert (or Malazgird) in 1071, in which the Seljuq Turks captured the Byzantine emperor Romanos I, the frontier was opened, and large numbers of Turks, who had already migrated into Iran, began to move into Anatolia and settle there. The ultimate result was that the Greek-speaking province of Anatolia was transformed into the land of the Turks, or *Turkey*. In later centuries the Seljuqs would be succeeded by other Turkish tribes. The most important were the Osmanlis or Ottomans, who would become a major world power in the fifteenth century.

The extraordinarily confusing situation in the Near East of the eleventh century, as Arabs, Persians, and Turks as well as Sunnis and Shiites fought among themselves, is epitomized by the revolt of Basasiri, a Turkish slave who had started his career as a military leader under the Buyids. When the Seljuq Turks—who were staunch Sunnis—arrived in Baghdad, Basasiri decided to transfer his allegiance to the Fatimid (i.e., Ismaili Shiite) caliph in Cairo. In return, the Fatimid caliph made Basasiri governor of a city along the Euphrates, and, as a result of Basasiri's efforts, the Fatimid caliph's name was pronounced in the Friday sermon at several cities in Iraq.

Naturally these developments incited the anger of Tughril, a staunch defender of Sunnism. Tughril set out from Baghdad with an army to attack Basasiri and took the important city of Mosul, located on the upper Tigris. Tughril left Mosul in the hands of his brother, Inal, but the treacherous Inal, who coveted his brother's sultanate, abandoned his post as governor, left Mosul to the Fatimids, and threw his lot in with Basasiri. When Tughril found out about the treachery, the enraged ruler took off in pursuit of his rebellious brother, leaving Baghdad ripe for Basasiri's picking.

On December 27, 1058, Basasiri, at the head of four hundred poorly equipped cavalrymen, took Baghdad. The muezzins of the city were instructed to give the call to prayer using the distinctive Shiite formula in which the phrase "Come to the best of works" is added and the last sentence, "There is no god but God" is repeated. For the first time, the Friday sermon in Baghdad was said in the name of the Fatimid caliph of Cairo. Basasiri was warmly welcomed not only by the substantial Shiite population of Baghdad but also by the many Sunnis there who hated Tughril's Turkish troops. Many of Basasiri's supporters were lured by the promise of riches they might pillage from behind the walls of the caliph's palace. Indeed, Basasiri and his troops sacked the palace and appropriated the caliph's turban and cloak, as well as a particular lattice screen behind which the Abbasid caliph used to sit in audience. These insignia were sent to the Fatimid caliph in Cairo as trophies. Tughril, having meanwhile triumphed over his brother Inal, returned to Baghdad. Basasiri fled but was overtaken by Tughril's cavalry and killed on January 15, 1060, his head delivered to the sultan.

History is written by the victors, so Basasiri's achievement has often been overlooked. For one year, however, Baghdad, the center of Abbasid Sunnism, had been forced to acknowledge Fatimid Shiite sovereignty and the Friday sermon was pronounced some forty times in the name of the Abbasids' most serious rivals for authority in the Islamic lands. Not only does the episode illustrate the continuing struggle between Sunnis and Shiites, but it also shows how both Seljuqs and Fatimids attempted to expand their spheres of influence. In the end, Tughril's success promoted the cause of Sunnism and Abbasid legitimacy, of which he was the chief defender. Nevertheless these internal struggles also symbolize the anarchy that made the Islamic lands of the Middle East particularly vulnerable to outside attack.

ON NOVEMBER 27, 1095 AT THE COUNCIL OF CLERMONT IN FRANCE, Pope Urban II delivered a rousing address in which he exhorted a militant Christendom to recover the Holy Sepulchre, Christ's tomb in Jerusalem, from the "Saracens"—what the Greeks and the Romans had called the nomads of Arabia and Syria even before the rise of Islam. At the conclusion of Urban's speech, the crowd shouted *Deus vult* ("God wills it") in support of the Pope's call. At this dramatic moment, the Bishop of Le Puy knelt before the Pope, took the vow to recover Jerusalem, and received the papal blessing. Many others in the crowd followed his example. Urban then continued his speech, urging volunteers to sew crosses onto their clothes as a sign of their commitment to the cause. "Crusaders" who died en route to the Holy Land were promised remission of their sins and a crown in Paradise, as well as papal protection for their families and properties. Those who failed to fulfill their vows, however, would be anathematized. With this speech, Pope Urban initiated the Crusades, the military venture to the Near East that occupied the heart and soul of Christian Europe for the next two centuries.

Unlike Muslim pilgrims, whose religion demanded that they make the pilgrimage to Mecca, Christians volunteered or vowed to make a pilgrimage for personal reasons. For medieval Christians, Jerusalem was one of the three most important destinations for pilgrims, the other two being the tombs of St. Peter in Rome and of St. James (Santiago) at Compostela in northwest Spain. The trip to Jerusalem had always been arduous and long, but Muslims in the Levant had rarely prevented Christians from reaching their goal. Indeed, it was said that

Harun al-Rashid's treaty with Charlemagne gave the latter rights of protection over Jerusalem. Following the Seljuq invasion of Anatolia and the Muslim capture of Antioch (now the Turkish city of Antakya) from the Byzantines, however, pilgrimage to Jerusalem became increasingly difficult. At the same time, these Muslim victories dealt a sharp blow to Byzantine prestige, and in the late eleventh century the Byzantine emperor Alexios I Comnenos swallowed his pride and appealed to his fellow Christians in the West to help him expel the Saracens from his territories.

The Roman and Byzantine churches had been on divergent courses for centuries and in 1054 mutually excommunicated each other, but Christians temporarily put aside their conflict as European knights set out for the East by land and sea. French, Norman, and Flemish commanders led armies that eventually amassed at Constantinople and crossed the straits into Anatolia in May 1097, a year and a half after Pope Urban's initial call. The Crusaders scored their first success when the Byzantine city of Nicaea (now Iznik), which had been taken by the Seljuqs, surrendered on June 19, 1097. During the heat of summer, the Crusaders then pushed across the Anatolian plateau, arriving at the walls of Antioch in October.

Soon, however, the Crusaders broke with their Byzantine allies and decided to go it alone. A Crusader contingent took the city of Edessa (now Urfa in Turkey) and established the County of Edessa on March 10, 1098. The main Crusader army took Antioch in June 1099 and founded a principality there. The Crusaders then moved on to Jerusalem, which had been occupied in August 1098 by a Fatimid army from Egypt. On July 15, 1099, after a forty-day seige, the Crusaders triumphantly entered Jerusalem, having achieved their goal in less than three years since Urban's ringing call. Tancred, the leader of the Crusader army, promised the inhabitants protection, but his orders were disobeyed, and virtually all Muslims and Jews—men, women, and children—perished in the general slaughter that followed.

In 1100, just after the conquest of the city, an elderly Jewish pilgrim to Jerusalem wrote a letter to a relative:

> The Franks arrived and killed everybody in the city, whether of Ishmael or of Israel; and the few who survived the slaughter were made prisoners. Some of those have been ransomed since, while others are still in captivity in all parts of the world. Now all of us had anticipated that our sultan—may God bestow glory upon his victories—would set out against the Franks with his troops and chase them away. But time after time our hope failed. Yet to this very present moment we do hope that God will give the sultan's enemies into his hands. For it is inevitable that the armies will join in battle this year; and if God grants us victory through the sultan and he conquers Jerusalem—and so may it be with God's will—I for one shall not be among those who linger, but shall go there to behold the city . . .

Clearly the Jews felt they had more to fear from the Christians than from their traditional rulers, the Muslims.

The triumphant Crusaders established the Latin Kingdom of Jerusalem, and Baldwin of Boulogne was elected its king. He was supported by the Knights Templar, who took over the Dome of the Rock and made the surrounding Haram al-Sharif or Temple Mount their headquarters, and by the Hospitalers, who maintained a large hospice for pilgrims near the Holy Sepulchre. Within a decade, the Crusaders added the County of Tripoli (1109) to their territories in Syria and Palestine.

There were several reasons for the Crusaders' unexpected success in capturing the Holy Land from the Muslims. Surely their fanatical determination to wrest Christ's tomb from the "infidel" played no small part in their victory. Europeans also enjoyed several military advantages, among them the use of chain mail armor, which was unknown to the Muslims. In addition, the Crusaders had naval support, which proved crucial at several junctures. Most important to the Crusaders' success, however, was the sheer indifference of most Syrian Muslims to the threat these foreigners posed.

Syria, which had been the heartland of Umayyad imperial power several centuries earlier, had come to be divided into innumerable small principalities which served as buffers between the conflicting imperial ambitions of the Fatimids, the Abbasids, the Seljuqs, and the Byzantines. None of the Syrian princes had the resources, let alone the desire, to mount a unified defense against the new European invaders. In any event, Syrian Muslims did not initially consider the Crusaders to be significantly different from any of the other strongmen who had previously muscled their way into the area to set up principalities. That the Crusader states were Christian was not exceptional, for the Christian Byzantines had long ruled northern Syria and there was still a substantial, if not a majority, Christian population in Palestine. In any event, Muslims had a relatively low opinion of the "Franks," deeming them to be people from a cold, damp land shrouded in fog who had never produced anything culturally worthwhile.

Eventually the Muslims mounted a successful counterattack. In the first half of the twelfth century, it was spearheaded by the Turkish rulers of Mosul. Recruiting large numbers of Kurds who lived in the region, these rulers attempted to expand their territory at the expense of anyone else in the vicinity, whether Muslim or Christian. In 1144 the Kurdish leader Zangi captured Edessa from the Crusaders and put them on the defensive for the first time.

Over the next thirty years, the Crusaders, supported by fresh troops arriving from Europe during the Second Crusade (1147–49), attempted to capture Damascus from the Turks, who had taken it from the Fatimids at the end of the eleventh century. The inhabitants of that city, unhappy with both the Turkish rulers and Frankish besiegers, turned it over to Zangi's son, Nur al-Din, instead. For the first time, Muslims came together in a new anti-Christian and anti-Crusader spirit, exemplified by a new veneration of Muslim holy places in Jerusalem, especially because they were now controlled by Christians. The Dome of the Rock, for example, was respecified as the site where Muhammad had ascended to heaven, as mentioned in Chapter 17 of the Koran. In 1168–69 Nur al-Din ordered the ablest woodworkers in Aleppo to begin work on a magnificent wooden minbar, or pulpit, which he planned to install in the Aqsa Mosque in Jerusalem, once he had taken the city back from the Crusaders.

The next phase of the Muslim counterattack was directed by Salah al-Din ibn Ayyub (known in the West as Saladin), the nephew of Nur al-Din's Kurdish general, Shirkuh. In 1169, fearing that the Crusaders would attack Egypt, which was then ruled by the moribund Fatimid dynasty, Nur al-Din sent Shirkuh and his nephew to take over the country before the Crusaders could get there first. After Shirkuh's unexpected death, his troops recognized Saladin as his successor, and two years later, Saladin was able to remove the last Shiite Fatimid caliph of Egypt and reestablish a Sunni regime there. In so doing, Egypt and Syria were joined in a unified Muslim state, which would endure—more or less intact—for the next eight centuries.

Saladin, now sultan of Egypt, returned to Syria. In 1174 he took Damascus from one of Nur al-Din's successors who had alienated the city's population by seeking a truce with the Crusaders. The cities of Aleppo and Mosul fell to Saladin in 1183 and 1186 respectively. From this strong Syrian base, he then turned against the Crusaders, decisively defeating them at the battle of Hattin on July 4, 1187. The poet Ibn Sana al-Mulk (d. 1211) addressed a rapturous panegyric to Saladin on this occasion:

> You took possession of Paradise palace by palace, when you
>   conquered Syria fortress by fortress.
> Indeed, the religion of Islam has spread its blessings over
>   created beings.
> But it is you who have glorified it . . .
> You have risen up in the darkness of the battle like the moon
>   when it climbs slowly in the night
> You have never shown yourself in battles without appearing,
>   O Yusuf, as beautiful as Yusuf [the biblical Joseph in the
>   Koran].
> They attacked en masse like mountains, but the assaults of
>   your chivalry have turned them into wool . . .
> Syria is not the only object of the congratulations addressed
>   to you, but it is also every region and country.
> You have possessed the lands from east to west.
> You have embraced the horizons, plain and steppe . . .
> God has said: Obey him;
> We have heard Our Lord and obeyed.

The victory at Hattin was followed by the easy reconquest of various Crusader lands and towns, above all the holy city of Jerusalem. Saladin waited to take possession of the city until October 2, 1187 because the date corresponded with the anniversary of the *miraj,* the Prophet's miraculous ascension to heaven. Some sixty letters, a dozen poems, and several Friday sermons were dedicated to this triumphal moment.

In contrast to the Christians, who had indiscriminately slaughtered the city's inhabitants, the Muslim conquerors decided to accept a ransom of ten gold dinars for men, five for women, and two for children. (A lower-middle-class family could survive on about two dinars a month.) Those who could pay within forty days were free to leave the city with their possessions. According to the contemporary chronicler Ibn al-Athir, when the Muslims entered the city they found a great gilded cross, which the Templars had left on top of the Dome of the Rock. Some of Saladin's troops climbed to the top of the dome to remove it, at which point the Muslims of the city cried out *Allahu akbar* ("God is great!") while the Christians groaned. At that time, Saladin also installed the minbar that Nur al-Din had ordered made eighteen years earlier.

Five years later, after the siege of the seaport of Acre, Saladin himself concluded a truce with the Crusader king Richard the Lionheart, as a result of which the Crusaders were able to maintain a foothold on the coast of Palestine and Syria for another century. Shortly after the truce, on March 4, 1193, the most celebrated hero of the Muslim counterattack died in Damascus. Both Muslim and Christian writers extolled Saladin's virtues. The Crusader historian William of Tyre, for example, portrayed him as a generous, energetic, and ambitious ruler whose policies presented a real threat to the Crusader states. In due course, however, the historical Saladin became a mythic figure of chivalric romance. This romanticized view of him continued well into the nineteenth century, most notably in Sir Walter Scott's novel *Ivanhoe*.

Despite—or perhaps because of—Saladin's successes, Europeans mounted several other crusades. The Fourth Crusade, for example, was launched in 1202 against Egypt, which was now ruled by Saladin's successors, who were known as the Ayyubids. The Crusaders hoped that subjugating Egypt would be a substitute for recovering Jerusalem. The Crusaders got sidetracked, however, and, led by the Venetians, they conquered and pillaged the Byzantine capital of Constantinople instead. On April 13, 1204, Baldwin, count of Hainault and Flanders, was elected emperor of the Latin Empire of Constantinople, which lasted until the Byzantines retook the city in 1261. Meanwhile, all subsequent crusades in the first half of the thirteenth century were directed against the Ayyubids, who were themselves embroiled in their own family squabbles. Seeking allies wherever they could find them, the Christian leaders, such as Louis IX of France and Pope Innocent IV, tried to strike a deal with a new power in the region, the Mongols, who, at this very moment were marching across Iran toward Iraq, Anatolia, and Syria.

MUSLIMS CALL ALL THE LANDS OF NORTHERN NORTH AFRICA BEYOND Egypt (including present-day Tunisia, Algeria, and Morocco) the West, or *maghrib* in Arabic, the land of the setting sun. Libya was of little account in medieval times, and the Muslim territory in the Iberian peninsula was known as al-Andalus, from which Spaniards have derived the regional name "Andalusia." In the seventh and eighth centuries, Muslims had conquered this entire region from the indigenous North Africans, who are known as Berbers, but the region's distance from the centers of Islamic power in the Near East meant that it was always a place apart. This feeling was only strengthened by the political and religious differences between the central powers and the nonconformists the region attracted. For example, in the tenth century the Shiite Fatimids had risen to power in North Africa—an area not previously known as a center of Shiite power—by channeling Berber dissatisfaction with the status quo and their belief in a messiah-like figure who would usher in a new age of prosperity.

The Fatimids ultimately changed little for the Berbers, but they set the precedent for the rise of two other Berber dynasties, the Almoravids (r. 1062–1147) and the Almohads (r. 1130–1269). While both of these movements were staunch in their Sunni beliefs, they, like the Fatimids, were able to channel Berber dissatisfaction and belief in a prophetic figure into revolutionary movements. The first started in what is now Senegal, the second out of a comparable movement in the High Atlas mountains. Both were spearheaded by Berber tribesmen who, rather like the Turks in the lands far to the east, were converts to Islam and somewhat separate from the mainstream religious culture of the cities. These Berber dynasties, which expanded to rule both Morocco and Spain, fought fiercely but ultimately unsuccessfully against the expanding Christian kingdoms in the north.

The Christian conquest of the Iberian peninsula took place at approximately the same time as the Crusades in the Near East. It is one of the very few instances where a land that had been conquered by Islam and heavily Islamized reverted to Christian rule. (The only other notable example is the island of Sicily, which had been conquered by the Muslim Aghlabids in the early ninth century and reconquered by the Christian Normans in the late eleventh.) Spaniards called this historical process the *Reconquista* ("reconquest"), thereby implying that the peninsula was returned to the fold of Christian civilization.

As much as later Spanish monarchs tried to eradicate all traces of the Muslim "cancer" from the historical record, in reality Spanish civilization is deeply indebted in many ways to the long and glorious centuries of Muslim rule there. Muslim thinkers brought books and ideas to the cities of Spain, where Christian monks learned about subjects ranging from neo-Platonic philosophy to Arabic numerals and algebra. Many Spanish words beginning with the letters AL come from Arabic—albatros, alcatraz, alcázar, alcoba, alcohol, algodón, almacén, almirante—and the troubadour, the quintessential musician of medieval European chivalry, was someone who knew the Arabic verb *taraba,* to "entertain with music." The troubadour played a lute, the ancestor of the guitar and mandolin, whose name is a contraction of the Arabic name *al-oud.* Many of the foods associated with Spain, whether Valencian rice or Seville oranges, were introduced by the Arabs. Ideas fostered under "Islamic" rule remained important even after Spain became a Christian country and continue to characterize Hispanic culture in both Spain and the New World.

7

City and Country

PERHAPS THE MOST NOTABLE FEATURE OF THE GOLDEN Age of Islam was the extraordinary growth of towns and cities within the vast region between Spain and Central Asia. Many old cities, such as Jerusalem, Alexandria, Damascus, Hamadan, Merv, and Samarkand, continued to flourish under the aegis of Islam, and many new ones, including Fez, Tunis, Cairo, Baghdad, Basra, Isfahan, and Nishapur, were founded by Muslims. Not only were there now more cities, but more people lived in them.

This was no easy feat. Cities and their inhabitants only survive on the excess agricultural production of a hinterland, but most of the region in which Islam traditionally flourished is arid, and much of the land is mountain, steppe, or desert unsuitable for cultivation. A few mighty rivers—the Nile in Egypt, the Tigris and Euphrates in Iraq, the Oxus (Amu Darya) and Jaxartes (Syr Darya) in Central Asia—bring huge amounts of water from distant snowcapped mountains and tropical forests. For millennia these rivers had been harnessed to increase the amount of cultivated land and support larger populations and governments, and this pat-

tern continued in Islamic times. In Egypt, the annual flood of
the Nile caused by tropical rains to the south was measured in
a building in Cairo called the Nilometer. It allowed farmers to
know when to break the dikes and let the water flow into
canals and flood the fields. In Mesopotamia and Transoxiana,
governments constructed huge networks of canals to channel
the water to outlying fields as well as drains to prevent the ac-
cumulation of salts in irrigated fields.

The great rivers of the Near East are generally slow moving
as they cross broad expanses of relatively flat terrain. Where
possible, waterwheels and watermills were built along rivers
to raise water for irrigation, grind grain for flour, and crush
materials for various industrial processes. The great *norias* on
the Orontes River at Hama in Syria are wooden water-raising
machines over sixty feet high. The hydrography of the Near
East differed markedly from the situation in Europe, with its
swiftly moving rivers and streams. In the later Middle Ages engineers there were able to harness this water power for industrial development, thereby helping to fuel the rebirth of the
European economy.

The vast arid region of the traditional Islamic lands shared a
common climate, with relatively short wet winters and long hot
summers. Water was not always available when and where it
was needed, so people developed ingenious ways of storing
and transporting this precious resource. In some places drinking water was collected in cisterns where it was saved for the
dry season. In ninth-century Tunisia the Aghlabid rulers built
huge cisterns outside Kairouan to store water for the city. As in
Roman times, above-ground aqueducts carried water to these
holding tanks. Elsewhere, water for drinking and irrigation was
supplied by an underground aqueduct, called a *kahriz* or *qanat*
in Iran and a *khattara* or *foggara* in Morocco and Algeria. An almost horizontal underground conduit—often many miles

long—brings water from a waterbearing stratum below ground (known as an aquifer) to the place where it is needed on the surface. These conduits are built by laboriously digging a series of parallel well shafts and connecting them at the bottom by a tunnel, which is sometimes lined with tiles or bricks to keep it from collapsing. Such systems have been known in the region since the second millennium B.C.E. and are still used today.

The construction and maintenance of *qanats*, like other major irrigation projects, requires not only great skill but also large outlays of capital. With regular maintenance, *qanats* and canals will last for centuries. If not maintained, however, they can silt up or collapse and prevent water from reaching the fields. These systems are also vulnerable to attack, either directly or indirectly. When the Mongols invaded Iran, many peasants fled from the land, and the character of Mongol rule did not encourage them to return quickly. Without the skilled labor to maintain the *qanats*, the agricultural land they had watered reverted to desert. The economy of a village or even an entire region supplied by *qanats* could therefore be destroyed easily.

Because of the widespread scarcity of water in the lands of the Near East, only a few regions, such as the Nile Valley, Mesopotamia, or the Farghana Valley in Transoxiana, could support large populations in great cities such as Cairo, Baghdad, and Samarkand. Baghdad may have had as many as 840,000 inhabitants in its Abbasid heyday, while Cairo probably had somewhere between 300,000 and 450,000 at its maximum in the fourteenth century. Most other Islamic cities were smaller—perhaps 10,000–20,000 inhabitants—but there were many of them. The biggest European cities were significantly smaller than the metropolises of the Islamic world: in the fourteenth century before the Black Death, it is estimated that Paris had only 210,000 people, Venice 180,000, and London 40,000.

Because it was difficult to transport food over long distances, most settlements in the Islamic lands were surrounded by fields where people grew the crops needed to support urban life. In general, settlements were scattered amidst vast empty expanses inhabited by nomads who raised sheep, goats, and camels, which provided meat to the cities and transportation for the settled population, as well as the wool to make cloth and furnishings. After the harvest, animals grazing on the stubble also provided fertilizer for the fields. The relationship was always symbiotic, as settled populations made goods and provided markets for the nomads.

Wheat, which had been domesticated during the seventh millennium B.C.E., remained the main food crop in the Islamic Near East, where virtually everyone ate wheat bread, usually in the form of flat bread baked in an oven. Whereas the Greeks and Romans had grown emmer, or soft summer wheat, the Arabs introduced the cultivation of hard durum wheat to the Mediterranean basin. The high gluten content of durum wheat meant not only that it could be stored for a longer period against famine but also that it could be made into different foods, such as pasta and couscous, which could also be stored. In medieval Europe, by contrast, even the upper classes ate bread made from barley or rye, both grains with little gluten.

Yet one of the most striking phenomena in the medieval Muslim world was the spread of crops from one region to another. The most important were rice and sugarcane, which were native to India and carried by Muslims across Iran to the Mediterranean region. Where rice was grown, as in northern Iran or lower Iraq, it became a common item in the diet of the poor, but elsewhere it remained a luxury. By the tenth century the Arabs had introduced the cultivation of rice and saffron to Sicily and Spain. (Without them there would be no *paella*.) Sugar (our word comes from the Sanskrit via the Persian *shakar* and the Arabic *sukkar*) was always expensive because the cane had to be crushed and the juice extracted and then boiled down into syrup and crystallized. The refining of sugar-cane was an important state monopoly in Egypt under the Mamluks: one author mentions that there were fifty-eight sugar factories in Cairo alone. The wealthy used it in their food, but the poor could afford to use it only as medicine. Like Europeans, they normally used honey or fruits for sweetening.

The Arabs also introduced such fruits as oranges (from the Persian *naranj*), lemons, apricots, mulberries, bananas, and watermelons and such vegetables as eggplants and artichokes. Oil was produced from olives in the Mediterranean region and from various seeds in Iran where olives were not grown. Food was preserved by pickling and salting, fresh milk was preserved as yogurt and cheese. Luxuries were imported from afar: dried and salted fish, honey, and hazelnuts came from Russia and other Slavic countries. Melons from Transoxiana were brought to Baghdad packed inside lead boxes in ice. Spices such as pepper, ginger, cinnamon, cloves, cardamon, mace, betel, musk, and nutmeg were imported from China, the Sunda islands of Indonesia, India, and East Africa.

Beverages varied widely. *Sharbat* (from which our "sherbet" derives) was a popular drink of iced fruit juice and water. Even in the deserts of southern Iran, ice was made when the night-time temperatures fell below freezing and then stored in heavily insulated ice-houses. Coffee (from the Arabic *kahwa*, originally meaning "wine") comes from the berries of a shrub native to Ethiopia. By the fourteenth century it was cultivated in Yemen. Coffee drinking then spread throughout much of the region, at first probably through Sufis, who appreciated the "intoxicating" qualities of this beverage. Tea, which is now enjoyed from India to Morocco, was unknown until it was introduced, largely by Europeans in relatively recent times.

Wine, although prohibited by the Koran, was widely made by Christians and Jews, and many people who considered themselves observant Muslims, especially the rich, drank it regularly. One of the rooms in the Abbasids' palace at Samarra was littered with wine jars broken after nights of revelry of the kind practiced by their Umayyad predecessors. Painted labels even specify the vintage. The Spanish traveler Clavijo also reported on the prodigious quantities of wine that the Mongol conqueror Timur and his court consumed in the early fifteenth century, and Timur's grandson Baysunghur, like many Mongols, was reported to have died of cirrhosis of the liver. The delights of wine was one of the standard images in classical Arabic poetry, and Sufis often celebrated the joys of intoxication in their poetry (although one can never be sure whether the intoxicating wine is an actual liquid or the love of God).

Medieval Muslim city dwellers often did not cook at home, and houses, especially the crowded apartments of city dwellers, did not have large kitchens. European visitors to medieval Cairo remarked on the thousands of cookshops along the streets, for they said that the "Saracens" scarcely did any cooking at home. The rich and powerful, however, had huge kitchens staffed by famous cooks who prepared elaborate meals of many courses.

A cookbook written in 1226 by Muhammad ibn al-Hasan al-Katib al-Baghdadi gives some idea of the kinds of food available in medieval Baghdad. Here is his recipe for apricot stew (*mishmishiyya*), a recipe remarkably like a stew made in present-day Iran known as *khoresh-e zardalu*:

> Cut fat meat into small pieces, put it into a saucepan with a little salt, and cover with water. Boil, and remove the scum. Cut up onions, wash, and throw in on top of the meat. Season with ground coriander, cumin, mastic, cinnamon, pepper and

ginger. Take dry apricots, soak in hot water, then wash and put in a separate saucepan and boil lightly. Take out, wipe in the hands and strain through a sieve. Take the puree and add it to the saucepan to form a broth. Take sweet almonds, grind fine, moisten with a little apricot juice, and throw in to thicken. Some cooks add a trifle of saffron to color the stew. Spray the saucepan with a little rosewater, wipe its sides with a clean rag, and leave it to settle over the fire.

The growth of agriculture in early Islamic times allowed commerce and urban centers to flourish in the Golden Age. Muhammad and the religion of Islam had emerged in urban environments, first at the shrine and trading city of Mecca and then in the oasis town of Medina. Islam enjoins Muslims to gather every Friday for communal worship. This practice had evolved in Medina, where Jews had gathered on Friday for the weekly market before the Saturday Sabbath. Unlike Jews and Christians, who celebrate a weekly Sabbath, or day of rest, Muslims deem it necessary only to stop work during the time of communal prayer, not for the entire day. A shopkeeper might only put a stick or a cloth across the entrance to his shop to signal that it was closed while he went to the mosque for prayer. Only in modern times has the Thursday–Friday "weekend" emerged in some Muslim countries such as Iran and Kuwait as an equivalent to the Saturday–Sunday weekend celebrated in the West.

The congregational mosque, located in the center of the city, was often set amidst a large market, called a *suq* in Arabic and a *bazar* in Persian (whence our word "bazaar"). The markets were made up of small shops, often only the size of a small room or large closet, set next to each other along a street. The network of streets constituting the market was often covered to provide shade from the sun and had gates or doors that allowed the entire street to be locked after the market had closed for the night. Similar types of goods were normally sold in adjacent shops along one street, so that shoppers could find goods of one kind—shoes, textiles, hardware—in one area of the market. Shops selling the most precious commodities, such as spices, gold, silk, and books, were usually clustered in the most prestigious part of the market, normally in the vicinity of the congregational mosque in the center of the town. Often even the space along the outer walls of a mosque was rented out as shops, and the rents in turn helped pay for the mosque's upkeep. Modern urban developers have often torn down the shops and structures along a mosque's exterior, giving such buildings as the great mosques of Damascus and Kairouan a free-standing monumental aspect they would never have had in the Middle Ages.

Small shops selling daily necessities, bakeries, and bath houses were normally found throughout the city. Shops selling bulky agricultural products, such as grain, vegetables, and fibers, were usually located near city gates for easy access. Manufacturing processes that polluted the water and the air, such as dyeing fibers for textiles, tanning hides to make leather, and firing pottery in smoky kilns, were placed on the downstream and downwind sides of a town. In Fez, the tanneries and dye houses were located at the bottom of the city, so that their waste water flowed directly into the fields beyond the city's walls and did not contaminate the city's drinking water.

The driving force of the medieval Islamic economy was the textile industry. It was based on the production and trade of different types and qualities of cloth—ranging from canvas to gauze—out of four major fibers—wool, linen, cotton, and silk—which were raised or grown by farmers and nomads. Dyes to color the cloth, which were usually extracted from plants, were also traded widely, as were many other substances used in textile production. Chemicals known as mordants were needed to make dyes colorfast. Alkali (from the Arabic word *al-kali,* "ashes"), for example, helped fix the color of saffron (from the Arabic *zafaran*), a bright and expensive yellow dye made from the stamens of autumn crocuses. Other products connected with the textile trade included bleaches, niter and quicklime for degreasing wool, and starches for finishing and glazing the fabric. While some textiles, such as felts and carpets, were prepared by nomad tribeswomen in their camps, most others, ranging from the finest brocaded silks to the coarsest canvases for sails, were woven by men in urban workshops, and cities became known for the particular type of textiles they produced. The textile industry was comparable in importance to the automobile industry in modern times. The preeminence of the Islamic textile industry and the importance of its products in the West is evident in the many European words for fine textiles derived from Arabic and Persian place names and terms. The word *damask* derives from the name of the city of Damascus, *muslin* from the city of Mosul, and *organdy* from the city of Urgench in Central Asia. *Mohair* comes from the Arabic word *mukhayyir* (meaning choice, select), and *taffeta* from *taftan,* the Persian verb "to spin."

Among the many other industries practiced in and around cities and towns were metalworking, glassblowing, and pottery. These industries not only supplied utilitarian pots, pans, and dishes for local townspeople but also produced works of great craft and skill, which were prized possessions and traded across vast distances. As with textiles, particular towns often became known for their craft products. The city of Mosul, for example, was renowned for fancy bronze vessels inlaid with gold and silver, and several cities in Syria were famous for their fine blown glass. The rough-and-tumble Crusaders were knocked off their feet by the luxuries they found for sale in Near

Eastern bazaars. Hugh of Lusignan, King of Cyprus and Jerusalem in the early fourteenth century, ordered a magnificent bronze washbasin made especially for his own use. Many examples of "Islamic" metalwork were decorated with Christian scenes—such as Christ's Nativity and saints—to appeal to Frankish tourists.

Goods of all kinds were shipped from city to city. Ports like Basra, Alexandria, Tunis, and Seville flourished on the profits from international trade. Elsewhere, inland cities were linked by caravans across the deserts, and one of the distinctive features of medieval Islamic times is the phenomenal growth of caravan cities, such as Kairouan in North Africa and Merv in Central Asia. Already before the rise of Islam, wheeled vehicles, such as carts and chariots, had been deemed impractical in much of the region. They were abandoned in favor of beasts of burden, particularly camels which could cross long stretches of arid desert. City streets therefore had only to be wide enough to let two fully laden animals pass side by side. There was no need for wide avenues and plazas where wagons could pass and turn around. Hence the medieval Islamic city developed a distinctive character with narrow winding lanes and culs-de-sac. In a hot climate, these narrow streets also helped to keep houses cool.

A typical caravan could travel about twenty-five miles a day. To encourage trade and protect merchants, rulers often built caravansaries, the medieval equivalent of motels for commercial travelers, spaced along the major routes a day's journey apart. The typical caravansary was located near a permanent source of water—well, cistern, or *qanat*—and consisted of a walled building with a single entrance large enough to admit laden animals. The building could be locked at night. Inside, the courtyard was surrounded by rooms on two floors. The first had stables for the animals and storerooms for goods. Upstairs were bedrooms for merchants and caravaneers. The building might also have a small mosque near the entrance or in the courtyard.

Once in town, merchants would unload their goods at an urban caravansary, which was known variously as a *khan, wakala,* or *funduq.* Usually located in the heart of the market area, the urban caravansary not only served the weary traveler to store his goods but also functioned as a wholesale market where local merchants could buy large quantities of imported goods for resale. European merchants often resided permanently in *funduqs*, which not only offered protection for them and their wares but also served as a sort of proto-consulate. As early as 1157, the Pisans had a *funduq* in Tunis, and in 1236 the merchants of Marseilles established one in Ceuta on the Moroccan coast. The contacts went beyond the commercial: the Pisan merchant Leonardo Fibonacci, who had lived in the Pisan *funduq* in Tunis, returned to Italy where in 1202 he wrote his treatise on Arabic numerals.

Urban caravansaries were often adjacent to the public bath, known in Arabic as a *hammam.* Like the baths of Roman antiquity, the typical *hammam* had several connected rooms heated by fires under the floor. There was a cold room for undressing and dressing, a warm room for washing and relaxing, and a steamy hot room for sweating and washing. Unlike Roman baths, *hammams* rarely had plunge pools, for this was seen as a waste of water. Steam baths were very practical, as they made the most of this precious resource. They also served a public health function, as travelers were encouraged to wash their bodies—and their clothes—upon entering a town, thereby reducing the transmission of diseases and pests. Baths also served an economic function, since their revenues—like those of the caravansary next door—were often used to support the nearby mosque or theological school. To mark his conversion to Islam in 1296, the Mongol ruler Ghazan ordered a mosque and bath constructed in every town in his realm.

The central role of merchants in medieval Islamic society is documented by an unusual treasure trove now known as the Geniza documents. This cache of three hundred thousand documents was found at the end of the nineteenth century in the Geniza, or storeroom, uncovered when the Palestinian Synagogue in Old Cairo fell into disrepair. Among the documents put there for safekeeping centuries earlier were letters, court records, deeds, orders of payment, and trousseau lists. Dating between the tenth and the fifteenth centuries, most of the documents were written in Judeo-Arabic, the vernacular Arabic spoken by most people in medieval Cairo but written by the Jewish community in Hebrew script. Because Jews—like Muslims—thought that any piece of writing containing the name of God was sacred, they saved these old scraps of paper for honorable burial. In the case of the Geniza documents, however, the papers seem to have been forgotten and walled up when the synagogue was remodeled in the Middle Ages. Although produced by the Jewish community, the Geniza documents have provided unparalleled evidence for the bustling activities of merchants involved in trade between the Atlantic coast of Europe and India.

Judging from the Geniza material, the economy of the period was largely a paper economy, for both wholesale and retail commerce was often conducted on credit. Orders of payment, the equivalent of modern checks (indeed, the Persian word *sakk* is the origin of our word "check"), were drawn in amounts upwards from one dinar. They were written on relatively small pieces of paper cut from larger sheets, since paper was still expensive. Letters of credit drawn upon well-known merchants or bankers enabled traders traveling far from their homes to avoid transporting large sums and quantities of gold coin. In the western Sudan, the tenth-century geographer Ibn Hawqal saw a certified check for 42,000 dinars drawn by a man from Sijilmasa, the great trading city in southern Morocco. Such commercial paper was used not only by merchants: an Egyptian scholar who traveled to Spain brought along 5,000 dirhems (a silver alloy coin nominally worth 1/40 dinar) in cash for expenses as well as a letter of credit to local bankers. The story is also told of a ninth-century poet who received a generous check from an admirer. When he tried to cash it, however, the banker refused, which led the poet to compose a satirical verse to the effect that he would gladly pay someone a million dinars on the same plan.

THE WEALTH ON WHICH MEDIEVAL ISLAMIC CIVILIZATION RESTED WAS produced by economic activities like agriculture, manufacturing, and trade, which not only allowed the population to grow and flourish, but also supported cultural and intellectual activities on an unparalleled scale. Good rulers, such as the early Abbasid caliphs, invested heavily in infrastructure by building canals and roads, and their successors reaped the benefits. Bad rulers, such as the worst of the Mamluk sultans of Egypt, plundered the country's resources and watched idly while the economy stagnated and declined.

Nowhere was this sophisticated urban life more evident than the city of Cairo. Whereas the legendary city of Baghdad, the capital of the caliphate, represents the ideal city of the Islamic middle ages, Cairo exemplifies the practical reality. In contrast to Baghdad, about which we know relatively little, Cairo is one of the best-documented cities of medieval times. In addition to the Geniza documents, there are numerous histories and topographies of the city. Furthermore, Cairo was never destroyed the way Baghdad was, and hundreds of buildings still survive from the medieval period. Cairo traces its origins in the Islamic period to al-Fustat, the garrison that the first Muslim conquerors established in 641 to administer the country and provide a base for further conquests in North Africa. The settlement grew quickly as it attracted a large population of indigenous Coptic (Egyptian Christian) artisans, merchants, and administrators, who worked alongside their Muslim brethren.

The city expanded in the eighth century under the Abbasids, who established a new army quarter, and again in the ninth century under the semi-independent dynasty of the Tulunids, who built the beautiful Mosque of Ibn Tulun (879). But it was under the Fatimids, the Shiite dynasty from North Africa, that Cairo reached its apogee. The Fatimids conquered Egypt in 969 and established, like their predecessors, a new garrison settlement as a base for the further conquest of Syria and Arabia. Named al-Qahira, "the Victorious," the garrison soon housed the caliph's palaces as well as all the attributes of a major metropolis. Enclosed within massive mudbrick walls about two and a half miles long and protected by a moat and a canal, the city was bisected by a broad avenue running roughly north-south between the caliph's two palaces. In the middle of the city, between the palaces, the street—still visible today as the Sharia Muizz li-Din Allah—opened out into a large processional square. Great gates, three of which still exist, gave access to the interior of the city, which, like Baghdad, contained not only the caliph's palaces but also administrative offices and the congregational mosque. This mosque, known as al-Azhar, "the Radiant," was founded in 970 and became a major center of Shiite learning. After the fall of the Fatimids in 1171, the mosque retained its position as the foremost intellectual center of Arab Islam. Many consider it to be the oldest university in the world.

The Persian traveler—and Ismaili spy—Nasir-e Khusraw, who visited Cairo in the middle of the eleventh century, left an eyewitness account of urban life there. Although written almost a millennium ago, it seems remarkably modern:

I estimated that there were no less than twenty thousand shops in Cairo, all of which belonged to the sultan. Many shops are rented for as much as ten dinars a month, and none for less than two. There is no end of caravansaries, bath-houses, and other public buildings—all property of the sultan, for no one owns any property except houses and what he himself builds. I heard that in Cairo and Old Cairo there are eight thousand buildings belonging to the sultan that are leased out, with the rent collected monthly. These are leased and rented to people on tenancy-at-will and no sort of coercion is employed. . . .

In the midst of the houses of New Cairo are gardens and orchards watered by wells. In the sultan's harem are the most beautiful gardens imaginable. Waterwheels have been constructed to irrigate these gardens. There are trees planted and pleasure-parks built even on the roofs. . . . These houses are so magnificent and fine that you would think they were made of jewels, not of plaster, tile and stone! All the houses of Cairo are built separate one from another, so that no one's trees or outbuildings are against anyone else's walls. Thus, whenever anyone needs to, he can open the walls of his house and add on, since it causes no detriment to anyone else.

In the eleventh century, the Crusaders, emboldened by their successes in Palestine and Syria, attempted to take Egypt as well, but Saladin refortified Cairo's walls and built the huge citadel that still dominates the city's skyline. After the fall of the Fatimids, the new rulers moved their palace to the citadel, and the land occupied by the old palaces was taken over by the sultans and their cronies, who used the land to build their charitable and educational foundations.

8

The Flowering of Intellectual Life

THE PREEMINENT INTELLECTUAL ACTIVITY IN THE Islamic lands was religious science or theology,
which focused on jurisprudence *(fiqh)* and is known
as *ilm al-kalam,* "the science of the Word." Students—mainly but not exclusively boys—began
learning the Koran as children in an elementary
school, where they also studied such subjects as the
Muslim creed. Pupils entered elementary school between the ages of five and ten and usually stayed
for two to five years. Only a few pupils went on to
secondary education, which expanded from the
Koran to include study of the Traditions of the
Prophet *(hadith)* and jurisprudence.

Learning at virtually all levels was aural, as the students listened to the teacher and then committed
what he had said to memory. Some people memorized the entire Koran, and others also memorized
Traditions of the Prophet and legal decisions. Most
authors memorized the books they had written and
dictated them to their students who made copies and
then memorized the books on their own. The great
theologian al-Ghazali (d. 1111), for example, is re-

ported to have been robbed of his books while traveling. He cried out to the robber to take everything but leave him his precious books. The robber retorted, "How can you claim to *know* these books when by taking them, I can deprive you of their contents?" Al-Ghazali took the robber's words as a warning from God and spent the next three years memorizing his notes.

Since paper was precious, students learned to write with a reed pen and ink on a wooden tablet which could easily be washed (a method still used today in many places in the developing world). In general, more people knew how to read than to write, and, although hard evidence is difficult to gather, it seems likely that the general level of literacy was greater in the medieval Islamic lands than in Byzantium or western Europe. Writing was found everywhere in this culture of the word—on buildings, swords, textiles, works of art, and even objects of everyday life, such as lamps and dishes. The words inscribed range from quotations from the Koran on mosques to poetry on fancy ceramics or simple good wishes on coarse pottery. Even if some people could not *read* the words, they recognized that they were words and were often able to infer the message from the context and style.[4]

IN EARLY ISLAMIC TIMES ALL SCHOOLING TOOK PLACE IN THE MOSQUE, where teachers of particular subjects would lecture to gather-

---

4. For example, a group of earthenware bowls and plates made in the tenth century in northeastern Iran and Transoxiana, when the Samanid dynasty controlled the region, are largely decorated with Arabic proverbs written in elegant and elaborate scripts. On one, the text reads, "Blessing to its owner. It is said that he who is content with his own opinion runs into danger." Others read, "Planning before work protects you from regret; patience is the key to comfort," and "Knowledge is an ornament for youth and intelligence is a crown of gold." Apparently there was a clientele in tenth-century Iran and Central Asia who knew the Arabic language well enough to appreciate having their dinnerware decorated with moralizing aphorisms in Arabic.

ings of interested pupils who might come from far and wide to hear a particular lecturer. As the teacher would often sit on the floor of the mosque leaning against a column with his pupils before him in a circle, these groups came to be known as *halqa*s, or "circles," and a student was said to belong to a particular "circle." Students far from home would find their own lodgings nearby. By the eleventh century, however, separate institutions of higher education were established in the major cities, often, but not necessarily, built near the city's major congregational mosque. This type of institution, known as a *madrasa* (literally, "a place of study"), provided space for teaching and prayer, as well as for lodging students and faculty, and was supported by a charitable endowment. Each theological college normally specialized in one of the four main schools of Sunni law, usually the one followed by the founder, whose tomb might be incorporated in the complex. Considered a major weapon in the Sunni arsenal against Shiism, madrasas were often sponsored by the state and maintained by charitable endowments. Nizam al-Mulk (1018–92), for example, the powerful vizier to the Seljuq sultan Malikshah, founded madrasas known as *nizamiyya*s in all the major cities of the Seljuq realm.

One of the grandest madrasas was the Mustansiriyya in Baghdad, founded by the caliph al-Mustansir in 1233 for teaching the four orthodox schools of law. The chronicler Ibn al-Fuwati reported that for its inauguration, on Thursday, April 6, 1234, the caliph watched from a window while

> the deputy vizier came to the college with all the governors, chamberlains, qadis, teachers, religious notables, controllers of the household, Sufis, preachers, Koran readers, poets, and foreign merchants. Each of the four orthodox schools then chose sixty-two representatives, Muhi al-Din ibn Fadlan and

Rashid al-Din al-Faraghani were chosen as professors for the Shafiis and the Hanafis respectively, and two assistant professors were chosen for the Hanbalis and Malikis. Each of the professors was presented with a black gown and a blue mantle, as well as a riding mule with complete equipment ... while each of the assistant professors was presented with a heavy tunic and a red turban. Presents were also given to four Koran reciters from each of the four schools, and to the foremen, laborers, courtiers, and library assistants. Then a banquet was prepared in the courtyard of the College, and the tables loaded with all kinds of food and drink. After the company had feasted, further presents were distributed among the teachers, controllers of the household, Koran readers, poets, and foreign merchants, and poems were recited in honor of the occasion. Next, accommodation in the building was allotted to the four schools ... and the chambers and other lodging apartments were also allotted to their occupants. Sufficient allowance for their upkeep was made in accordance with the provisions of the founder.

The course of study in the madrasa was never fixed, but it always took place in Arabic. Students were expected to study not only the Koran and the Traditions, but also the Koranic sciences of exegesis and variant readings, the biographies of transmitters (so as to check the accuracy and authenticity of the Traditions they transmitted), the principles of religion and religious law, the laws of the school to which one belonged, the divergences of the law within one's own school and between schools, and dialectic or logical argumentation. The study of these "Islamic sciences" could be complemented by independent study outside the madrasa of philosophical and natural sciences, which might include medicine, mathematics, geometry, and astronomy, and of the literary arts, which included the Arabic language, prosody, grammar, and poetry. The core of legal and theological study was logical disputation, and students were supervised by professors until they had completed the course and were granted a degree, which was literally a license to teach.[5]

The madrasa graduate was well versed in the principles of faith and religious law and could follow several career paths, whether as a teacher, scholar, or lawyer. Religious law was administered by judges known as *qadis,* who heard complaints and offered judgments. At first qadis gave judgments based on the Koran, the *sunna,* or Tradition of the Prophet, and custom, but after religious law was systematized in the Abbasid period, the qadi reached his decision following the doctrines of the school of law to which he belonged. The judge as well as the parties in court might consult a *mufti,* a private scholar of high reputation, for his opinion, which was known as a *fatwa.* Since it was only an opinion, a *fatwa* was not binding on any of the parties as was the qadi's judgment. (The practice of delivering *fatwas* still exists, of course, as in the case of the opinion—not a judgment—Imam Khomeini gave regarding the writer Salman Rushdie.) Furthermore, the qadi's jurisdiction extended only to Muslims, because non-Muslims, such as Jews and Christians, had their own legal institutions, although they sometimes sought the sanction of Muslim courts.

---

5. The system of universities and colleges that began to develop in twelfth-century Europe was parallel in many ways to the madrasa system of the medieval Islamic lands. As the European system developed roughly a century after that in the Muslim world, it is highly probable that the Western universities were not spontaneous creations but modeled on Muslim institutions of learning, particularly since some of the earliest universities developed in regions such as southern Italy and Spain where connections with the Muslim world were strongest. Although the European university played a central role in the revival of learning that led to the Renaissance, their ultimate debt to Muslim institutions of learning remains largely unacknowledged.

The great fourteenth-century philosopher Ibn Khaldun distinguished the fields of religious learning, which are ultimately dependent on God's revelation, from *falsafa,* a term derived from the Greek word *philosophia,* or "love of wisdom." *Falsafa* applied to those fields of learning that are based on observation and deduction, including logic, arithmetic, geometry, astronomy, music, physics, medicine, agriculture, and metaphysics. These subjects were not taught in madrasas, which were exclusively schools of law. Whereas the religious sciences were grounded in knowledge of the Koran, the study of "philosophy" also depended on the knowledge of learning from cultures before and beyond the boundaries of Islam, including classical Greece and Rome, Sasanian Iran, Byzantium, and Hindu India. Medieval Islamic philosophers mined these sources in their work.

The rulers of the Islamic empire needed scientists and mathematicians who knew such subjects as geometry, surveying, algebra, and alchemy to survey the land and keep records of the taxes they collected and ensure that inheritances were divided fairly and equitably according to Koranic laws. Rulers were also responsible for public hygiene in the burgeoning cities of their empire and for the use of fair weights and good coins in the bustling marketplaces. Engineers needed knowledge of science to dig canals and *qanat*s to irrigate the fields and to build bridges and roads to connect the cities. Hence scientists and bureaucrats sought whatever applicable knowledge they could find in earlier Greek, Indian, and Persian science. They translated these texts into Arabic so that they could be used more easily.

The systematic translation and study of works from outside the Islamic tradition began at the end of the eighth century in the time of Harun al-Rashid and his son al-Mamun. The first translators were Assyrian Christian scholars who worked from

Syriac translations of Greek originals. Eventually the translators also translated other great works of Greek science, including Galen's book on medicine, Ptolemy's books on geography
and astronomy, and Euclid's work on geometry. By the end of
the ninth century, Abbasid mathematicians had access to the
works of Archimedes, Apollonius of Perga, and Ptolemy—all
translated from the Greek, as well as the Great Sindhind astronomical work translated from Sanskrit and the works of Iranian mathematicians translated from Middle Persian.

Perhaps the greatest polymath in al-Mamun's intellectual
circle was the mathematician and geographer Muhammad
ibn Musa al-Khwarizmi (ca. 800–ca. 847). Al-Khwarizmi, a
native of the Khwarizm region of Central Asia south of the
Aral Sea, had been drawn as a youth to Baghdad by the
caliph's House of Knowledge. There, he produced several
treatises of earth-shattering importance on mathematics and
geography. Although none of al-Khwarizmi's mathematical
works survive in the Arabic in which he wrote them, his book
On Calculation with Hindu Numerals, written about 825, was
principally responsible for the diffusion of the Indian system
of numeration in the Islamic lands and—in a Latin translation—in the West.

At first, the Arabs, like the Hebrews, Greeks, and Romans
before them, had used different letters of the alphabet to represent numbers (e.g., *alif* =1, *ba*=2), but the Indians—perhaps
as early as the fifth century—had developed an ingenious and
eminently simple system of representing any quantity by using
just nine symbols in decimal place value (there was originally
no zero). A Syrian bishop who lived just after the coming of
Islam was the first person in the Western world to mention this
system, and it seems to have been known in Baghdad by the
late eighth century, so it was probably brought to the Islamic
lands by merchants who traded with India.

The new system was far superior to the old ones, for it allowed people to multiply and divide easily, but it was not quickly accepted, primarily because people were used to calculating the old way—using a finger on a dustboard to record mental calculations and then writing down the answers—and were reluctant to change. Al-Khwarizmi and his tenth-century followers, such as the mathematicians al-Uqlidisi, Abu'l-Wafa al-Buzajani, and Kushyar ibn Labban, developed new ways of calculating with the "Hindu" numerals which were adapted to the use of pen on paper. Using these methods, a person could check his work step by step. These new methods were quickly disseminated throughout the Muslim world, and eventually they triumphed.

The new system of calculation seems to have reached Muslim Spain by the end of the tenth century. By the twelfth century, al-Khwarizmi's book had become quite popular, for many Hebrew and Latin translations and adaptations were made, particularly after the Castilians conquered Toledo in 1085 and the Aragonese took Saragossa in 1118. In this way, Christian scholars gained access to works of Islamic science and philosophy which were more sophisticated than their own. Just as Baghdad in the ninth century had been a center for the translation of Greek works into Arabic, so Toledo in the twelfth and thirteenth centuries became a busy center of translation of Arabic works into medieval Latin.

The consequent transfer of knowledge from Islam to Christendom involved a sudden growth in the use of numerals, and it appears that Europeans, who had since Roman times used a type of abacus with moveable dicelike counters known as apices, began to inscribe these counters with the new Hindu-Arabic numerals. As these counters could be moved and rotated, some of the Hindu-Arabic numeral forms inscribed on them—particularly the numerals for 1, 2, 3, 4, 7, and 9 written

a Gallery of Islamic art and Culture

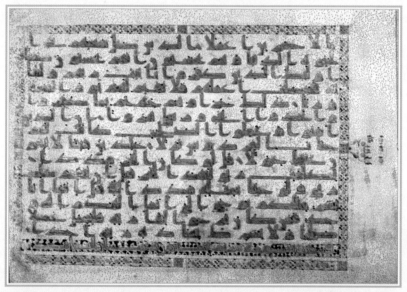

The Koran is the word of God as revealed orally to the Prophet Muhammad in the early seventh century. The text was soon transcribed into books, but none of the earliest copies survives. The reverence Muslims feel for the text is evident in the unusually lavish use of gold which was used to transcribe the entire text in this unique manuscript. [*See p. 39.*] *(Baltimore, MD, Johns Hopkins University Library, Garrett Collection)*

Muslims are required to worship God five times a day—at dawn, noon, mid-afternoon, sunset, and nightfall. Although individuals may pray anywhere, they often join together in communal worship. Worshipers line up in rows facing the Kaaba in Mecca and prostrate themselves while reciting certain phrases. This short ceremony constantly reinforces the sense of community among Muslims. [*See p. 36.*] *(Gardner Films)*

Islam makes few liturgical requirements on believers. They must face Mecca in prayer, and so most mosques have a mihrab, a niche in the wall facing Mecca. Male Muslims must also join together for noon worship on Friday, when a sermon is given from a pulpit normally located to the right of the mihrab. Both mihrab and minbar are visible in the mosque within the great complex built by the Mamluk sultan Hasan (d. 1362) in Cairo. [*See pp. 36–37.*] *(Gardner Films)*

Muslims are required to perform ritual ablution before prayer, and most mosques therefore provide pools or fountains in which people can wash their faces, hands and arms, head, and feet, as here in the Qarawiyyin Mosque in Fez, Morocco. *(Blair & Bloom)*

All Muslims are enjoined to make the pilgrimage to Mecca once in their lifetimes, if they are able. Today pilgrims arrive by jumbo jet, but in the Middle Ages they traveled by caravan, and the round-trip journey often took several months or even years. In this image from a thirteenth-century manuscript, the pilgrimage caravan departs with great fanfare. One of the camels carries a richly-decorated palanquin, presumably carrying a noble woman. [*See p. 38.*] *(Paris, Bibliothèque nationale, MS Arabe. 5847 fol. 94v/Bridgeman Art Library)*

Islam, which arose over fourteen centuries ago, continues to play a vibrant role in modern life. This busy street, once the center of medieval Cairo, continues its role as a commercial and religious center of Egyptian life. *(Gardner Films)*

Islam evolved in the harsh deserts of Arabia. Since it was impossible to use wheeled vehicles there, the camel became the major means of transport and beast of burden in the traditional heartlands of Islam. As Islam spread to other areas, the desert is no longer the quintessential Islamic landscape. *(Gardner Films)*

Gardens have always been important in the hot and arid lands where Islam flourished. Gardens were often planted inside the courtyards of buildings, thereby inte-

grating inside and outside spaces. The greenery and running water cooled and refreshed, the scents of flowers perfumed the air, and the fruits and vegetables that were produced graced the tables. These gardens also could symbolize the paradise promised to believers. [*See p. 43.*] *(Blair & Bloom)*

The Kaaba in Mecca is the focus of Muslim devotion. A cubic building of stone draped with a black veil, the Kaaba is believed to be God's house erected by Abraham. Muslims direct their daily prayers towards it and circumambulate around it during the rites of the pilgrimage. It now stands in the middle of an immense mosque. [*See p. 38.*] *(Robert Azzi/Woodfin Camp)*

Muhammad received the first revelation on Mount Hira outside Mecca around the year 610. This painting, from a multi-volume manuscript about the life and miracles of the Prophet made for the Ottoman sultan in 1594, evokes the awesome scene with its unworldly gold background and fiery halo around the Prophet. Muslims do not make religious images and have often disapproved of representing the Prophet. Here his face is veiled to underscore his sanctity. [*See p. 29.*] *(Istanbul, Topkapi Palace Museum, H1222, fol. 158b)*

Muhammad was regarded as a peacemaker in Mecca. According to tradition, he is said to have devised the ingenious solution of letting the chiefs of the various clans each hold a corner of his cloak to help place the Black Stone back in the Kaaba's walls. This incident is depicted in a fourteenth-century painting from a manuscript of Rashid al-Din's universal history, where the full figure of the Prophet is shown. [*See pp. 28–29.*] (*Edinburgh, Edinburgh University Library, Ar. Ms. 20*)

According to the first verse of chapter 17 in the Koran, Muhammad made a miraculous night journey from the nearest mosque to the furthest mosque. Later mystics elaborated this brief allusion into the account of the Prophet's ascension to heaven on the human-headed steed Buraq and to the presence of God. Such popular accounts may have inspired Dante's depiction of heaven in the *Divine Comedy*. [*See pp. 58–59.*] *(L.P. Winfrey/Woodfin Camp)*

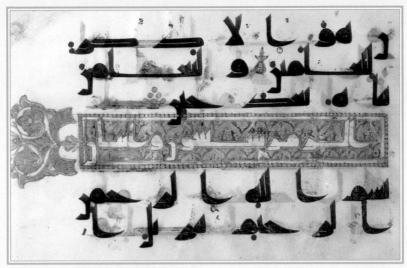

Large-format copies of the Koran were often made for mosques, where they would be read during the month of Ramadan. This page, from a manuscript made in the ninth century or earlier, shows the end of chapter 38 and the beginning of chapter 39, written in an angular script which is particularly difficult to read. As many Muslims knew the text of the Koran by heart, the written word would have served as an aid to memory. [See p. 154.] (Washington, DC, Freer Gallery of Art, Smithsonian Institution, F1930.60r)

The Dome of the Rock in Jerusalem, begun in 692, is the first work of Islamic architecture. It stands on the site of Solomon's Temple and is now believed to mark the spot from which Muhammad made his miraculous journey to heaven. Whatever its original purpose, it was surely meant to symbolize that Islam had come to stay. [See pp. 67–68.] (Blair & Bloom)

Muslims are enjoined to worship communally on Friday at noon, and every city—large or small—has at least one congregational mosque. The Mosque of Damascus, begun in 705, is one of the earliest and finest, although much of its original decoration in gold glass mosaic was lost in a fire at the end of the nineteenth century. [*See pp. 69–70.*] *(Gardner Films)*

Shiites venerate the family of the Prophet Muhammad. The grave sites of many of his descendants have been transformed into major shrines. The most important in Iran is the grave of the eighth imam, Ali Reza (d. 818), who was buried in a small village in northeastern Iran. The sanctuary, or *mashhad,* has become the center of the second-largest city in modern Iran and has given the city its name. His tomb, under a gold-plated dome, is adjacent to a large mosque. [*See p. 54.*] *(Blair & Bloom)*

The Prophet's grandson Husayn, who was martyred at Kerbala in Iraq in 680, is still revered in Iran. The day of his martyrdom, the 10th of Muharram, is commemorated by the festival of *Ashura*. Ashura is marked by public mourning, flagellation, and dramas recalling the terrible event. Husayn's idealized portrait is found all over Iran, as in this mosque at Kashan. [*See p. 52.*] *(Blair & Bloom)*

The Abbasid dynasty ruled from Iraq over an empire which stretched from the Atlantic coast to Central Asia. Their might is symbolized by the enormous congregational mosques they built in their capital cities in the ninth century. The spiral brick tower, or *minaret*, at the Great Mosque of Samarra, stands over 150 feet high and dominates the surrounding Mesopotamian plain. [*See p. 85.*] *(Estelle Whelan)*

Like their overlords, the Abbasids' provincial governors built mosques in their capital cities. The Aghlabid dynasty, which governed much of North Africa in the ninth century, is responsible for building the Great Mosque of Kairouan, now in Tunisia. Many of its elements, such as the marble columns and capitals, were reused from earlier buildings. [*See p. 86.*] (*Gardner Films*)

Water was always a precious resource in the dry lands of the Middle East and North Africa, and rulers had to make provisions to supply water year-round. The Aghlabids built great basins outside the city of Kairouan as part of an extensive system of waterworks. [*See p. 104.*] *(Gardner Films)*

In order to irrigate fields and bring water to cities from rivers, new and ingenious methods were developed in the Islamic lands. The *noria*, an undershot waterwheel, uses the flow of a river to raise water to an aqueduct, from which it is distributed. Norias were especially popular along the Orontes River in Syria, as here at Hama. [*See p. 104.*] *(Gardner Films)*

Ahmad ibn Tulun, the Abbasids' governor in Egypt, declared independence from his overlords and constructed a magnificent city on the banks of the Nile at the end of the ninth century. All that remains of its splendor is his gloriously serene mosque, whose courtyard is an oasis of tranquility in the bustling modern city of Cairo. [*See p. 86.*] *(Gardner Films)*

Books and learning were important aspects of Muslim life in the Middle Ages. Whereas medieval European libraries were lucky to have dozens or hundreds of volumes, some libraries in the Islamic lands had hundreds of thousands of volumes. This representation from a thirteenth-century manuscript shows scholars seated on the floor of a library examining a volume, with many other books stacked on the shelves behind them. [*See pp. 120–21.*] *(Paris, Bibliothèque nationale, MS Arabe 5847)*

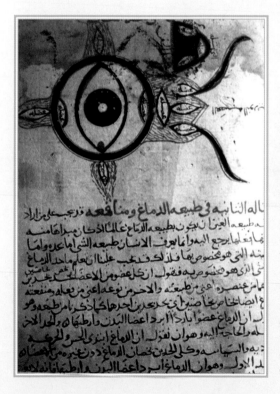

Scientists, mathematicians, and physicians in the Islamic lands built on the foundations laid by their Greek, Persian, and Indian predecessors. One branch of medicine that flourished, particularly in Egypt, was ophthalmology, perhaps because eye diseases were unusually common there. This drawing from a treatise on ophthalmology shows the parts of the eye. [*See p. 131.*] *(R/S Michaud/Woodfin Camp)*

Village and urban life is a cornerstone of Islamic civilization, for the mosque was the center of the community. In this painting from a thirteenth-century manuscript, the artist has shown the domed mosque and its minaret in the upper left corner as the backdrop for a domed bazaar in which various crafts are practiced. In front, several goats drink from a pool. [*See p. 109ff.*] *(Paris, Bibliothèque nationale, MS Arabe 5847, fol. 138/Bridge-man Art Library)*

Tents, or portable cloth structures, were used for millennia by the nomadic pastoralist. They inhabited much of the traditional Islamic lands while they tended herds of sheep, goats, and camels. The black tent made up of long strips of goat hair cloth sewn together is typical of many Arab nomads. [*See p. 24.*] *(Gardner Films)*

Dhows, or lateen-rigged sailing ships, were first used by sailors in the Indian Ocean and adjacent seas. They then spread, with Islam, to the eastern Mediterranean, where they were seen by Europeans at the time of the Crusades and named "Latin" sails. Their particular configuration al-

lowed lateen-rigged ships, unlike European square-rigged vessels, to sail against the wind, and their triangular shape meant that a shorter mast could carry much larger sails. With these advantages, Muslim sailors were able to master the seas. [*See p. 226.*] *(M/E Bernheim/Woodfin Camp)*

The market, whether known as a souk or a bazaar, was the center of commercial life in the medieval Islamic lands. Rows of small shops lined either side of the market street, which was often covered to provide shade from the hot sun. Here, in Marrakesh, Morocco, the street is covered with wooden slats to temper the harsh light and provide ventilation. [*See pp. 109–10.*] *(Blair & Bloom)*

The Crusader castle of Crac des Chevaliers was built in the twelfth and thirteenth centuries on the site of an earlier Kurdish fortress. As the main base of the Knights Hospitallers in the County of Tripoli, it was used to defend their eastern frontier and to serve as the administrative center of their great estates. They made it the finest and most elaborately fortified castle in the Crusader Levant. [*See p. 95.*] *(Gardner Films)*

The city of Córdoba in southern Spain was the most populous city in medieval Europe and a flourishing cultural center under the Umayyad caliphs. The Great Mosque was the focus of the city's religious and intellectual life, and in 976 the caliph al-Hakam II expanded the mosque and built a magnificent dome over the mosque's mihrab, or prayer-niche. Decorated with gold mosaics provided by the Byzantine emperor, the dome symbolizes the wealth and power of the Umayyad realm. [*See pp. 87–89.*] *(Blair & Bloom)*

The city of Isfahan in central Iran became prominent from the ninth century, but its first heyday came in the eleventh century when the Seljuk Turks made it one of their capitals. Under their patronage, the congregational mosque was enlarged to its present plan of a spacious open courtyard surrounded by arcades, with a vaulted open room (known as an *iwan*) in the middle of each side. Although this mosque was later redecorated, its plan became standard for Iranian mosques in later centuries. *(Blair & Bloom)*

The thirteenth-century mystic Jalal al-Din Rumi is the best-known Sufi poet. His works are still best-sellers in modern America. His blue-tiled tomb at Konya in central Turkey is home to an order of mystics whose observances involve slow turning to the plaintive music of a reed flute. This practice has given rise to their popular name, the "Whirling Dervishes." [*See pp. 62–63.*] *(Blair & Bloom)*

The Mongol capture of Baghdad in 1258 signaled the end of the classical age of Islamic civilization. No longer were all the Islamic lands under the rule, albeit nominal, of a single caliph. In the ensuing centuries, regional differences became stronger. This painting, detached from an unknown manuscript, probably shows the Mongol siege of Baghdad, with ballistae in the lower left and right center for bombarding the city with stones. A bridge of boats protected by a gate, defends the city. [*See p. 162.*] *(Berlin, Staatsbibliothek, Diez A. fol. 70, p.7)*

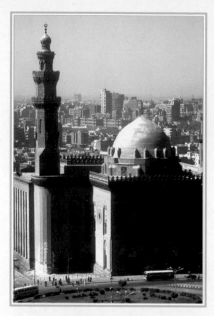

The Mamluk rulers of Egypt and Syria established charitable foundations to provide education and social services to the community. These complexes included the founder's tomb in an attempt to preserve the ruler's memory in uncertain times. The biggest of these was the complex of Sultan Hasan in Cairo, which comprised a congregational mosque and four schools of law, as well as associated service institutions, all set behind the enormous domed tomb intended for the ruler. The young and incompetent Hasan was never buried there after his death in 1361. [*See p. 172.*] (*Blair & Bloom*)

Invaders from the steppes of the east, the Mongols also brought many cultural innovations to the Islamic lands they ruled. Under their patronage the arts of the book flourished, and the *Shahnama*, the national epic of Iran, was illustrated with memorable scenes of Iranian heroes, as this one where the pre-Islamic king Bahram Gur slays a dragon. (*Cambridge, MA, Harvard University Art Museums*)

The Alhambra palace at Granada in southern Spain is the best-preserved and most familiar example of a medieval Islamic palace. The Court of the Lions, which takes its name from the lions supporting the fountain in its center, was a private palace for the ruler. Adjacent to it was a more formal palace for official receptions. [*See pp 178–80.*] *(Gardner Films)*

The Ottoman sultan Mehmed II was only nineteen when he began preparations for the conquest of Constantinople, a city that Muslims had coveted for over eight centuries. A true Renaissance prince, Mehmed was deeply interested in the history of his Muslim and Christian subjects; his court was a center for writers, scholars, and artists, including the Venetian painter Gentile Bellini, who painted this portrait of the sultan late in life. [*See p. 192.*] *(London, National Gallery)*

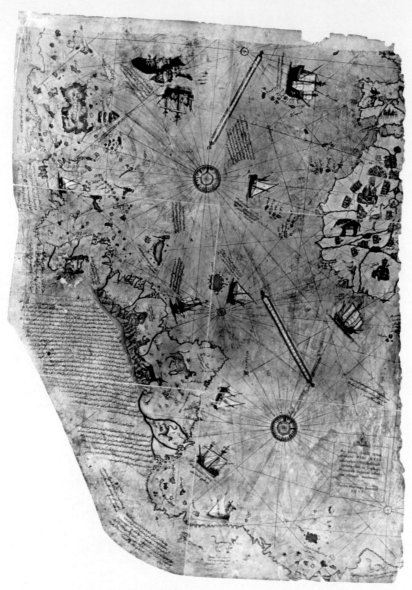

This copy of a parchment map shows the south Atlantic between Spain and West Africa (top right) and South America (bottom left). It is the only surviving fragment of a 1513 world map composed by the Turkish admiral Piri Reis. The Turkish legend inscribed on the South American mainland states that it was based in part on one of Columbus's maps of the "Western Parts," which the Turkish admiral acquired from a Spanish prisoner of war. It shows how quickly knowledge of the coast of the New World was disseminated throughout Europe. *(Washington, DC, Library of Congress, Collection of the Geography and Map Division)*

Suleyman the Magnificent, like other Ottoman sultans, commissioned a great mosque for his capital at Istanbul. Located on one of the seven hills of the city, the Suleymaniye mosque, with its soaring minarets and cascading domes, stands in the center of a great charitable complex which includes schools, hospitals, soup-kitchens, and the tombs of the founder and his wife. [See p. 192.] (Gardner Films)

Suleyman the Magnificent set out to conquer not only the Islamic lands of the Near East but also the Balkans and Italy in an attempt to recreate the ancient empire of the Romans. To symbolize his supremacy over the Pope and the Holy Roman Emperor, Suleyman commissioned Venetian goldsmiths to fashion him a bejewelled gold crown with four tiers to outdo the Pope's triple crown. Long since melted down, the crown is known only through this contemporary European engraving. [See p. 191.] (New York, Metropolitan Museum of Art, The Elisha Whittelsey Collection, 49.97.176)

SVLIMAN·OTOMAN·REX·TVRC· X·

The city of Isfahan enjoyed a second heyday after the Safavid shah Abbas
I transferred the capital there in the late sixteenth century. The centerpiece
of his new capital was a large open plaza, or *maydan*. From the bazaar portal on the north, one faced the new congregational mosque with its soaring
portal and minarets. To the left is the dome of the small mosque of Shaykh
Lutfallah; to the right is the Ali Qapu, the entrance to the royal palace
precinct and a viewing stand from which the ruler could watch the activities in the royal square. [*See pp. 203–06.*] *(Blair & Bloom)*

The Safavid palace precinct at Isfahan contained several pavilions set in
verdant gardens. The Chihil Sutun, or "Forty Column" pavilion, has a huge
reception hall decorated with murals of the Safavid rulers' triumphs (real or
imagined) over their Muslim neighbors. Here, Shah Tahmasp receives the
Mughal prince Humayun, who had been forced to abandon his kingdom in
India and seek refuge at the Safavid court. *(Gardner Films)*

The Mughal emperors of India traced their descent from the great Mongol warlords Genghis Khan and Tamerlane. They ruled over multi-ethnic and multi-confessional populations and were in diplomatic contact with the great contemporary powers of Europe and the Islamic lands. In this painting, the emperor Jahangir is shown presenting a book to the aged Sufi Shaykh Husayn, superintendent of an important shrine at Ajmer, and ignoring the Ottoman sultan and the English king. The painting is thought to symbolize the emperor's choice of a spiritual life over worldly power and allude to the source of Mughal dynastic power in

the Sufi orders. [*See pp. 218–19.*] *(Washington, DC, Freer Gallery of Art, Smithsonian Institution, F1942.15a)*

The Mughal emperor Akbar was eclectic in his beliefs, listening to many competing claims including those of Jesuit missionaries and Sufi saints. After a Sufi sage wisely predicted that the emperor would have three sons, he constructed a new capital at the site of Fatehpur Sikri. The centerpiece of the new city, which Akbar rarely inhabited, was an enormous congregational mosque with a massive portal rising above a great staircase. Inside the mosque's courtyard stood the Sufi's tomb. [*See pp. 214–15.*] *(Blair & Bloom)*

The Mughal rulers of India were the richest rulers of later times. They attempted to claim immortality, like their Mongol forebears, by constructing huge tombs set in lush gardens which were  meant to evoke paradise. The most famous of these tombs is the Taj Mahal at Agra, built by the emperor Shahjahan (d. 1666) for himself and his wife Nurjahan. Its sublime proportions and refined details have made it one of the landmarks of world architecture. [*See p. 215.*] *(Blair & Bloom)*

Learning flourished throughout the Islamic lands in state- or individually-sponsored schools known as madrasas. Probably the precursors of European universities, madrasas were typically large buildings with rooms for living and teaching set around a large open courtyard. The city of Bukhara, located on the ancient Silk Route in what is now Uzbekistan, became a center of learning for the eastern Islamic lands after 1500. Many students who spoke Persian flocked to madrasas like this one erected by the high-ranking military administrator, Nadir Divanbegi Arlat. It was finished in 1620. [*See p. 209.*] *(Blair & Bloom)*

Learning also flourished in madrasas erected at the opposite end of the Islamic lands. The city of Fez was the center of religious scholarship in the Maghrib, or western Islamic lands, but the largest madrasa found there is the Ben Yusuf Madrasa, built in Marrakesh by the Saadian ruler in 1564. [See p. 196.] (Blair & Bloom)

Islam was carried across the Sahara Desert as early as the tenth century by merchants and missionaries in search of gold, ivory, and slaves. Builders adapted local techniques to construct Muslim places of worship. The congregational mosque at Mopti, in Mali, was actually built in 1935 on the model of the much older mosque at nearby Djenne. [See p. 223.] (Betty Press/Woodfin Camp)

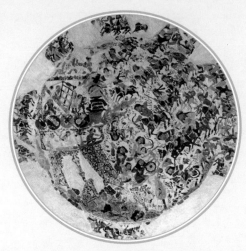

Many of the crafts practiced in the Islamic lands transformed humble materials into splendid works of art. This particularly large and elaborately decorated shallow bowl is painted with a battle scene. It shows a minor Iranian prince and his troops capturing an Assassin stronghold in the mid-thirteenth century. [See p. 112.] (Washington, DC, Freer Gallery of Art, Smithsonian Institution, 43.3)

Exotic brass vessels inlaid with silver and gold were some of the luxuries European Crusaders discovered in the souks of the Islamic Near East. This enormous canteen, in the shape of the ceramic flask traditionally carried by pilgrims to Jerusalem, was made in Syria during the thirteenth century. It is decorated with scenes from the life of Christ and saints and inscribed with good wishes in Arabic to an anonymous owner. It was probably made as a souvenir of the Holy Land for some wealthy crusader. [See p. 112.] (Washington, DC, Freer Gallery of Art, Smithsonian Institution, 41.10)

in Arabic as ١, ٢, ٣, ٤, ٧, and ٩ respectively—were rotated and changed into those "Arabic" numerals used almost universally today in the West. Other "Arabic" numerals, such as 5 and 6, were made by transforming the Roman numerals V and VI as they had been written in the Visigothic script used by Christians in Spain. The numeral 8, which bears no resemblance to the inverted "V" (٨) used by the Arabs, came from an abbreviation of the Latin word *octo* ("eight"), when the last letter is written above the first.

At first Europeans were as reluctant as their Muslim brethren to adopt the new system of numeration, and for more than a century the algorists, who manipulated the new numerals on paper, struggled against the abacists, who preferred traditional calculation with counters. In 1202 the Pisan merchant Leonardo Fibonacci, who had learned about Arabic numerals in Tunis, wrote a treatise entitled *Liber abaci* ("The Book of Abacus [pieces]"). Despite its name, the book rejected the abacus in favor of the Arab method of reckoning, and as a result, the system of Hindu-Arabic numeration caught on quickly in the merchant communes of Central Italy. By the fourteenth century, Italian merchants and bankers had abandoned the abacus and were doing their calculations using pen and paper.

In addition to his treatise on numerals, the Abbasid mathematician al-Khwarizmi also wrote a revolutionary book on mathematics entitled *Kitab al-mukhtasar fi hisab al-jabr wa'l-muqabila* ("The Book of Summary Concerning Calculation by Transposition and Reduction") in which he sought ways of resolving quadratic equations. The examples were given either as geometric demonstrations or as numerical proofs using an entirely new mode of expression, in which letters or words represented numerical values.

Al-Khwarizmi's work was widely known in the Islamic lands and soon translated into medieval Latin. The earliest known translation was made in 1145 by the Englishman Robert of Ketton. His translation of al-Khwarizmi's treatise on algebra, *Liber Algebras et Almucabola,* opened with the words *dixit Algorithmi,* "Algorithmi says." In time, the mathematician's epithet of his Central Asian origin, *al-Khwarizmi,* came in the West to denote first the new process of reckoning with Hindu-Arabic numerals, *algorithmus,* and then the entire step-by-step process of solving mathematical problems, *algorithm.*

Robert of Ketton's translation was followed shortly thereafter by that of the Toledan scholar Gerard of Cremona (c. 1114–1187) entitled *De Jebra et Almucabola.* The Arabic word for "transposition," *al-jabr,* gave the entire process its name in European languages, *algebra,* which is understood today as the generalization of arithmetic in which symbols, usually letters of the alphabet such as A, B, and C, represent numbers. Al-Khwarizmi had used the Arabic word for "thing" *(shay)* to refer to the quantity sought, the unknown. When al-Khwarizmi's work was translated in Spain, the Arabic word *shay* was transcribed as *xay,* since the letter *x* was pronounced as *sh* in Spain. In time this word was abbreviated as x, becoming the universal algebraic symbol for the unknown.

Although al-Khwarizmi's fame in the West was established by his books on Indian numerals and algebra, his geographical and astronomical works were equally—if not more—significant in the medieval Islamic world. No proof exists, but al-Khwarizmi was most likely one of the scholars working at the caliph al-Mamun's House of Knowledge in Baghdad who translated and improved on earlier Greek, Persian, and Indian geographical works, particularly the *Geography* written by the second-century Greek author Ptolemy. The great mathematician was most likely also one of the scholars chosen by the caliph to make a large colored map of the world, showing such features as its "spheres, stars, land, and seas, the populated and unpopulated areas, settlements, and cities." No trace of this map remains, but al-Khwarizmi wrote a book, of which one copy survives, containing tables that locate over two thousand localities by longitude and latitude. These tables corrected many values given by Ptolemy and gave the coordinates of many locations that were unknown to the ancients. Such geographical coordinates were an essential tool in helping Muslims locate themselves on the face of the globe and accurately pray toward Mecca five times each day; they also facilitated international trade.

With the help of maps and tables like these, Muslim scientists were able to determine the circumference of the earth. Al-Khwarizmi stated that a degree on the earth's surface was equivalent to 75 linear miles; therefore, the earth's circumference was 27,000 miles. This figure was remarkably accurate—only 41 meters off (less than 0.04 percent) from the modern reading of 110,959 meters at 36°—when one considers that al-Khwarizmi used a Roman mile of 1,480 meters. When converted to Arabic miles, the ratio of 75 is replaced by 56, which is close to the figure determined by the direct geodetic surveys commissioned by al-Mamun. A medieval account described how this was done:

> The Commander of the Faithful al-Mamun desired to know the size of the earth. He inquired into this and found that Ptolemy mentioned in one of his books that the circumference of the earth is so-and-so many thousands of *stades*. He asked the commentators about the meaning of the word *stade*, and they differed about the meaning. Since he was not told what he wanted, he directed Khalid ibn Abd al-Malik, Ali ibn Isa, the instrument maker, and Ahmad ibn Bukhturi, the surveyor, to gather a group of surveyors and skilled artisans to make the instruments they needed. He transported them all to a place in

the desert near Sinjar (in Syria). Khalid and his party headed north, and Ali and Ahmad headed south. They proceeded until they found that the maximum altitude of the sun at noon increased, and differed from the noon altitude which they had found at the place from which they had separated, by one degree, after subtracting from it the sun's declination along the path of the outward journey. There they put arrows. Then they returned to the arrows, testing the measurement a second time, and so found that one degree of the earth was 56 miles, of which one mile is 4,000 black cubits. This is the cubit adopted by al-Mamun for the measurement of cloth, for surveying fields, and for spacing way-stations along the roads.

Around the year 1000, the great polymath al-Biruni developed a new method for measuring the circumference of the earth, which "did not require walking in deserts," but involved determining the radius of the earth based on the observation of the horizon from a mountain peak. He stationed himself on a peak in the Salt Range, a mountain in the Punjab area of present-day Pakistan, and measured the dip of the horizon. Using trigonometry, he determined that a degree was equal to the figure reported by al-Mamun's surveyors.[6]

In the larger perspective, these empirical experiments indicate that Muslim scientists had learned that the ancient Greeks were not infallible, thereby initiating a new era of scientific inquiry. After reading the ancient texts, Muslim scientists had begun to discover that their own direct observations contradicted ancient wisdom. They began challenging the

---

6. Al-Biruni, however, must have fudged his numbers because the horizon was difficult to see through the haze and dust, and his measurements would have been inaccurate because of refractions. This was neither the first nor the last time, however, that an astronomer published fictitious results.

fundamentals of Greek science on the basis of their own direct observations, looking for alternatives to the old knowledge and attempting to build their science on a systematic and consistent basis according to physical models and mathematical representations.

While Muslim scientists did not wholly abandon the Greek tradition, they reformulated it by introducing a revolutionary new concept of how knowledge ought to progress, a concept that still governs the way science is done today. Better instruments and better methods, they reasoned, would bring about more accurate results. Such geographers as al-Biruni, for example, realized that Ptolemy had used instruments that were far too small to provide the necessary precision of observation his theories demanded.

This new scientific approach spilled over into other fields of inquiry. A scientist constantly checked the facts and theorized about them, questioning the authority that had produced the theories in the first place. Physicians, for example, began to question the inherited medical traditions and to distinguish one disease from another. Ibn al-Haytham (ca. 965–1039), the so-called father of optics, actually explained how human vision took place. He showed by physical analysis down to the last detail how rays travel and light is reflected, that light must be reflected off specific objects before the human eye can perceive something. His treatise, by integrating physical, mathematical, experimental, physiological, and psychological considerations, had an enormous impact on all later writers on optics, both in the Muslim world and through a medieval Latin translation in the West.

Similarly, the great Egyptian physician Ibn al-Nafis (d. 1288) discovered the minor, or pulmonary, circulation of the blood from the right ventricle of the heart through the pulmonary artery to the lungs, and from there through the pulmonary veins to the left ventricle of the heart. This discovery boldly contradicted the accepted ideas of the Greek physician Galen and anticipated the work of the English physician William Harvey by some three and a half centuries. In contrast to Harvey, whose discovery was based on experiment, Ibn al-Nafis derived his theory from abstract reasoning; unfortunately his remarkable theory remained virtually unknown.

IN SHARP CONTRAST TO MODERN PHYSICIANS, SCIENTISTS, AND ACAdemics, whose specialties have become increasingly narrow, the great intellectual figures of medieval Islamic times, such as al-Khwarizmi and al-Biruni, were polymaths, moving easily from practical considerations of mathematics and medicine to abstract speculation about the meaning of existence and the divine. The caliph al-Mamun's House of Knowledge provided a nurturing environment for new directions in the study of philosophy. As at other times in human history, philosophers dealt with such questions as the relative values of faith and works, the roles of free will and predestination, and the nature of God and His seemingly contradictory qualities. Some Muslims believed that the Koran could provide answers to all such questions, while some looked to other sources of knowledge, particularly the great traditions of Greek philosophy and Christian theology. Like other Muslims, these rationalists started from principles stated or implicit in the Koran and deduced logical consequences from them. Their theory of knowledge supported the power of the human intellect, which is known in Arabic as *aql.*

Needless to say, the traditionalists and the rationalists soon came into conflict. Matters came to a head in the middle of the ninth century in the crisis provoked by a group known as the *mutazilis*, literally "those who keep themselves apart," but who described themselves as "the party of unity and justice." The Mutazilites, who worked out their doctrines with much refinement, upheld God's unity and transcendence, but believed that the Koran was not part of God's actual essence. Rather, they deemed it a created message which God had inspired in Muhammad. As a corollary of God's power, the Mutazilites accepted man's moral freedom and responsibility for his actions. They maintained God's justice and goodness, but held man alone responsible for evil. If man were not morally free, they argued, then the merciful and compassionate God would be the cause of evil, something that was patently impossible.

The caliph al-Mamun was said to have been receptive to Mutazilite speculations and tried to impose the views of the Mutazilite rationalists over those of the traditionalists, who took as articles of faith the eternality and the uncreatedness of the Koran. Jurists were forced to swear an oath to the createdness of the Koran, but this "inquisition" foundered, particularly under the strong opposition of the Sunni legal scholar and traditionalist Ahmad ibn Hanbal. By 848 the inquisition had ended, and the authority of the *sunna* of the Prophet and the doctrine of the eternality of the Koran had been firmly reestablished.

The Mutazilite crisis deeply affected the career of the first Muslim philosopher, Abu Yusuf Yaqub al-Kindi (ca. 800–ca. 870). Born at Kufa, he was educated there, at Basra, and at Baghdad, the three centers of learning in medieval Iraq. A companion of the Abbasid caliphs al-Mamun and al-Mutasim, al-Kindi fell from favor during al-Mutawakkil's reign, probably due to the philosopher's Mutazilite leanings, and his personal library was seized. Only a few of his works have survived, but he is said to have written 240 books on philosophy, theology, logic, astronomy, astrology, alchemy, arithmetic, geometry, optics, medicine, pharmacology, and music. He set the stage for a long line of Islamic philosophers who combined their theoretical speculations with practical applications as physicians and scientists. Al-Kindi took Platonic, Aristotelian, and neo-Platonic concepts from Greek philosophy (not from the Koran) and tried to recast them in a perspective consistent with the Islamic view about the creation of the world.

Unlike al-Kindi, who spent all his life in Iraq, most later philosophers traveled from city to city in search of learning and patronage in increasingly unsettled times. For example, Abu Nasr Muhammad al-Farabi (ca. 873–950), who became known in the medieval West as Alfarabius or Avennasar, was born in the city of Farab in Transoxiana, and later studied and taught at Baghdad and Aleppo. His father may have been a Turkish guard in the caliphal entourage, but al-Farabi made his career as a philosopher and musician independent of caliphal patronage, being neither a secretary nor a member of the court. In his philosophical work, al-Farabi gave direction to the philosophy pioneered by al-Kindi. He gained such a high reputation as an Arabic commentator on Aristotle that he became known as the Second Teacher, the first of course being Aristotle himself. Al-Farabi was also a logician and the first to put the study of logic on a firm basis. His *Survey of the Sciences* became known in the West through medieval Latin translations by Gerard of Cremona and John of Seville. In addition, al-Farabi was the foremost scholar of music in the history of Islam. Of the 160 works attributed to him, 8 deal with music. In the most important, the *Grand Book of Music,* he not only formulated musical theories based on Greek concepts but also related them to contemporary performance.

Like the philosophy of al-Farabi, that of Ibn Sina (980–1037), who is known in the West as Avicenna, synthesizes Aristotelian and later Greek theories with his own original views. He tried to harmonize the writings of Aristotle and the Neoplatonists with the unitary teachings of the Koran and Islamic monotheism. In attempting to unite philosophy with the study of nature, he followed the encyclopedic conception of the sciences traditional since ancient Greece. Born in Bukhara, Ibn Sina was extraordinarily precocious and was said to have mastered the Koran and religious sciences at an early age. He was acknowledged as a practicing physician by the age of sixteen. After curing the Samanid ruler of Bukhara of an illness, Ibn Sina was granted access to the extensive Samanid royal library, where he mastered all the known sciences without a teacher. After the Turkish warlord Mahmud of Ghazna conquered Bukhara in 1001, Ibn Sina was forced to leave his hometown. He moved westward across Iran from city to city, serving either as a court physician or a government clerk at Nishapur, Rayy, Qazvin, Hamadan, and Isfahan.

Despite his peripatetic life, Ibn Sina produced an immense corpus of scientific writing, which remained important for centuries. He purportedly wrote some 276 works in Arabic as well as his native Persian, which was just resurfacing as a literary language at this time. Among his works were the *Book of Healing* and the *Canon of Medicine,* perhaps the most famous book of medicine in the East or West. It was translated eighty-seven times, mostly into medieval Latin, but also into Hebrew and other languages. The Latin translation, made between 1150 and 1187 by Gerard of Cremona, formed the basis for the teaching and practice of medicine in Europe from the twelfth century to the sixteenth. It appeared, for example, in the oldest extant syllabus of teaching given to the school of medicine at Montpellier—a bull of Pope Clement V dated 1309—and remained in all subsequent syllabi until 1557. The Arabic text was edited at Rome in 1593, showing that it was still useful well into the Renaissance. Ibn Sina cast a long shadow: on the millennary of his birth in 1954, his works were republished and restudied, and an imposing tomb was built over his grave at Hamadan in Iran.

The work of al-Farabi and Ibn Sina was not devoid of controversy. The writings of both men were condemned by the great philosopher al-Ghazali. After studying at the madrasa founded by Nizam al-Mulk in Nishapur, al-Ghazali became a professor in Baghdad where he attacked many of his predecessors' views as contrary to the teachings of Islam. He particularly disliked his predecessors' denial of the creation of the world in time, of God's knowledge of particulars, and of man's corporeal resurrection. A spiritual crisis in 1095 led him to adopt many Sufi ideas, and after that time, his writings began to emphasize inward and practical aspects of belief, while cautiously drawing on Aristotelian ethics and neo-Platonic mysticism. All these ideas were fused together in his monumental work, *Revivification of the Religious Sciences,* which remains influential among Muslims to this day. Discussing the Koranic prohibition (4:43) against worshiping while intoxicated, "O you who believe, do not approach ritual prayer while you are intoxicated; [wait] until you can comprehend what you are saying," al-Ghazali interpreted the text by observing:

> Some say that the word "intoxicated" means inebriated by many anxieties, while others say it means drunk on the love of this world. According to Wahb [a famous Traditionalist], the meaning is obviously a caution against world attachment, since the words "until you can comprehend what you are saying" explain the underlying reason. Many are those who pray without having drunk wine, yet do not know what they are saying in their prayers.

An important philosophical tradition also developed at this time at the other end of the Muslim world in Spain and North Africa. It drew in part on the works of eastern philosophers and provided the conduit through which these works and those of the ancients were made available to European Christians. This school was exemplified by Ibn Sina's contemporary Ibn Hazm (994–1064), who attempted to unite philosophy and theology. Born in Córdoba to a wealthy family of viziers, Ibn Hazm, who was sometimes known in the West as Abenhazam, spent his youth on the family estate, where he received an exceptionally wide-ranging education. He mastered many disciplines, including history, grammar, poetry, genealogy, and logic. The collapse of the Spanish Umayyad caliphate in 1009 forced the family to move from estate to estate until they settled near Valencia in 1013. In the following years Ibn Hazm repeatedly held various jobs in several short-lived governments, but before long he withdrew completely from public life to devote himself to his scholarship.

In his writings Ibn Hazm applied literalism to theology in a logical and sweeping fashion that allowed no other source of religious truth than revelation. Whereas Greek logic or metaphysics might help to *explain* this truth, they were not, according to Ibn Hazm, independent sources of knowledge. Even after the Christians took Toledo, scholars there translated the works of Ibn Sina and other Muslim and ancient Greek philosophers, particularly under the enlightened patronage of Alfonso X, "the Wise," king of León and Castile from 1252 to 1284. As a result of these translations, medieval scholastics had access to many more sources than did their predecessors.

There was also parallel activity in Toledo translating from Arabic into Hebrew, underscoring the inter-confessional intellectual life that often goes by the Spanish name of *Convivencia*. Two works by the great Jewish philosopher Moses Maimonides (1135–1204), the *Mishna Torah* and *The Guide of the Perplexed,* were first translated into Hebrew in 1204 from the Judeo-Arabic in which they had been written. Maimonides, who was known in Arabic as Ibn Maymun al-Qurtubi (from

Córdoba), had been born in that city to a scholarly Jewish family long established in Muslim Spain. They had fled in 1148 after the invasion of the Almohads, who were hostile toward non-believers in their midst. As he moved around southern Spain and North Africa, Maimonides acquired both religious and secular knowledge. Although he settled in Fez in 1158, he resumed wandering in 1165, going first to Palestine, at that time embroiled in the Crusades. Passing through Acre, Jerusalem, and Hebron, Maimonides eventually settled in Cairo. At first he earned his living there importing precious stones from India, but after his brother was killed in a shipwreck and the family business foundered, Maimonides was obliged to practice medicine. He became a protégé of the chief qadi of Cairo and then court physician to the Ayyubid ruler there. Maimonides also served as head and representative spokesman (called *nagid*) of the Jewish community to the Muslim rulers, and his descendants continued in this position until the fourteenth century.

Maimonides' writings on logic were closely related to those of al-Farabi, who was his chief source of inspiration among Muslim philosophers. He also drew on the writings of Ibn Sina and al-Ghazali. In addition, Maimonides wrote twelve books on medicine, and these works were transmitted in both Hebrew and Arabic. Maimonides' *Guide of the Perplexed* was designed to calm the troubled minds of intellectuals who, because of their scientific and philosophical knowledge, might be confused about religious teachings concerning God, the origin of the world, and the validity of religious law. Maimonides held the work of his Spanish contemporary Ibn Rushd (1126–1198) in great esteem, but learned about it too late to incorporate it in his own writings.

Ibn Rushd, who was known in the West as Averroës, was also born in Córdoba, just a few years before Maimonides. Ibn

Rushd, however, came from a Muslim family of judges and received a traditional training in law, theology, Arabic grammar, and poetry. As a Muslim he did not have to flee the Almohads; indeed, by 1153 he was making astronomical observations in the Almohad capital at Marrakesh. A decade later, he met Abu Yaqub Yusuf, the Almohad ruler, who commissioned the scholar to write Arabic commentaries on all the translated works of Aristotle. The task took Ibn Rushd the rest of his life. While writing, he was also appointed qadi in his hometown of Córdoba as well as in the second Almohad capital of Seville. Like Maimonides, Ibn Rushd served as chief court physician. He wrote on Islamic law, medicine, and philosophy, specifically defending philosophy against the attacks of al-Ghazali. (Ibn Rushd's work has not entirely survived in Arabic, but much of it is known through medieval Latin and Hebrew translations.) Ibn Rushd's commentaries on Aristotle contained many original ideas, and his own philosophy was a revived Aristotelianism, which had been purified of late Greek and early Islamic accretions.

Towards the end of his life, Ibn Rushd found himself out of favor, as the Almohad ruler was engaged in a war against the Christians of Spain. To rally the support of the orthodox, the ruler denounced Ibn Rushd, who had previously attacked powerful theologians in his writings. Ibn Rushd was condemned for heresy and exiled, although he was rehabilitated at the very end of his life in Morocco, away from the sensitive Christian frontier.

Despite the growing disapproval of philosophy, the Aristotelian tradition of Ibn Rushd was kept alive by the extraordinary figure of Ibn Khaldun (1332–1406), arguably one of the greatest minds of all time. Born in Tunis to a family who had been forced to flee the Christian advance in Spain, Ibn Khaldun studied religious subjects, such as the Koran, Traditions, Islamic law, and grammar, along with secular and rational sciences, such as logic, mathematics, and philosophy. He intended to pursue a career as a scribe, and his first major post, at the age of twenty, was in the chancellery in Tunis, where he signed official papers with the name and titles of the Hafsid sultan.

Ibn Khaldun's temperamental personality, however, meant that he could not keep a job for long, and he soon embarked on a second career as a peripatetic government official and scholar. After traveling across North Africa for two years, he arrived at the Marinid court in Fez, where he soon got embroiled in factional rivalries. In 1362 he moved to Spain, where he was sent as ambassador from the Nasrid court in Granada to the court of Pedro the Cruel (1350–69), king of Castile and León, in Seville. In 1365 court rivalries in Granada forced Ibn Khaldun to leave for Bijaya (now Annaba in Algeria), where he was appointed chamberlain and part-time preacher and teacher of law. The brief period in Bijaya marked the culmination of Ibn Khaldun's career as an administrator, courtier, scholar, and philosopher. It ended abruptly when the Hafsids conquered the city in 1366. Facing uncertain prospects, Ibn Khaldun retired to an intellectual life first at Biskra, then at the Sufi hospice of Abu Madyan outside of Tlemcen in western Algeria. By 1372 he had returned to Fez and by 1375 he was back at Granada, but he soon resettled with his family at Tlemcen. Between 1375 and 1378 he lived near Oran where he worked on his masterpiece, the *Muqaddima* ("Introduction [to History]"). Returning again to Tunis in December 1378, he began a new career as a scholar.

In 1382 Ibn Khaldun decided to leave for Egypt, where he was based for his last twenty-four years as a professor and judge. After spending his first forty years in the small and provincial Muslim courts of Spain and North Africa, he was dazzled by the cosmopolitan life in Cairo, seat of the Mamluk sultans. His great reputation as a scholar had preceded him, and students flocked to his courses at al-Azhar, the mosque founded by the Fatimids that now functioned as a university. Ibn Khaldun's happiness in Egypt was marred when his wife and family died in a shipwreck near Alexandria on the way to join him. In 1387 he made the pilgrimage to Mecca. Immediately upon his arrival in Cairo, he had been appointed chief Malikite qadi, but true to form, he became embroiled in local rivalries and was soon dismissed. He held, lost, and regained several prestigious academic and legal positions before his death in 1406.

Toward the end of his life Ibn Khaldun met one of the greatest military figures of his time, the Mongol conqueror Timur, who had swept from Central Asia to conquer most of the eastern and central Islamic lands and was now threatening the Mamluk sultanate. At the end of 1400 Ibn Khaldun accompanied the Mamluk sultan on an expedition to relieve Damascus from the threat of Timur's invasion, and Ibn Khaldun played a role in the eventual surrender of the city. He left a vivid account of his interviews with the extraordinary figure of Timur, whom he may have seen as the man of the age who possessed enough of the ancient spirit of solidarity, for which he used the old Arabic term *asabiyya*, to reunite the Muslim world and give a new direction to history.

Ibn Khaldun is considered the creator of a new science of culture or social science, although he was deeply dependent on his predecessors, including Ibn Sina. Ibn Khaldun put this theory of society forward in the *Muqaddima,* which he intended as a prologue to a much longer work, his universal history, which is somewhat uneven in quality and more important for the history of the Muslim west than other regions. Rational in approach, analytical in method, and encyclopedic in detail, his *Muqaddima* represented an almost complete departure from traditional Muslim historiography, for he ignored conventional clichés and sought to establish a philosophy of history. Ibn Khaldun tried to understand the connection between worldly activity and religious concerns and discern the patterns in the changes that occur in man's political and social organization. He made the study of history a comprehensive study of human experience, thereby raising it from the knowledge of particular incidents to a comprehensive understanding of the whole of human civilization. From this study it was possible to generate theories about the rise and fall of empires, for history, in the view of Ibn Khaldun, was cyclical.

LIKE THE SCIENCES, THE ARTS CAME OF AGE UNDER THE ABBASIDS. The capital at Baghdad became the center of arts and literature, and, as one Arab historian put it, "the market to which the wares of the sciences and arts were brought, where wisdom was sought as a man seeks after his stray camels, and whose judgment of values was accepted by the whole world." Traditional poetic forms that had been favored in the early Islamic period—notably the *qasida* or ode of nostalgic longing for the free life of the desert and the *ghazal* or love-lyric— were replaced by new types of literature, new approaches to new subjects, and new languages in this Golden Age. Poetry remained the principal form of art patronized by the powerful and educated, and poets always had to temper their desire for self-expression with the need to win a purse from a wealthy patron. Poets were constantly held to high standards. Al-Thaalibi (961–1038), a scholar and author of an important literary anthology, for example, judged the chief merits of poetry to lie in elegant expression, subtle combination of thoughts, fanciful imagery, witty conceits, and striking use of rhetorical figures.

The most famous poet of the early Abbasid period was the licentious Abu Nuwas. Born around 750 at Ahwaz in southwestern Iran, he became a boon companion at the court of the Abbasid caliph Harun al-Rashid and died ca. 810. According to contemporary critics, he represented the modern school of poets, and his collected works, or *diwan,* comprise some 1,500 poems. For the first time in Arabic literature, he included a special chapter of hunting poems, in which he used a remarkably rich vocabulary to describe hounds, falcons, and horses as well as various other kinds of game. This work was modeled on descriptions of animals from old Bedouin poetry, but Abu Nuwas turned the subject into an independent genre.

Abu Nuwas was at his best, however, in his songs on wine and pederasty. He reveled in the delights of both and depicts his adventures in these fields with humorous realism. One of his *Khamriyyat* or wine songs, reads, in the translation by R. A. Nicholson, the pioneering English Orientalist who introduced much of Arabic literature to a Western audience in the early twentieth century:

> Ho! A cup, and fill it up, and tell me it is wine
> For I will never drink in shade if I can drink in shine!
> Cursed and poor is every hour that sober I must go,
> But rich am I whene'er well drunk I stagger to and fro.
> Speak, for shame, the loved one's name, let vain disguise
>   alone:
> No good there is in pleasures o'er which a veil is thrown.

The Abbasid court at Baghdad was not the only source of patronage for poets, many of whom, like contemporary philosophers and scientists, moved from place to place in search of work. This was the case with the great tenth-century poet Abu'l-Tayyib Ahmad ibn Husayn, universally known by his nickname al-Mutanabbi, meaning "he who pretends to be a prophet." Born in Kufa in southern Iraq, he moved to Baghdad and then to Syria, finding work as a wandering singer. He became a panegyrist in Damascus and Aleppo, and the nine years that he spent there at the court of the Hamdanid prince Sayf al-Dawla (r. 944–67) are considered the peak of the poet's career. Court intrigue forced al-Mutanabbi to move, first to Egypt, then back to Baghdad, and finally further east to Persia, but he was no longer considered successful. On his return journey in 965, he was attacked by Bedouins and killed.

Al-Mutanabbi's work epitomizes Abbasid panegyric and classical verse. He was an outstanding panegyrist, and his eulogies served as prototypes of the genre. He was often called upon to produce poems for specific events. One particularly graceful example of his encomia was composed on the occasion of Sayf al-Dawla's departure from Antioch:

> Whither do you intend, great prince? We are the herbs of the
> hills, and you are the clouds;
> we are the ones time has been miserly towards respecting
> you, and the days cheated of your presence.
> Whether at war or at peace, you aim at the heights, whether
> you tarry or hasten.
> Would that we were your steeds when you ride forth, and
> your tents when you alight!
> Every day you load up afresh, and journey to glory, there to
> dwell;
> and when souls are mighty, the bodies are wearied in their
> quest.
> Even so the moons rise over us, and even so the great seas
> are unquiet;
> and our wont is comely patience, were it with anything but
> your absence that we were tried.
> Every life you do not grace is death; every sun that you are
> not is darkness.

Al-Mutanabbi was also a master of philosophical verse, love poetry, and other traditional genres. He wrote in a subtle but forward-looking style.

The unsettled times of the later Abbasid period forced artists to seek different life styles. For example, one of the finest poets of the succeeding century, al-Maarri, was born in 973 at Maarrat al-Numan, a town in northern Syria from which he takes his nickname. Blind from childhood, he became a famous panegyrist at the Hamdanid court in Aleppo, but eventually abandoned court life to live as an ascetic, surrounded by disciples and sought out by scholars, until his death in 1057. In contrast to the light-hearted Abu Nuwas, al-Maarri was deeply religious, disturbed by the shallowness of life and the uncertainties of his age. For him, the world was a prison and death the ultimate goal, the end of all existence. An inventive poet, he often forced his ideas into the straitjacket of artificial forms. His most famous work is his volume of mature verse *Luzum ma la yalzam* ("The Necessity of That Which Is Not Necessary"), the term for his self-imposed limitation to difficult rhymes. He is generally reckoned to be the finest Arab writer of philosophical poetry.

Al-Maarri's poems reverberate with his philosophy about his own faith and other religions. They are shot through with pessimism, asceticism, and fatalism, as in this verse:

> O Death! be thou my guest; I am tired of living,
> and I have tried both sorts in joy and sorrow.
> My morrow shall be my yesterday, none doubts it;
> My yesterday nevermore shall be my morrow.

Among the new types of literature fostered by the elevated levels of Abbasid society was *adab* (generally translated by the term belles lettres), which came to imply the sum of intellectual

knowledge that makes a man courteous and urbane. Adab was
based first on pre-Islamic poetry, the art of oratory, and the historical and tribal traditions of the ancient Arabs, as well as on
the corresponding sciences of rhetoric, grammar, lexicography,
and metrics. As Islam increasingly became a civilization of
writing, scholars began to study and write down the oral poetry
of pre-Islamic Arabia in order to understand the language used
in the Koran, for the old poems were seen as repositories of the
pure classical Arabic spoken at the time of the Prophet Muhammad. Originality of expression was initially condemned, but the
great Sunni polymath Ibn Qutayba (828–89) introduced the
revolutionary idea of the qualitative ranking of poets. These
collections were usually accompanied by commentaries speci-
fying under what conditions a particular poem was composed
and often ran to many volumes. As a result of increased contact with other cultures, from the early Abbasid period this Arab
concept of adab gradually broadened to include a knowledge of
non-Arab literatures.

The best-known compilation of early Islamic poetry was the
Kitab al-Aghani ("Book of Songs"), assembled by Abu'l-Faraj
al-Isfahani (897–967). His work was based on an earlier compilation of the hundred best poems made for the Abbasid
caliph Harun al-Rashid. Abu'l-Faraj extended the collection by
giving the melody for each song and a biography of the author.
These subjects led him to expound on events of the author's
time and comment on the content of the poems, adding ex-
planatory poems by other poets, which in turn provoked an
account of the events mentioned there. The resulting work
stretched to an astonishing twenty volumes. Abu'l-Faraj
quoted long passages from earlier Arab writers whose works
have not survived, so his book became a major source for trac-
ing the development of Arabic literary and poetic style. It also
provided a treasure of information, encapsulating Arab civi-

lization from the pre-Islamic "period of ignorance" to the end of the ninth century.[7]

Adab literature also included works ostensibly composed for instruction, either handbooks for secretaries in the chancellery or encyclopedic guides for polite forms of behavior and erudite or elegant conversation. Some of the best examples are the works by Ibn Qutayba, who wrote about adab as well as theology. He composed his *Adab al-katib* ("Belles Lettres for the Scribe") as a manual on style, orthography, and lexicography to help secretaries draft official letters and documents which had to be composed in conventional forms. His *Uyun al-akhbar* ("Choice Histories") was addressed to scribes to give them advice and direction in conducting official, social, and private affairs.

Another genre comprised manuals known as mirrors for princes, which contained advice given in the form of anecdotes, moralistic tales, and alleged historical examples. One of the best-known and longest-lived is the book of animal fables entitled *Kalila and Dimna* after the two jackals who are its protagonists. The tales can be traced back to the popular Indian fables, the *Panchatantra,* which had been translated from Sanskrit into Pahlavi, or Middle Persian, at the time of the Sasanian king Khusraw Anushirwan (r. 531–79) by his physician Burzoe. The now-lost Pahlavi version was in turn translated into Syriac ca. 570.

Some two centuries later, the Pahlavi version of these ani-

---

7. Often cited by modern Arabists, the *Kitab al-Aghani* has long been popular in the Arab world as a prerogative of princes. For example, Badr al-Din Lu'lu', regent of Mosul in the early thirteenth century, had a splendid copy prepared between 1217 and 1220. Each of the twenty volumes had a frontispiece showing the book's patron engaged in princely pursuits, thereby underscoring his position as an enlightened intellectual and patron of the arts.

mal fables was translated into Arabic. Although a stylish work intended for literary connoisseurs, it soon became widely popular. The earliest illustrated manuscripts of Arabic prose are copies of the *Kalila and Dimna* fables made in Syria in the opening decades of the thirteenth century. The Arabic version of the *Kalila and Dimna* fables eventually passed to the West. By the late tenth century it had been translated into Greek, and at the beginning of the twelfth century, it was translated into Hebrew. Between 1263 and 1278, the Hebrew version was translated into Latin. This Latin text served as the basis for later translations into Western European languages such as Italian and French, which in turn inspired La Fontaine to write his fables.

Like the *Kalila and Dimna* fables, much medieval Arabic adab literature was meant to entertain sophisticated audiences. The *Maqamat,* usually translated as "Assemblies" or "Seances," involved a wandering scholar who lived by his wits roving through the land, a Muslim counterpart of the medieval European *Fahrende Schüler* or *Vagans Clericus.* The narrator of the *Maqamat* encountered this wandering character wherever he went and entertained his audience with tales of the traveler's erudition and the anecdotes he recounted. Each seance dealt with a separate topic, but the whole work was unified by the twin protagonists of narrator and traveler. Written in rhymed Arabic prose, the *Maqamat* was witty and full of learned allusions, which presupposed a knowledgeable audience.

The *Maqamat* genre was created by Badi al-Zaman al-Hamadani (969–1008), whose work revolved around the travels of one Abu'l-Fath of Alexandria. Al-Hamadani's work was soon eclipsed, however, by his more famous successor, al-Hariri (1054–1122), whose *Maqamat* is the story of fifty adventures of the rogue Abu Zayd of Saruj as recounted by the merchant al-Harith. Al-Hariri's version of the *Maqamat* enjoyed enormous popularity among the educated bourgeoisie of the Arab lands, primarily for its linguistic ingenuity and punning style. Although the verbal pyrotechnics of the text did not lend themselves easily to illustration, illustrated versions were repeatedly made. The illustrations in these manuscripts emphasized another aspect of the text—Abu Zayd's adventures across the contemporary Islamic world—and the paintings thereby provide rare glimpses of daily life in medieval times. The most famous manuscript of the *Maqamat,* copied and illustrated by Yahya al-Wasiti at Baghdad in 1237, shows contemporary villages, houses, mosques, and even dhows, the lateen-rigged ships used to cross the Persian Gulf and sail in the Indian Ocean.

Some Arabic literature was also pitched at a more popular level. The legends of the pre-Islamic prophets known as *qisas al-anbiya* were a web of fantasies woven around heroes and caliphs, travelers, and scholars. These tales related the lives of the Prophets of the Old Testament, the story of Jesus, and various other events involving pious heroes or enemies of God. The origins of the genre can be traced back to pre-Islamic Arabia, but it was given a new meaning in Islamic times, when people saw parallels between these tales and events in the life of the Prophet Muhammad. From the Muslim point of view, the lives of the pre-Islamic prophets are awful examples *(ibar),* warning against the evil fate of those who are disobedient to God and His messengers. These tales thus became part of universal history, as history in general was considered as a series of awful examples. Several different versions of the legends were gathered by al-Kisai, a Persian poet who lived in the Central Asian city of Merv (now in Turkmenistan) in the late tenth century.

The best examples of popular Arabic literature from this period, however, are the stories in the book that later came to be known as *Alf Layla wa Layla,* or the *Thousand and One Nights.* In its frame story, which gives the work its name, the princess

Shahrazad (Sheherezad) saves her life by telling her murderous husband King Shahrayar a series of interconnected tales over three years. The earliest evidence for the Arabic text is a small paper fragment (now in the Oriental Institute at the University of Chicago) thought to be from ninth-century Syria and containing the opening tale. The stories, some of which were set in a mythical Baghdad of the early ninth century, became particularly popular in later centuries, and combined traditional tales from a variety of sources, including Persian and Indian folklore. The tales came to Europe in the seventeenth and eighteenth centuries, and were first published there by the French scholar and traveler Jean-Antoine Galland (1646–1715). A born storyteller, he adapted his translation to the taste of his European readers. His translation enjoyed widespread popularity in Europe and stimulated an investigation into the ultimate origins of these popular tales.

Despite its great importance as the language of Islam, Arabic was not the only literary language used in this period. New Persian (as distinct from Middle Persian) also came to the fore. With the Arab conquest and gradual conversion of Persians to Islam, Arabic had become the main language of administration and religion in Iran. People continued to speak Persian, but New Persian surfaced as a literary language in the late tenth century when it began to be written in the Arabic script. Since Persian, an Indo-European language, has several sounds not found in Arabic (G, P, and V, for example), new letters had to be devised by adapting the Arabic letters. Many Arabic words also entered Persian at this point, much as many French words entered English after the Norman Conquest in 1066.

The emergence of New Persian marks the beginning of a thousand-year tradition of classical Persian poetry, with one set of forms and one metrical system, both rigidly defined from the outset, and recognized by all, practitioner and audience alike. These verses were penned by professional poets, who produced poetry just as their Arab counterparts produced work on demand for the ruler. At the beginning of his discourse on poets composed in the mid-twelfth century, Nizami Arudi of Samarkand set forth the purpose of poetry:

> Poetry is a craft by means of which the poet arranges in order premises that produce an image in the mind and knits together arguments that lead to a conclusion in such a way that he makes the meaning of an insignificant thing significant and the meaning of a significant thing insignificant, and he displays a beautiful thing in a hideous robe and an ugly thing in a gorgeous raiment. By means of such ambiguousness, he stirs up the irascible and concupiscent faculties so that people experience contractive and expansive moods and thereby cause great affairs in the order of the world.

Thus, the art of Persian poetry resided not in innovation but in the refinement of existing conventions. The stereotypes of lover and beloved—the miserable, suffering, and unrequited lover constantly seeking the aloof, unconcerned, and unapproachable beloved—and the conventional metaphors or *topoi* that exemplified these relationships—the moth and the candle, the nightingale and the rose, the lovers Farhad and Shirin— were immutably fixed in this tradition.

The short quatrains, or *rubais*, composed by Abu'l-Fath Umar ibn Ibrahim Khayyami of Nishapur (d. ?1132), held no great place in Persian literature until the nineteenth century when Edward FitzGerald's translations of them, the *Rubá'iyyát of Umar Khayyam*, became best sellers. In his own time Umar Khayyam was far better known as a philosopher, mathematician, astronomer, and musician, and in any event, the authorship of many of the quatrains FitzGerald ascribed to the poet is "uncertain as that of an English limerick." Perhaps the most famous translation in FitzGerald's version is

> Here with a Loaf of Bread beneath the Bough
> A flask of Wine, a Book of Verse—and Thou
> Beside me singing in the Wilderness—
> And Wilderness is Paradise enow.

Even this lyrical translation, however, rests on a misreading of the Persian original, for the word used is not *kitab,* book, but *kabab,* roast meat. The two words look very much the same in Persian.[8]

After decades and even centuries of repetition, poetic images of lips as red as rubies became so hackneyed that eventually the simile was jettisoned and ruby lips became simply rubies. Similarly, tears that rolled down the cheeks like pearls became simply pearls, and tears that glistened like stars became stars. Much of Persian poetry was pervaded by a spirit of mysticism, for Sufis quickly figured out that they could "express the ineffable" more easily in poetry than in prose. Actual wine was transformed into the wine of union with the divine, and beautiful cupbearers became *shahids,* or witness-bearers to the dazzling beauty of that which truly existed.

The most famous Persian poet of this period was Abu'l-Qasim Firdawsi, whose poem, the *Shahnama* ("Book of Kings"), has been considered the national epic of Iran since its completion in 1010. His work exemplified the spirit of Persian independence

---

8. The reading *kabab* also makes more sense, since *kitab* generally refers to the Koran, which is patently unsuitable reading beneath a bough with a flask of wine and the beloved! Had the poet intended a book of poetry, he would have used a different word.

that arose at this time, for his fifty-thousand-verse narrative chronicled Iranian kingship and the victories of Iranians over their perennial enemies, the Turanians. In it Firdawsi glorified the heroes and legitimate lines of kings down to the Arab invasion of Iran. Tales from the *Shahnama* inspired the Victorian poet Matthew Arnold to compose his epic *Sohrab and Rustum.*

Persian, like Arabic, poetry was often accompanied by music, which flourished in many milieux. Performances on the *oud* (the ancestor of the lute) are shown in contemporary miniature paintings illustrating the courtly love story of Bayad and Riyad. The narrative takes place in northern Syria where the hero, Bayad, a poetically inclined merchant from Damascus, falls in love with Riyad, handmaiden of a noble lady who was the daughter of a chamberlain. One painting shows Riyad strumming her lute before her lady; another shows Bayad in a similar scene, serenading his beloved Riyad, her lady, and the other handmaidens, all of whom listen spellbound, wine goblets in hand. The *oud* was an attribute of courtly life, for in most of the paintings Bayad wears an elegant turban, the lady sports a tall gold crown, and the scenes are set in a garden with belvederes. Both the style of the calligraphy and the motifs in the paintings suggest that the manuscript was made for an aristocratic milieu in Spain or Morocco in the thirteenth century.

The traditional musical modes known as *maqam* also began to appear in treatises written at the end of the Abbasid period. The name, meaning "place" or "station," may derive from the place assigned to the musician in interpreting a given musical mode, but each mode also has a defined place and a position on the fingerboard and fingering of the *oud*. Although the philosopher al-Farabi mentioned a system of musical notation based on the letters of the Arabic alphabet, he did not use it in his writings, and we have little idea of what music of the Golden Age actually sounded like.

The visual arts also came to the fore in this period. In medieval Europe, the Church was the main patron of the arts, and the great churches and cathedrals of Europe are architectural testimony to ecclesiastical patronage. In the Islamic lands, mosques, although they did not have the same corporate identity that churches had, played a similar role, and every town and city boasted a splendid congregational mosque, which was often expanded and embellished to meet the growing size and wealth of the community.

So, too, one can draw a parallel between the fancy liturgical books—hymnals, missals, breviaries and the like—ordered by the Church and the many splendid manuscripts of the Koran. The oldest extant, dating to the ninth century or possibly earlier, were transcribed on sheets of parchment and commissioned for public reading at Friday prayer and other times in the mosque. Of course, most "readers" would have already known the text by heart, so that they would have had little difficulty in reading the extremely stylized script in which these manuscripts were copied.

By the ninth century, paper had been adopted for copying scientific and other types of utilitarian texts, but it took longer for people to accept the use of paper as a fitting support for God's word. The first paper manuscript of the Koran to survive dates from 972, but from this date paper soon became standard. To judge from the dedications and colophons in these paper manuscripts of the Koran, many were made for private individuals as personal copies to be read and studied at home.

Many of the other arts important in the Islamic lands—ceramics, glass, and metalwork—can be subsumed under the rubric "arts of fire," for they use fire to transform humble minerals extracted from the earth into beautiful things. Ceramics were used for storage, cooking, and serving food; glass for lighting, storing and serving foods, and storing perfumes and unguents; metalwares for weapons, tools, and utensils as well as jewelry and coins. In Islamic times these techniques of craft production became major artistic vehicles, and the "decorative arts" show a concern for transforming the accouterments of ordinary life into works of great beauty. Unlike the Christian West, where vessels of silver and gold were used in church liturgy, Islam required no such luxury objects in the mosque. Indeed, the use of gold vessels was officially prohibited, although this prohibition, like many others, was often obeyed more in the breach than in practice.

Unlike medieval music, which has scarcely left a trace, the visual arts of Islam have survived in quantity, and museums around the world proudly display the finest pieces created during this Golden Age. Cases of luster-glazed plates and bowls jostle with those filled with carved ivory caskets, rock crystal vials, and inlaid metal jugs, basins, and candlesticks. Compared to poetry and music, however, these beautiful objects seem to have played relatively unimportant roles in their own time beyond their function as practical objects used in everyday life. There is no word for "visual art" in classical Arabic, and the word most commonly used today, *fann,* is a neologism, for it traditionally meant "craft" or "skill." (The same is true of the Persian and Turkish words *hunar* and *hüner.*) In addition, most artists did not enjoy high status in Islamic society, and in this period there were few, if any, personalities comparable to Michelangelo or Rembrandt whose lives became the stuff of legend. Rather than objects, it was ideas and words that mattered in the Golden Age of Islam.

Part III

The Age of Empires

1250–1700

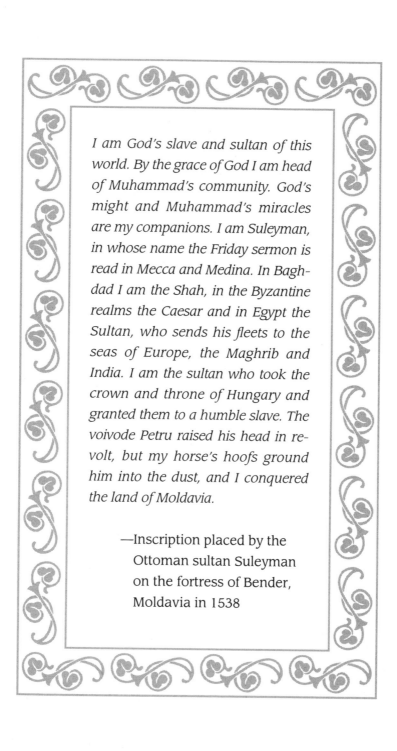

I am God's slave and sultan of this world. By the grace of God I am head of Muhammad's community. God's might and Muhammad's miracles are my companions. I am Suleyman, in whose name the Friday sermon is read in Mecca and Medina. In Baghdad I am the Shah, in the Byzantine realms the Caesar and in Egypt the Sultan, who sends his fleets to the seas of Europe, the Maghrib and India. I am the sultan who took the crown and throne of Hungary and granted them to a humble slave. The voivode Petru raised his head in revolt, but my horse's hoofs ground him into the dust, and I conquered the land of Moldavia.

—Inscription placed by the Ottoman sultan Suleyman on the fortress of Bender, Moldavia in 1538

9
Regional Powers

THE GOLDEN AGE OF ISLAMIC CIVILIZATION WAS brought to an abrupt end in the early thirteenth century by a series of cataclysmic invasions. The Muslims of Syria and Egypt had successfully withstood the European Crusaders and ejected them from the heartlands of Islam, but they did not anticipate that an even stronger force would arrive from the opposite direction, the steppes of Central Asia, and change the very nature of Islamic civilization. For centuries, Turkish tribes had migrated from the grasslands of Inner Asia westward into the Islamic lands, transforming Islamic society as they settled, became Muslims, and adopted the norms of Islamic urban life. Anatolia (now modern Turkey), which had only been opened to Muslim settlement after the battle of Manzikert in 1071, emerged as a new center of Islamic power and culture and the staging-post for the expansion of Islam into the Balkans and southern Russia. In much the same way, India, which had had a sporadic and limited Muslim presence in coastal Gujerat and Sind from the eighth century, became a center of Muslim power when other Turks estab-

lished the Delhi sultanates in the heart of the subcontinent in
the thirteenth century.

The invasions of the thirteenth century were different from
what had come before. They were far more brutal, and by taking Baghdad in 1258 and killing the last Abbasid caliph, the
Turco-Mongolian invaders seemingly destroyed the very foundations of Arab Islamic civilization. In truth, however, they established a new paradigm in which political legitimacy derived
neither from descent from the Prophet Muhammad nor from a
consensus within the Islamic community but from descent
from the Mongol warlord Genghis Khan. In the wake of these
invasions, the embracing Arab-Islamic caliphate of the Golden
Age was replaced by regional powers in which a new Persian-
Islamic culture emerged as the international standard. Within
the traditional heartlands of Islam, three regional powers
emerged: the Mongols in Iran, the Mamluks in Egypt and Syria,
and a series of dynasties in the Maghrib. The western Islamic
lands were located far away from the Mongols and Turks, and
quite naturally were the least affected by these events in the
east. Hence a distinctive Islamic culture developed in the
Maghrib in this period. This was also the age of the Persian
poet Jalal al-Din Rumi, widely revered as one of the greatest of
all mystic poets, and Hafez, one of the greatest of all lyric poets.
It was the age when the art and culture of Persia became the
standard against which those of virtually all other Islamic countries were measured.

The Mongol conquests opened the frontier between the Islamic lands of western Asia and the Far East, enabling the easy
passage of men, ideas, and merchandise, from pepper to
firearms, across Eurasia. The inland Mediterranean Sea, which
had linked Europe, western Asia, and northern Africa in a
nexus of trade and ideas since ancient times, was shifted to the
periphery of a new world trading system centered in the cara-

van cities located in the heart of the great Eurasian landmass. Meanwhile western Europe had awakened from the long slumber of the Middle Ages, and adventurous merchants like Marco Polo embarked on long journeys to seek the fabled luxuries of the East in Muslim bazaars and beyond.

Such trade was so lucrative that from the fifteenth century European navigators attempted to circumvent Muslim middlemen and reach the sources of oriental luxuries directly. Christopher Columbus's inadvertent discovery of the New World in 1492 and Vasco da Gama's rounding of the Cape of Good Hope in 1498 signaled yet another momentous shift in world trade patterns. From the sixteenth century the trans-Eurasian overland system was superseded by an oceanic system, in which the rulers of the great Islamic empires now had to deal with newly empowered European states, made wealthy by merchants transporting goods in tall ships around the world. Muslim merchants, particularly in this later period, were responsible for introducing Islam into new areas, such as tropical Africa and southeast Asia, which eventually became the areas with the greatest Muslim populations.

THE MONGOLS, NOMADIC PEOPLE WHO HAD ORIGINALLY LIVED IN THE forests around Lake Baikal in Siberia and Mongolia, first conquered the eastern part of the steppe, the great grassy plain that stretched from Central Asia to Hungary, in the twelfth century, where they intermingled and intermarried with the Turkish tribes of the region. They were great herders: their flocks comprised mainly sheep and horses, although they also used oxen and camels. All these animals were able to convert the proteins in the grass they ate into proteins that could support human life, as in milk and meat. The Mongols were shamanists, believing that priest-doctors were able to control the unseen world of gods, demons, and ancestral spirits. They

displayed a traditional steppe tolerance—or even indifference—
toward organized religion, giving an ear to Christians of all
stripes, Muslims, Buddhists, and Confucianists.

The Mongols had entered recorded history when they began
systematically conquering the world under the leadership of
Genghis Khan. Born around 1167, he was originally called
Temujin (blacksmith), but after defeating his rival chiefs, or
khans, he acquired the title of Chingiz, meaning "oceanic" or
"universal," a title that has been anglicized as Genghis Khan.
Genghis was acclaimed supreme chief of the Turco-Mongolian
peoples at an assembly of chiefs in 1206. He then set out on
campaign. By the end of it, he had conquered most of Eurasia
from the China Sea to the banks of the Dnieper in Ukraine.

According to Mongol custom, territory was divided among
family members after the ruler died, and this is exactly what
happened after Genghis's death in 1227. One line of his descendants ruled Mongolia and northern China as the Yüan dynasty, another ruled southern Russia as the Golden Horde,
while a third ruled Central Asia as the Chaghatayids. In the
fall of 1253 Genghis Khan's grandson Mongke, who was
supreme ruler of the Mongols in China, dispatched his brother
Hulagu at the head of an army against his enemies to the
west. Hulagu moved speedily across Iran, conquering and
devastating whatever areas did not capitulate. Hulagu over-
came the Ismailis in northern Iran and took Baghdad from the
Abbasid caliph in 1258. This date marked the official establishment of the fourth line of Mongol rulers, which was centered in Iran and known as the *Il-khans* or "subordinates" (to
the great khan in China).

Although Arab historians, who were always hostile to the
Mongols, reported that the invaders burned Baghdad to the
ground, the reports were clearly exaggerated, for the city remained a cultural center as well as the Mongols' winter capital.

Following Mongol tradition, the Ilkhanids continued the nomadic practices of the steppe. They wintered in the warmer lands of Mesopotamia and summered on the grassy plains of northwestern Iran, often moving their capital as they made the transition from tents to buildings. At its greatest extent, the Ilkhanid domain encompassed lands from the Oxus River almost to the Mediterranean Sea and from the Caucasus Mountains to the Indian Ocean, territory that once was ruled by the Sasanians and now covers modern Afghanistan, Iran, the Central Asian republics, Turkey, and Iraq. The Mongols' spread was limited only by the extent of the grasslands on which their herds could graze, for once they reached the limit of the steppe, Mongol horsemen could extend their sway no further.

The Pax Mongolica imposed on this vast tract of land in east, central, and western Asia dramatically facilitated communication and trade between Europe and Asia along the cities of the ancient Silk Route. Christian missionaries trekked to the Great Khan's court in China, in search of the legendary Christian king Prester John and bearing messages from the Pope intended to rouse an attack on the Mamluk rulers of Syria and Egypt who had evicted the Crusaders from the Holy Land. For their part, the Mongol khans, especially in Iran, maintained active correspondence with European rulers, principally in the hope of an alliance against these same foes. Meanwhile, merchants were busy buying and selling whatever they could along the way in cities like Sultaniyya and Tabriz, which became active commercial entrepôts.

The Venetian merchant Marco Polo (1254–1324) journeyed across the Mongol domains with his father and uncle. He left Italy in 1271 and arrived at Xanadu (Sheng-du), the Mongol capital north of the Great Wall of China, four years later. Entering the service of the great Kublai Khan, the young Venetian traveled as far as the Chinese province of Yunnan and Indochina. He then accompanied a Mongol princess to Iran, where she was to marry the local Ilkhanid ruler. Marco returned to Venice in 1295, after an absence of twenty-four years, and dictated the story of his travels, a book that became one of the best-selling travel accounts of all time. Marco described Tabriz, one of the Ilkhanid capitals in northwestern Iran, as the most splendid city in the province. He mentioned the cosmopolitan populace of Armenians, Nestorians, Jacobites, Georgians, and Persian Muslims, but what really impressed the Venetian merchant was the city's commercial possibilities:

> The people of Tabriz live by trade and industry; for cloth of gold and silk is woven here in great quantity and of great value. The city is so favorably situated that it is a market for merchandise from India and Baghdad, from Mosul and Hormuz, and from many other places; and many Latin merchants come here to buy the merchandise imported from foreign lands. It is also a market for precious stones, which are found here in great abundance. It is a city where good profits are made by traveling merchants.

This cosmopolitan world of Ilkhanid Iran was exemplified by the extraordinary rise and fall of the statesman and historian Rashid al-Din Tabib (ca. 1247–1318). The son of a Jewish apothecary in Hamadan, the ancient city of Ectabana whose Jewish community went back to the times of the biblical Esther and the Achaemenid king Xerxes, Rashid al-Din was trained as a physician, hence his epithet, *tabib*, "doctor." He converted to Islam around the age of thirty, entering the Ilkhanid bureaucracy, and rising to the position of chief vizier, or prime minister. He attained great wealth, with enormous agricultural estates and economic interests spread across the Ilkhanid domains. He built large philanthropic foundations in the capital

Tabriz, Hamadan, and elsewhere, combining mosques with hospitals, schools, hospices, and soup kitchens for the poor.

Rashid al-Din is best known, however, for his work as a historian. He compiled the *Compendium of Chronicles,* a multi-volume history of all the world's people, with sections on the Mongols, Chinese, Indians, Europeans, Jews, and the Muslim dynasties. He also wrote books on Islamic theology and practical science, including agriculture, mineralogy, civil and naval architecture, as well as translating works on Mongol and Chinese medicine, pharmacology, and government. At the peak of his power, his arch-rival, a wily jeweler turned bureaucrat, accused him of having poisoned the sultan. Rashid al-Din was tried, convicted, and executed, and his vast wealth confiscated.

The other Mongol capital in northwestern Iran was the city of Sultaniyya, "the Imperial." Whereas Tabriz was an old city, Sultaniyya was founded by royal fiat in the midst of a grassy plain where the Mongols pastured their herds. It was a large city with sixteen massive towers, stone gates, and walls broad enough for four horses to ride abreast. The only thing that has survived, however, is the colossal blue-tiled tomb of Sultan Uljaytu (r. 1304–16). Baptized with the name of Nicholas and raised as a Christian by his Nestorian mother, Uljaytu eventually converted to Islam, taking the Arabic name Muhammad and the Persian name Khudabanda (servant of God) and wavering between various Sunni and Shiite sects. His enormous tomb, towering to the height of 160 feet over the surrounding mud-brick village, was the center of a complex that included a mosque, a madrasa, a hospice for Sufis, a hospital, and many subsidiary buildings. Like the buildings at Xanadu of Uljaytu's great-great uncle Kublai Khan, which inspired the nineteenth-century Romantic poet Samuel Taylor Coleridge to write of the stately pleasure dome there, Uljaytu's magnificent tomb at Sultaniyya passed into the collective memory of Muslims, inspiring a line of massive royal tombs down to the Taj Mahal.

While the Mongols were active in northwest Iran, the southern province of Fars remained relatively calm, and its beautiful capital city of Shiraz nurtured many poets and writers. The most famous of them was the great Shams al-Din Muhammad Shirazi (1326–89), a lifelong resident of the city, who enjoyed the patronage of several local rulers. He received a thorough classical Islamic education and by an early age had memorized the Koran, thereby earning the nickname *hafiz,* or "memorizer [of the Koran]" by which he is universally known and loved.

Hafez's *ghazals,* or odes, are the most celebrated in all Persian literature, blending human and mystical love with balance and proportion in some of the world's most sublime and technically exquisite poetry. In the opening couplets from one of his odes, *Love's Awakening,* Hafez evoked many of the standard images of Persian poetry:

> Ho, saki, haste, the beaker bring,
> Fill up, and pass it round the ring;
> Love seemed at first an easy thing—
> But ah! the hard awakening.

> So sweet perfume the morning air
> Did lately from her tresses bear,
> Her twisted, musk-diffusing hair—
> What heart's calamity was there!

> Within life's caravanserai
> What brief security have I,
> When momently the bell doth cry,
> "Bind on your loads; the hour is nigh!"

Rebels and heretics as well as the pious have died with the beautiful poems of Hafez on their lips, and many Persian-speakers today often quote one of his lines to clinch an argument. The rose garden containing his tomb in Shiraz is still revered, and fortune-tellers use his verses to predict the future.

Within a century of their arrival in Iran, the power of the Ilkhanids had dissipated, and a second Mongol conqueror appeared onstage. Timur, known to the West as Tamerlane from his nickname "Timur-leng" (Timur the Lame), was a military adventurer from the Barlas tribe. Born in the 1320s or 1330s, he came to power in Central Asia by building up loyal bands of followers and defeating other chiefs. To enhance his prestige and gain legitimacy, he married a princess of the Chaghatayid branch of the Mongols, thereby acquiring the important title of *gurgan* or "royal son-in-law" (i.e., to Genghis Khan). Descent from Genghis Khan continued for several centuries to be the prime means of legitimacy in this part of the world.

In 1370 Timur made the ancient city of Samarkand his capital and began reassembling the lands of central, western, and southern Asia into a vast military empire like the one Genghis Khan had assembled a century and a half earlier. Timur's campaigns were decisive: he quickly conquered Iran, Afghanistan, and Mesopotamia, where the city of Baghdad received a final blow from which it never recovered. In 1394–96 Timur advanced through the Caucasus Mountains and went as far as Moscow. By 1398 he had about-faced into India, sacking the Muslim capital at Delhi. During the winter of 1400–1401, he attacked Syria, capturing Aleppo and Damascus and carrying its finest artisans off to Samarkand, where he put them to work beautifying his capital. In the summer of 1402, he engaged and defeated the Ottoman army near Ankara, where he captured sultan Bayezid himself. Timur put him in a cage, intending to carry him home to Samarkand, but the Ottoman ruler died en route.

Returning to Samarkand, in 1404 Timur staged a great council at which he received ambassadors from China, Egypt, and Europe. One was Ruy González de Clavijo, who had been sent in 1400 by King Henry III of Castile. Henry had feared that the Ottoman Turks were about to conquer Byzantium and flood into Christian Europe, so he sought to make an alliance with his enemy's enemy. However, by the time Henry's ambassador arrived at Timur's court, Timur had already defeated the Ottoman army and the Byzantines were spared an Ottoman conquest for another fifty years.

Clavijo left a vivid and detailed account of his travels and stay in Timur's capital, including a firsthand portrait of the aged and nearly blind ruler:

> His Highness had taken his place on what appeared to be small mattresses stuffed thick and covered with embroidered silk cloth, and he was leaning on his elbow against some round cushions that were heaped up behind him. He was dressed in a cloak of plain silk without any embroidery, and he wore on his head a tall white hat on the crown of which was displayed a balas ruby, the same being further ornamented with pearls and precious stones. . . . Three chamberlains came forward, and taking each of us ambassadors by the arm, advanced with us to come stand immediately before the place where Timur sat, and here again they made us kneel. His Highness, however, commanded us to arise and stand close up to him that he might the better see us, for his sight was no longer good, indeed, he was so infirm and old that his eyelids were falling over his eyes and he could barely raise them to see.

In the fall of 1404, despite his age and ill health, Timur decided to embark on a campaign against China to complete his dream of restoring Genghis Khan's empire. Early in 1405, having set off for China, Timur worsened and died. His body was returned to Samarkand for burial.

Timur's tomb at Samarkand, with its imposing turquoise dome, was inspired by Uljaytu's tomb at Sultaniyya and became the emblem of the conqueror's new capital in Central Asia. Unlike the Ilkhanid fiat city, Samarkand was located in a naturally advantageous position that guaranteed its commercial prosperity over the centuries. Set at the intersection of the Silk Route with the Zerafshan (gold-sprinkling) River, Samarkand may have been founded by Alexander the Great. Under Timur and his successors a millennium and a half later, it became one of the greatest cities of the world, as they embellished it with mosques, madrasas, palaces, markets, caravansaries, and other buildings, all enveloped in webs of glittering blue tile.

As was the case with earlier Mongol rulers, Timur's lands were partitioned among his sons and grandsons, none of whom was ever able to reassemble his empire or acquire his stature and prestige. One branch of the family continued to rule in Samarkand, another in the province of Khurasan in northeastern Iran and northwestern Afghanistan, and a third in western Iran and Iraq, where it came into constant conflict with two confederations of Turkmen tribesmen who had settled in the region, the Aqqoyunlu (White Sheep) and the Qaraqoyunlu (Black Sheep). Although the Timurid empire was much reduced in size, the Timurid capitals at Herat and Samarkand remained splendid centers of Islamic and Persianate culture until the end of the dynasty in 1507.

The effects of Mongol rule were felt well into modern times. Timur's grandson Ulughbeg, governor of Transoxiana from 1409 and supreme Timurid ruler from 1447 to 1449, brought the famous mathematician Ghiyath al-Din Jamshid Kashi to

Samarkand. There the ruler built an observatory including a huge meridian arc or sextant dug into the ground. The astronomical tables composed there for Ulughbeg, known as the *Gurkhanid Emphemeris,* after the Timurid title of *gurgan* or "son-in-law," is a masterpiece of observational astronomy, with sections on diverse computations and eras, the knowledge of time, the course of the stars, and the position of the fixed stars. A century later, the Mughal prince Babur reported that Ulughbeg's tables were "used all over the world," and indeed they were long celebrated in Europe. John Greaves, professor at Oxford, called attention to them in 1665; the Latin translation was revised in 1767; French and English translations were made in the nineteenth century; and a Persian and Arabic glossary of the star-names used in the tables was published in Washington, D.C., in 1917.

THE MONGOLS' GREATEST AND PERENNIAL RIVALS IN THE WEST WERE the Mamluks, who stopped the Mongol advance into Syria at the battle of Ayn Jalut (the Spring of Goliath) in 1260. For the next two hundred and fifty years, the Mamluk sequence of sultans continued to rule over Egypt, Syria, western Arabia, and parts of Anatolia from their capital at Cairo. They had a peculiar political system, epitomized by their name, which comes from the Arabic word for "slave." Most of them had actually been slaves, either Kipchak Turks from southern Russia or Circassians from the Caucasus Mountains. As youths, they were captured or sold by their families, enslaved, transported to Egypt or Syria, converted to Islam, educated in the arts of war and peace, and attached to the service of a sultan or other notable. These slaves rose in the ranks, were freed, served as emirs or army commanders, and eventually became members of the governing class. Ultimately they acknowledged one among them as sultan.

The sons of Mamluks occupied a lesser social status: as free-born Muslims, they could not be enslaved by Muslims. They were therefore excluded from the Mamluk corps and consequently unable (at least in theory) to inherit their fathers' high political rank. In practice, however, the descendants of the powerful sultan Qalawun (r. 1280–90) reigned for much of the fourteenth century. In the inherently unstable Mamluk system, many sultans reigned only for months, while others reigned several times successively. The able al-Nasir Muhammad ibn Qalawun reigned the first time as a child from 1293 to 1294, the second time as a youth from 1299 to 1309, and a third time from 1310 to 1341, when his enormous talents as a ruler were realized and he was able to occupy the throne for three decades. Wisely, he also married his daughters to powerful Mamluk commanders. To bolster their prestige and enhance their legitimacy in the eyes of the Muslim world, these upstart rulers resurrected one of the few Abbasids to have survived the sack of Baghdad in 1258 and brought him to Cairo to reestablish the line, if not the power, of a puppet caliphate there.

On the western front, the Mamluks conquered the last Crusader stronghold at Acre in 1291, forcing a retreat from the Holy Land to the Mediterranean islands of Cyprus, Rhodes, and Malta. In retaliation, the pope again stirred up Latin Christendom against the sultans of Cairo and attempted to discourage the growing trade between southern Europe and the Mamluks. However, European merchants, who during the Crusades had come to depend on the luxuries available in Near Eastern bazaars, returned again and again to Mamluk emporia where they traded arms, timber, iron, paper, and woolens for Indian spices, Near Eastern textiles, and great quantities of cotton. Trade was so important that the Mamluks allowed Venetian, Genoese, Pisan, and Marseillais merchants to establish permanent trading hostels in Alexandria and other Mamluk cities.

In these turbulent times family fortunes were always subject to confiscation by the state, and many wealthy Mamluks insured the survival of their estates and perpetuated their names by establishing charitable foundations. Money and property placed in trust for a charitable foundation (known in Arabic as *waqf*) were protected by religious law from confiscation, so many Mamluks established such trusts in which their descendants served as executors and beneficiaries. The foundation was often given physical presence by the tomb of the founder, which was surrounded by religious and charitable institutions dedicated to his memory. These might include a mosque, theological college, hospital, Sufi hospice, drinking-water dispensary, or elementary school. Such multi-functional complexes were intended not only to appease the native population by providing social services from the foreign rulers, but also to allay the disapproval of the conservative religious establishment, who regarded fancy tombs over the graves of rulers as so much impious display. The various activities were housed in large and impressive architectural ensembles which, like corporate skyscrapers in New York, Chicago, Dallas, or Atlanta, vied for space along the main streets of such Mamluk cities as Cairo, Damascus, and Aleppo.

With the fall of Baghdad to the Mongols, the Mamluk capital at Cairo became the metropolis of Arab Islamic civilization, attracting scholars and artisans from east and west. The juristic schools attached to the charitable foundations were a haven for some of the best minds of the time. The constant construction required corps of builders and decorators, including calligraphers, metalworkers, glassblowers, and weavers, to furnish the foundations as well as the palaces of the wealthy. Refugees from Spain, where Christians were conquering large portions of the peninsula from Muslims, also flocked to Cairo, further enhancing its cosmopolitan character.

Although the attractions of Cairo were great, other cities, such as Damascus, were also intellectual centers, and many scholars went back and forth between the religious foundations established by Mamluk sultans and emirs. The great Hanbali theologian and juris-consult Ibn Taymiyya (1263–1328), who had been raised in Syria, spent most of his life in Damascus and Cairo. As the Mamluk sultans and emirs were recent and superficial converts to Islam, Ibn Taymiyya believed his mission was to remind them of the meaning of their faith. He perceived widespread and dangerous trends in contemporary Islam, most notably Shiism and Sufism. He reasserted the middle Hanbali path in a doctrine of synthesis and conciliation, a "happy mean" that accorded each school of law its rightful place in a strongly hierarchical whole in conformity with the precepts of the Koran and the *sunna* of the Prophet. Ibn Taymiyya wrote:

> The Prophet has said, "The Muslim is brother of the Muslim." . . . How then can it be permitted to the community of Muhammad to divide itself into such diverse opinions that a man can join one group and hate another one simply on the basis of presumptions or personal caprices, without any proof coming from God? . . . Unity is a sign of divine clemency, discord is a punishment of God.

Ibn Taymiyya's philosophy epitomized the trend to make the ulema, or professional religious class, the focus of all religious and community life.

Hundreds of thousands of people lived in the bustling metropolis of Cairo, where space was so tight that developers, including the Mamluk commanders themselves, built up rather than out. Many buildings reached six stories high. Caravansaries and shops were surmounted by blocks of multi-storied apartments rented out by the month. Most apartments were duplexes, with bathrooms, kitchens, and reception halls on the first floor and sleeping areas above.

Italian travelers to Cairo in 1384 described the city in glowing terms. Leonardo Frescobaldi noted that "the imperial city of Cairo is rich and abounds with all sorts of sugars, spices, and food from all places. . . . The city has a population greater than all of Tuscany, and there is one street more populated than all of Florence." His companion, Simone Sigoli, showed more enthusiasm, if less accuracy in measurement, in noting that "the city of Cairo is more than twelve miles long and its circumference thirty miles around. In the city there is a great abundance of merchandise of all kinds, above all spices of all varieties, which come from the Indies by the Ocean Sea, entering into the Red Sea and being discharged at the port of St. Catherine [Suez]."

Under the unstable and sometimes corrupt Mamluk regime, however, Egypt, which for centuries had had a prosperous economy based on the wealth generated by the rich agricultural lands along the Nile as well as by manufacturing and commerce, suffered an economic decline. Owners of businesses saw no point in reinvesting their wealth when it might be confiscated so easily. Manufacturing languished from a shortage of capital and consequent technological stagnation, and commerce shifted into the hands of Europeans, desperate to find profitable manufactures, rather than gold and silver coins, to trade for eastern spices and other luxury goods. By the fourteenth century Europeans began to export woolen broadcloth and rag paper to Egypt, severely damaging the local textile and paper industries, which were already in sorry shape.

This decline was also exacerbated by natural disasters, including recurrent drought and repeated occurrences of plague. The Black Death, as it is known in European history, began during the early fourteenth century in the Asiatic steppes, where a permanent reservoir of plague infection existed among the wild rodents of the region. Like the Mongol invasions a century earlier, the pandemic spread from this region to the south and west, fostered by the easy communications of the Pax Mongolica. It first descended on China and India, and then moved westward to Transoxiana, Iran, and finally the Crimean peninsula on the north shore of the Black Sea. From the Crimean ports, merchant ships brought plague to Constantinople in mid-1347 and then to other ports around the Mediterranean basin. Egypt was infected by the autumn of 1347 and Syria by the spring of 1348. The effects of the Black Death were even more severe in the Near East than in Europe, for it reappeared more frequently and more severely. It also lasted longer; whereas the plague disappeared from most parts of Europe by the seventeenth century, it routinely reappeared in the Near East until the late nineteenth century.

The great Egyptian historian al-Maqrizi (1364–1442), a pupil of Ibn Khaldun, lamented the sorry state of Cairo after the Black Death had ravaged the city. The number of victims, he wrote, surpassed a thousand people a day:

> A man would sense that he had fever in his body. Then he would feel nauseated and spit blood, with death following. One after another the people of his household would go after him until all of them had perished. As everyone left alive was sure that he would die of the disease, all of the people prepared themselves for the end, increasing their charities, making expiation and turning to worship.

The streets and marketplaces, he said, were piled high with unburied corpses. Cairo had become so desolate that "a person might walk all the way from one end to the other without ever being jostled. Alas, it is all gone, except for very little . . . deteriorated . . . ruined . . . deserted . . . What remains of it pains me to see."[9]

The final blow to Mamluk power at the end of the fifteenth century was the European discovery of a sea route to India that bypassed Egypt and reoriented global trading patterns. For centuries, Egypt had flourished as the entrepôt between the Indian Ocean and Red Sea on the one side, and the Mediterranean on the other. The Portuguese discovery of a sea route around Africa in the fifteenth century and the Spanish discovery of the New World in 1492 shifted the global economy away from its traditional Mediterranean center to focus on long-distance trade directly with India, the Far East, and the Americas. Portuguese ships venturing into the Red Sea were chased out by Mamluk fleets in an attempt to protect Cairo's preeminence as a trading center, but to no avail. By the early sixteenth century, the Mamluk state was effectively dead: its monopoly on the India trade was broken, and in 1517 the city easily fell into the grasp of the Ottoman Turks.

THE ISOLATION OF THE ISLAMIC LANDS TO THE WEST OF EGYPT ONLY increased in this period. In early Islamic times, the Maghrib region had been integrated into a pan-Islamic system which had its capital at Baghdad in Iraq, but after the year 1000 this was no longer the case. The Turkish invasions of the eleventh and twelfth centuries and the Mongol conquests of the thirteenth had no direct effect on North Africa and Spain, but the centers of political and cultural power shifted from Iraq to Iran and Central Asia, and the indirect effect was to isolate almost all the lands west of Egypt. At the same time, resurgent Christian

---

9. Al-Maqrizi's vivid account, however, may be somewhat overdramatized since he was born fifteen years after the Black Death had struck Cairo.

power in Spain put the glorious Islamic civilization there on the defensive. Travelers and scholars, such as Ibn Khaldun or the indefatigable globe-trotter and freeloader Ibn Battuta (d. ca. 1370), may have moved between the west and the center, or even the east, but they were only individuals swimming against the current.

In 1212 King Alfonso VIII of Castile trounced the Almohad caliph al-Nasir Muhammad at the battle of Las Navas de Tolosa in Spain. This defeat rang the death knell to the empire of the Almohads, the Berber line of staunch Sunnis who had governed Morocco and Spain for nearly a century. Four regional powers emerged as successors: three rival Berber dynasties partitioned North Africa from Tunisia to Morocco while an Arab dynasty ruled in southern Spain. Over the course of the eleventh, twelfth, and thirteenth centuries, the great Muslim cities of Toledo, Córdoba, and Seville fell to the Christians, but the mountainous province of Granada in southeastern Spain held out. It came under the control of the Nasrids (1230–1492), who were caught between their powerful Christian neighbors to the north and their squabbling Muslim neighbors to the south. Despite its precarious position, the Nasrid court at Granada remained a brilliant center of Islamic civilization until 1492, when Ferdinand and Isabella, the Catholic monarchs of the combined kingdoms of Aragon and Castille, brought all of the Iberian peninsula under Christian control and put an end to nearly eight centuries of glorious Islamic civilization there.

Meanwhile urban life flourished in the prosperous cities of North Africa, such as Fez, Tlemcen, and Tunis. Fez enjoyed its most splendid period when it served as the capital of the Marinids (r. 1217–1465), during which time it was embellished with many buildings, notably madrasas and mosques. In 1276 the Marinids created a new quarter called the White City or New Fez on a plateau that still dominates the old city from the west.

Enclosed within a double wall to keep out marauders, the new city included palaces, administrative quarters, a congregational mosque, markets, caravansaries, baths, and a Jewish quarter.

The Alhambra, in the Nasrid capital at Granada, the best surviving example of a medieval Islamic palace, gives a good idea of the rich court life in this period. It was founded as a fortress on a spur of the Sierra Nevada range as early as the ninth century, but under the Nasrids it was enlarged until it became a veritable city in itself, containing palaces, mosques, baths, tombs, gardens, and quarters for artisans. The enclosing walls and towers were a distinctive reddish tone that gave the complex its name, the Alhambra, from the Arabic word for "red." Although now considered a single palace, the complex actually comprised several adjoining palaces connected to the Generalife, a summer palace set in gardens on an adjacent slope, whose name comes from the Arabic "Gardens of the Overseer." The first palace, known as the Palace of the Myrtles after the shrubs planted in the courtyard, abuts the second, known as the Palace of the Lions after the fountain in its courtyard which is supported on twelve stone lions. Both palaces are arranged around courtyards with verandas and alternating long and square rooms, but they were originally separate and served different functions. The Palace of the Myrtles, an inflated version of a typical urban house, was designed for official receptions, whereas the Palace of the Lions, based on a grand country house, was for private pleasure.

Most of the buildings in the Alhambra palace are structurally simple, and it is the lavish and glittering decoration that creates the overall effect. Walls and ceilings are completely covered with glazed tile, carved plaster, and carved or joined wood in a myriad of patterns. The so-called Hall of the Ambassadors, the large square room at the end of the courtyard in the Palace of the Myrtles, has a particularly elaborate wooden ceiling made of thousands of pieces of wood joined together to represent the seven heavens, an appropriate canopy for the ruler's audience-hall. Perhaps the most magnificent ceilings are the two plaster vaults suspended over rooms in the Palace of the Lions. Like the wooden ceiling over the Hall of the Ambassadors, these stucco vaults were meant to symbolize the dome of heaven. As sunlight passes from window to window in the drum of the vault, the movement of shadows creates the effect of a rotating starry sky. This image was underscored by verses commissioned from the fourteenth-century court poet Ibn Zamrak and inscribed on the walls of the rooms below:

> And how many arches rise up in its vault supported by
>   columns which at night are embellished by light!
> You would think that they are the heavenly spheres whose
>   orbits revolve,
> overshadowing the pillar of dawn when it barely begins to
>   appear after having passed through the night.

This opulent setting was made all the more splendid when furnished with rich silk hangings, soft carpets, and glittering ceramics. Outside and inside were commingled. Walled gardens opened to the sky, and interior fountains fed rivulets which flowed from room to courtyard. The ubiquitous sound of running water, brought to the palace by aqueducts from the surrounding hills, blurred the distinction between inside and out, this world and the next. Windows and loggias commanded extensive vistas over the gardens and city below, bringing outside and inside together and emphasizing the ruler's command over all he surveyed .

Although today the Alhambra is the most popular tourist site in all of Spain, in its own day it was much less important. The Nasrids were a relatively minor power at the western fringe of

the Islamic world at a time when the Mediterranean was beginning to wane in importance. Timur, by contrast, was far
wealthier and his palaces far more splendid, to judge from the
fragmentary remains of his gargantuan palace at Shahr-i Sabz
in Central Asia. The Spanish ambassador Clavijo was awed by
Timur's tent palaces, huge pavilions of bejeweled gold cloth set
in verdant gardens watered by streams, which were far more
magnificent than the mountaintop jumble of buildings that
make up the Alhambra.

10

Consolidation

B Y THE YEARS FOLLOWING 1500 THE IDEA OF ONE
Muslim community united under a single ruler
had become only a golden memory. The regional
powers had now consolidated into larger states
with distinct identities centered in Turkey, Iran, Central Asia, India, and Morocco. Some of them, such
as the Ottomans of Turkey and the Mughals of India,
were veritable empires, controlling vast territories,
amassing great wealth, and lasting for several centuries. Others, such as the Uzbek state in Central
Asia and the Sharifan state in Morocco, were
smaller and more ephemeral. These Muslim powers waged war against each other as often as they
fought the infidel. Nearly a thousand years had
passed since the revelation of the Koran, and
distinct doctrinal and regional variations had developed within the vast Muslim community. Nevertheless all believers were linked in a community of faith
and had to respond to the major developments
going on in the world around them, notably the
growing power of Europe and its commercial and
political expansion into south and east Asia and the
Americas. Arabic remained the language of religion,

and Persian the language of literature and the court, even though most of the rulers, except in North Africa, were ethnically Turks. All these powers expressed their identity by creating monumental capitals, such as Istanbul, Isfahan, Bukhara, Delhi, and Meknès, and to many today, these cities and their glorious buildings exemplify some of the greatest achievements of Islamic civilization.

THE OTTOMANS (1281–1924) WERE THE LONGEST LASTING OF ALL Muslim empires to rule in later times. They were originally part of the wave of Turkmen who came from the east and gradually pushed back the Byzantines in Anatolia, intermarrying with the indigenous Greek population of Anatolia and Thrace. The exact origins of the Ottoman family are obscure. The Ottomans, calling themselves Osmanlis, claimed descent from a Turkish ruler active in northwest Anatolia at the end of the thirteenth century. Later generations may have changed his name to Osman, the Turkish form of Uthman, to associate him with the prestigious third of the "rightly guided" caliphs who had succeeded Muhammad in the seventh century. (The term "Ottoman" in European languages ultimately derives from the Italian pronunciation of *Uthmani,* but there were other variants.) Whatever their origins, the Ottomans were the most powerful of several dozen independent principalities, known collectively as the *beylik*s, that arose in western Anatolia in the twelfth and thirteenth centuries. Inspired by love of plunder as well as religious fervor, these groups filled the vacuum left as Saljuq authority waned.

The Ottomans became particularly important after the fall of the Ilkhanids in 1335. A series of able sultans rapidly expanded the Ottoman state, first to the east over the Turkish principalities of Anatolia and then to the west, as Ottoman forces crossed the straits separating Asia from Europe and settled in

Byzantine territory in Thrace and the Balkans. The first Ottoman capital was at Iznik (ancient Nicaea, where important church councils had been held in 325 and 787), but after the Ottomans captured Bursa (ancient Prusa), a splendid site on the northern slopes of Ulu Dag in 1326, it became their capital as well as an important center for the silk industry. In 1402, after Timur and his troops had captured sultan Bayezid and burned the city, the Ottomans pulled back their capital from the frontlines to Edirne (ancient Adrianople) in Thrace. Nevertheless Bursa always remained important to them. The move to Edirne signaled their growing interest in expanding their power into Europe, and the legacy of their double focus on Europe and the Near East remains to this day in the dual role of the Republic of Turkey as a European and a Near Eastern Islamic country.

By the mid-fifteenth century the Byzantine empire consisted only of the city of Constantinople—itself largely abandoned—and its European suburbs, and an Ottoman conquest was inevitable. The Byzantines, who had been abandoned by Christian powers in Europe, began to meddle in Ottoman internal affairs, particularly because the reigning sultan, Mehmed II, was only a youth and could not control his squabbling advisers. The Byzantine emperor even harbored Mehmed's chief rival for the throne.

In 1451, the nineteen-year-old Mehmed (whose name is the Turkish form of Muhammad), advised by his tutor, the Greek renegade Zaganos Pasha, began to make preparations for the conquest of Constantinople, the city that Muslims had coveted for eight centuries. In the middle of March Mehmed left Edirne for Gallipoli, where he set sail up the Dardanelles and across the Sea of Marmora with six fully equipped galleys, eighteen galleons, and sixteen supply ships. He constructed a new fortress to guard the Bosphorus and control access to the city from the Black Sea. Mehmed also hired a Hungarian expert to cast the most powerful cannons ever made. His troops were intended to quickly breach Constantinople's legendary walls, which had successfully withstood eleven centuries of attack. Speed was of the essence, for a long siege might have provoked the European powers to come to Byzantium's aid, something Mehmed wished to avoid at all costs.

The most dramatic moment in the two-month siege came when the Ottomans found themselves unable to enter the Golden Horn, the narrow body of water protecting Constantinople on the north, because the Byzantines had strung a boom across the harbor. Mehmed's advisers, or perhaps the sultan himself, came up with the ingenious idea of moving part of the fleet overland to the harbor on greased planks. Seventy-two ships were rolled from the Bosphorus to the Golden Horn and launched, much to the consternation of the city's defenders, who thought their fortress impregnable.

Early on the morning of May 29, 1453, Ottoman troops entered the city through a breach in its walls. They fought their way across the city to Hagia Sophia, the great church of Holy Wisdom built by Justinian in the sixth century. Mehmed, anxious to establish the city as his new capital, ordered the fighting halted and took a brief tour. On the following day, he made a ceremonial circuit of the city and entered Hagia Sophia, proclaiming that it should be transformed into the city's congregational mosque and that henceforth the city should be his capital. Although the city would continue to be known in official Ottoman documents and on coins by its traditional Arabic, Persian, and Turkish name of Qustantiniyya ([city] of Constantine), it was popularly known as Istanbul, a name that had already been used in Byzantine times.

In order to quickly repopulate his capital city, Mehmed proclaimed a general amnesty. Any fugitive who returned within a specified time could reinhabit his home and practice his religion freely. The Greeks were invited to elect a patriarch to serve as the religious head of their community. Mehmed also forcibly resettled peoples from various parts of his empire in his new capital, which became the flourishing center of an empire straddling Europe and Asia.

Mehmed also founded an imperial mosque surrounded by charitable institutions. In doing so, he continued the long tradition begun by his predecessors in Bursa of erecting a building complex centered on a large mosque and the intended tomb of the sultan. Mehmed's foundation differed from its predecessors because the mosque was frankly modeled on the Byzantine church of Hagia Sophia, with a huge dome buttressed by semidomes. The twenty-five-acre site on the fourth of Istanbul's seven hills had formerly been occupied by the Church of the Holy Apostles, the second largest church in the city and the burial place of the Byzantine emperors. The choice was no accident, and like Abd al-Malik's construction of the Dome of the Rock in Jerusalem eight centuries earlier, Mehmed's mosque in Istanbul was intended to symbolize the presence of Islam in a city newly conquered from the Christians.

Not content with the conquest of Constantinople alone, Mehmed wanted to complete his mission by establishing the rule of Islam over all the lands once held by the Roman Empire, especially Italy. To this end he conducted an incessant series of campaigns against Venice and Hungary, extending the Ottoman empire from the Euphrates to the Danube. He also established the ideological basis of the Ottoman state in the concept of an absolute sovereign whose wishes were executed by an extensive bureaucracy. Mehmed promulgated two law codes that remained the basis of subsequent Ottoman law for two centuries. They dealt with state organization, penal law, and the relations between the state and the military class on the one hand, and its taxpaying subjects on the other.

Mehmed also took a personal interest in the figural arts and learning of Europe, Byzantium, and the Latin West, as well as the traditional arts and literature of Islam. He mastered the principles of Christianity, European history, and geography and supported the works of eminent scholars. He commissioned Kritovulos of Imbros to write his biography in Greek, and hired epic poets to extol his accomplishments in Italian. Mehmed personally visited the site of Troy in 1462, and commissioned a copy of the *Iliad* soon thereafter.

After trouncing his Turkmen enemies in 1473, Mehmed turned against his rivals to the west. He died on May 3, 1481 while on campaign, ostensibly against the Hospitaler Knights of Rhodes but probably against the Mamluks of Egypt. The most cosmopolitan and in many ways the most interesting of all the Ottoman sultans, Mehmed "the Conqueror" was the true founder of the classical Ottoman Empire.

Fraternal struggles framed the succession of Mehmed's son Bayezid II (r. 1481–1512) and grandson Selim I (r. 1512–20). Bayezid's accession was challenged by his younger brother Jem (d. 1495), who sought alliances against Bayezid with both Muslim and Christian princes. Bayezid's policy against the Mamluks in Egypt, Syria, and northern Mesopotamia was not successful, and he was sorely challenged by the rise of the Shiite Safavids on the eastern frontiers of his empire. His European policy was more successful: in 1484 he established control of the land route to the Ottoman vassal state in the Crimea, and during his reign the economy expanded significantly. At the end of his life, Bayezid saw his sons Ahmed and Selim struggling to succeed him; Selim, appropriately known as the Grim, won and forced the aged Bayezid to abdicate a month before his death. Selim expanded the Ottoman state to the south and east: his conquests in Syria, Egypt, the Hijaz, Iraq, and Iran made the Ottoman sultan the undisputed power in the Levant and protector of the holy cities in Arabia. It also brought him and his successors the title of caliph, which conferred undisputed prestige on the Ottoman sultan and raised him—at least in Ottoman eyes—above all other claimants to universal Islamic sovereignty.

During his stay in Damascus, after the Egyptian campaign of 1517, Selim ordered the rebuilding of the tomb over the grave of the great Sufi shaykh Ibn Arabi (1165–1240), whose writings had become textbooks in Ottoman madrasas. The structure was converted into a *tekye,* or Sufi convent, while Kamal Pashazada, chief religious figure of the Ottoman realm and the greatest of Ottoman historians, issued a *fatwa* praising the mystic. Born in Murcia, Ibn Arabi traveled throughout Spain and North Africa, the Levant, and Anatolia before eventually settling in Damascus. His writings represent the culmination of centuries of Sufi gnostic and philosophical contemplation. His main doctrine was *wahdat al-wujud,* or "the unity of being," in which he claimed that everything that exists is God and that the divine reality transcends all manifestations, but the manifestations are encompassed by and plunged in God. His works had a profound effect on later Sufi practice. His book, the *Fusus al-hikam,* or *Bezels of Wisdom,* synthesized hermetic, neo-Platonic, Ismaili, and Sufi strands into a religious vision supposedly dictated to the author by God through the angel Gabriel himself.

The forty-six-year reign of Selim's son Suleyman (r. 1520–66) marked the apex of Ottoman political, economic, and cultural development. Often known in English as "the Magnificent" (because of the splendors of his court) and in Turkish as *kanuni,* or "law-giver" (because he issued a second set of laws which harmonized traditional Islamic and Ottoman legal codes), Suleyman considered himself a worthy successor to his namesake, the biblical king Solomon celebrated in the Koran and Muslim lore. One of his major architectural projects was the refurbishment of the Dome of the Rock in Jerusalem, which was believed to stand on the site of the Jewish temple built by King Solomon. Suleyman ordered his court architect to replace the crumbling Umayyad-period mosaics on the exterior with the multicolored glazed tiles (restored in the twentieth century), that give the building its characteristic bejeweled appearance we see today.

Suleyman inherited a vast empire and an efficient administration. His reign was punctuated with military campaigns toward the east and west, and the sultan became a major protagonist in European and Mediterranean affairs. At the time of Suleyman's accession to the Ottoman throne, the Hapsburg king of Spain, Charles V, and the Valois king of France, Francis I, were fighting over the crown of the Holy Roman Empire. When Charles was elected emperor, war broke out between the two rivals. Suleyman took advantage of their conflict to launch his first western campaign, marching into Hungary (which was allied with the Hapsburgs) in 1521. Suleyman personally led an impressive series of campaigns, including ten in Europe and three in Asia. His spectacular successes sent shock waves throughout Europe. Entering into an alliance with France, Suleyman besieged the Hapsburg capital of Vienna in the fall of 1529 but was forced to retreat because of the onset of winter. In 1534–36 he embarked on the first of his three campaigns against Iran, during which he took Baghdad (now a diminished provincial center), as well as the Shiite shrines in southern Iraq, which had come to be very important to Iran's rulers.

This period of spectacular military victories was followed by another two decades of more modest successes. In this period, the Ottoman fleet, under the command of Khayr al-Din Barbarossa, became increasingly active in the Mediterranean. The Ottoman navy defeated the combined Venetian-Spanish fleets under the command of the Genoese admiral Andrea Doria at the battle of Preveza in September 1538. After waging several campaigns in Hungary, Suleyman finally signed a five-year peace treaty with the Hapsburgs in 1547, which freed him to take up arms again against Iran in 1548–49 and 1553–55.

By September 1555 Ogier Ghislain de Busbecq, ambassador from the Hapsburg emperor to the court of Suleyman, reported that the sultan was

> beginning to feel the weight of years, but his dignity of demeanor and his general physical appearance are worthy of the ruler of so vast an empire. He has always been frugal and temperate, and was so even in his youth. . . . Even in his earlier years he did not indulge in wine or in those unnatural vices to which the Turks are often addicted. . . . He is a strict guardian of his religion and its ceremonies, being not less desirous of upholding his faith than of extending his dominions. For his age—he has almost reached his sixtieth year—he enjoys quite good health, though his bad complexion may be due to some hidden malady; and indeed it is generally believed that he has an incurable ulcer or gangrene on his leg. This defect of complexion he remedies by painting his face with a coating of red powder, when he wishes departing ambassadors to take with them a strong impression of his good health; for he fancies that it contributes to inspire greater fear in foreign potentates if they think that he is well and strong.

Suleyman's favorite wife, Hurrem, a Ruthenian slave known in the West as Roxelana, who occupied an unusually important place in his court, died in 1558. His love for her was, by all accounts, extraordinary, and his love poetry to her, written under the pseudonym Muhibbi, was copied and illuminated by court artists. The year after her death, civil war broke out between

Suleyman's sons, who were positioning themselves to succeed the ailing monarch. Recurrent problems on the Austrian frontier led the aged ruler to mount his seventh attempt to secure Hungary in 1566. Suleyman died during the seige of Szigetvar, a few hours before the city fell on September 7, 1566. Fearing that news of the sultan's death would undermine state security, the grand vizier ordered an officer to impersonate the sultan for forty days, giving Suleyman's son Selim time to arrive in Belgrade and assume command.

Relations between the Ottomans and the Europeans were not entirely bellicose. European visitors to the Ottoman empire brought back carpets, silks, ceramics, and flowers. The tulip, for example, so thoroughly identified today with Holland, is actually native to eastern Anatolia and the Iranian plateau. Busbecq, the Hapsburg ambassador to Suleyman, first brought tulip bulbs back to Austria, and Charles de L'Écluse, professor of botany at the University of Leiden in Holland, encouraged their cultivation. The taste for tulips spread rapidly through Europe in the early seventeenth century, culminating in the great tulip mania of 1636–37. Fortunes were made and broken on the price of a single bulb on the Amsterdam exchange. The flower's name in European languages reveals its origin, for the word "tulip" derives from the Turkish *tulband* and the Persian *dulband,* or "turban."

The classical Ottoman empire represented a new type of Islamic society in which the state was the dominant institution, bringing the religious elites, nomads, and the settled subject masses all under state control. Ottoman society was based on the idea of a small ruling class governing a much larger subject population, which was organized into mostly self-governing ethnic, social, and professional groups. Membership in the Ottoman ruling elite was achieved through loyalty to the sultan, acceptance of Islam, and adherence to Ottoman social norms.

Thus, membership was theoretically open to everyone with ability and ambition.

This open-admission system was most successfully realized in the institution of the *devshirme,* the practice of regularly collecting subject Christian boys from provinces throughout the empire. Like the Mamluks, these youths were converted to Islam, brought to the capital, and instructed in the arts of war and peace. Unlike the Mamluks, the youths were never manumitted and remained the sultan's property. The ablest rose to great heights in Ottoman society: some were turned into crack soldiers in the Janissary corps, while others joined the bureaucracy. Both Suleyman's grand vizier Rustem Pasha and his great court architect Sinan were products of the devshirme system. Successful graduates often remembered their roots, bestowing the favors of the capital on the families, villages, and provinces from which they had come.

The Ottomans, because of the geographical location of their empire, had more contact with Christian Europe than any other Islamic empire, yet they maintained traditional Islamic values as well. Their cosmopolitan culture had its roots in Turkish, Arab, Persian, Byzantine, and European soil. Suleyman, for example, was a caliph who wore the turban, the traditional "crown of the Arabs," but he also commissioned Venetian goldsmiths to make him a four-tiered crown to outdo the pope's, whose crown had only three tiers. The Ottomans reacted to military technology with similar ambivalence. Like the Europeans, they began to realize the importance of field artillery in the middle of the fifteenth century, and used it to decisive advantage in their conquest of Constantinople. By contrast, they were less ready to accept the superiority of firearms, which, when carried by individual foot soldiers, had become decisive in western European warfare by the end of the sixteenth century.

Ottoman visual culture was equally turned toward east and west. Mehmed II, for example, brought the Venetian painter Gentile Bellini to do his portrait, now in London's National Gallery, and Italian and other European craftsmen and artists were employed at the Ottoman court in Istanbul. Ottoman architects, like their contemporaries, were mesmerized by the example of Hagia Sophia, and the series of great domed mosques that each sultan commissioned would have been inconceivable without the model of the great Byzantine church. Far from slavish imitation, however, the architects' great achievement was to reinterpret the model for new purposes, transforming the great domes of Byzantine architecture, which had glorified the altar, into canopies, which embraced the Muslim congregation of believers. The ability to absorb and reinterpret ideas from a wide range of sources was the great strength of the classical Ottoman state.[10]

Suleyman's failure to capture Vienna led to a period of stagnation and decline that dominated Ottoman history from the seventeenth century. Apart from the battle of Cyprus in

---

10. Considering Mehmed's interests in European culture, and particularly his interest in European books and book-learning, it is surprising that he did not welcome what was perhaps the greatest invention of fifteenth-century Europe: printing with moveable type. This decision can be explained in several ways. First was the difficulty of making type for the Arabic script in which the Ottomans wrote. Compared to the 250 individual sorts, or pieces of type, needed for a Latin font, a complete Arabic font needs at least 600 individual sorts. The practical problems were probably less important than the cultural obstacles, for the Ottomans, like many generations of Muslims before them, revered the calligrapher's art as the only acceptable means of transcribing the word of God. Printing, therefore, was not introduced to Istanbul until the eighteenth century, when it was used for reproducing secular works, although the minority communities in the Ottoman empire began printing somewhat earlier.

1570–71, the Ottomans won no great victories after Suleyman's reign. Rather, they fought exhausting wars against the Persians in the east and the Hapsburgs in the west. The empire became too great to maintain, particularly in the face of a Europe increasingly unified against the Ottoman threat.

The battle waged between the Ottoman navy and the combined Venetian-Spanish fleet at Lepanto on the Gulf of Corinth in Greece in October, 1571 was the greatest combat ever fought on the Mediterranean. The Ottomans lost over 200 ships, or half their fleet, and although they were able to rebuild it, they never regained control of that sea. (The Ottomans' loss of control over the Mediterranean was also due to their continued use of oar-powered galleys, while Europeans had adopted tall ships with sails, which were able to fire broadsides from rows of cannon on board.) Furthermore, the Portuguese circumnavigation of Africa and the opening of direct trade between Europe and India meant that the Ottoman Levant could no longer control the flow of luxuries from the Orient to Europe. At the same time, Iran was also expanding its international contacts, establishing direct trade with Europe through the ports along the Persian Gulf and thereby bypassing the Ottomans entirely. By the seventeenth century the Ottoman empire had stopped expanding and became a regional power confined to Asia Minor, the Balkans, and the Arab lands.

Later Ottoman rulers also moved away from the cosmopolitan attitudes of the fifteenth and sixteenth centuries to adopt more conservative and inward-looking policies. Administration was increasingly decentralized, encouraging parts of the empire to break away. The remaining core underwent a period of Westernization in the eighteenth century when, starting with sultan Ahmed III, the Ottomans began to turn to Europe for solutions to their problems. This attempt to adapt European institutions, however, did not keep the Ottomans from becoming politically and economically dependent on Europe throughout the nineteenth century.

To the north of the Ottoman domains as they expanded in Anatolia and the Balkans lay three Tatar khanates: the Khanate of Kazan which controlled the rich grain fields of the middle Volga, the Khanate of Astrakhan which controlled the lower Volga, and the Khanate of the Crimea on the Black Sea. Successor states to the Golden Horde which had ruled the region since the death of Genghis Khan in the early thirteenth century, these Muslim principalities emerged in the fifteenth century in the area straddling the border between Europe and Asia. The Ottoman expansion north into the Crimea precipitated Russian expansion to the south: Ivan the Terrible annexed Kazan in 1552 and Astrakhan in 1556, but the Russians were able to take the Crimea, which lay much closer to Ottoman lands, only in 1783. Russian domination provoked strong resistance among the local Muslim population, especially in Kazan, as the Russians attempted to consolidate their power and restructure the society by distributing Muslim lands to Russian nobles, importing Russian peasants, and forcing Muslims to convert to Russian Orthodox Christianity.

IN THE WESTERN ISLAMIC LANDS, WHICH AFTER 1492 AND THE FALL OF Granada consisted only of North Africa, the descendants of Genghis Khan held no sway, and legitimacy there still depended on traditional sources, particularly descent from the Prophet. The Ottomans, who had taken Egypt in 1517, expanded their power westward across North Africa in the following decades. The Ottoman conquest of Cairo sealed the city's fate as it became a provincial capital in the Ottoman empire, a status it retained for three centuries. Political disintegration and economic disruption across North Africa led the Ottomans to establish provincial governorates in city-states along the coast, which were supported largely by piracy. Although Spain in the sixteenth century was concerned mostly with its colonies in the New World, it was enticed to protect its southern and eastern coasts by extending its power to the Moroccan and Algerian coasts of the Mediterranean. In response, the Ottomans extended their influence across the Libyan, Tunisian, and Algerian coasts through the intermediacy of the corsairs. Despite the recognition of Ottoman suzerainty in Algiers (1529), Tripoli (1550s), and Tunis (1574) and the establishment of Ottoman governors there, the high culture of the Ottoman court at Istanbul was seen only through a distant lens.

In the fifteenth century many Muslim refugees from Spain had set themselves up in Algiers as corsairs, and to suppress them in the early sixteenth century the Spanish occupied the islets *(al-jaza'ir)* that give the city its name. The inhabitants appealed for help from a Turkish corsair, who established his base of operations there in 1510. After his death in 1518, his brother Khayr al-Din (Barbarossa), assumed power but was pushed back by the Spanish. In 1529 Khayr al-Din finally captured the town, dismantled the Spanish fortress on the largest of the islets, and used the materials to construct a breakwater connecting the islets with the mainland. After Khayr al-Din bequeathed his territories to the Ottoman empire, Algiers became the major Ottoman center of power in the Maghrib and the seat of the most important Janissary force outside Istanbul. Although nominally the capital of a Turkish province, Algiers increasingly enjoyed de facto independence from Istanbul, and its rulers, known successively as beys, pashas, aghas, and finally deys, maintained direct relations with European states.

The Ottoman navy was never able to extend its power into the western Mediterranean or the Atlantic, and the Ottoman government could not implant itself along the western Mediterranean coast or in the mountains and plateaux of Morocco, so the situation developed entirely differently in Morocco from elsewhere in North Africa. Power was concentrated in the hands of figures whose authority derived from affiliation with Sufi fraternities organized around the veneration of local saints. The Christian reconquest of Spain and the expulsion of the Muslims in 1492 increased the appeal of leaders who would defend the contracting frontiers of Islam. In 1511, the Saadian family of sharifs, who claimed descent from the Prophet, founded a state in southern Morocco and took control of Marrakesh. This was a time of increasing prosperity: in the northern cities the Andalusian emigrants brought industrial skills and international contacts, and in the south the Saadians extended their power over the Saharan trade routes bringing gold and slaves. The Saadian sharifs, however, were unable to establish firm control, and by the mid-seventeenth century they were replaced by another family of sharifs from the Tafilalt oasis, the Alawis.

During this period, in contrast to earlier times, Morocco became increasingly isolated from developments in the rest of the Islamic world and in Europe. Muslim refugees from Spain encouraged indigenous tendencies toward conservatism and traditionalism. The few Moroccans who traveled to the central Islamic lands were primarily pilgrims; even fewer visitors came to Morocco from the east. Fez remained a regional center of learning, but it was much smaller than Cairo and less than half the size of Tunis, which was more closely tied to Europe. In contrast to earlier times, when Fez had been the undisputed center of intellectual and artistic life, under the Saadians Marrakesh became the center. The Alawis made their capital at Meknès, although the sultan and his court made regular progressions from one capital to another to collect taxes and reaffirm their sovereignty over the indigenous Berber tribes.

The greatest of the Saadian rulers of Morocco was Ahmad al-Mansur (r. 1578–1603). He established trading relations with

Christian powers as far away as England, and the English Barbary Company received commercial privileges within Morocco. Ahmad's desire to expand his realm in the north was frustrated by the Ottomans, so he turned south, expanding across the western Sahara as far as the Niger Valley. Claiming to be the true caliph, or leader of all Muslims, he defeated the Muslim ruler of Gao (in modern Mali), thereby extending Moroccan domination over the savannah belt of West Africa from Senegal to Bornu. In this way he came to control both the salt mines of Taghaza, on which all west Africans depended, as well as the gold paid as tax for every load of salt extracted from the mines. The wealth which accrued to al-Mansur from this expedition earned him the epithet "the Golden," and he spent the spoils of this campaign on beautifying his capital at Marrakesh.

The greatest of the Alawi rulers was Ismail (1672–1727). He had been sent by his brother, the founder of the dynasty, to govern Meknès, a pleasant town in a fertile agricultural region near Fez. When Ismail succeeded his brother, he made the city his capital. During his long reign Mawlay Ismail created the form of government that Morocco retained until the twentieth century, with a royal household of black slaves, a ministry drawn from the leading families of Fez or the Berber tribes, and an army of European converts, former black slaves, and Berber tribesmen.

Mawlay Ismail's policies extended far beyond Morocco: He established diplomatic relations with Louis XIV, whose assistance he wanted to enlist against the Spanish, and tried to cement the alliance by marriage with the Princesse de Conti, Louis's illegitimate daughter. In return for great commercial benefits, French merchants supplied arms and munitions, including the artillery used against the Berbers and the Turks of Algiers, the other major power in the western Mediterranean. The French also assisted in Mawlay Ismail's grand building program, which included roads, forts, and palaces. These projects were supported by brutal taxation, a levy on the corsairs, ransoms from European captives, and generous gifts from foreign ambassadors, who were received with a mixture of buffoonery and splendor.

Dr. Thomas Shaw, chaplain to the British consulate at Algiers from 1720 to 1732, traveled extensively in North Africa during Mawlay Ismail's reign. A classical scholar who went on to become Regius Professor of Greek at Oxford, Shaw wanted to compare the topography of the present country to the descriptions of ancient Greek and Roman geographers. As a doctor of theology, he interpreted the life of the locals with reference to the Bible, and as a European of the Enlightenment, he described what he found with scientific enthusiasm and considerable sympathy:

> During the long Reign of the late *Muley Ishmael, These*, as well as the Parts of It more immediately influenced by the *Capital*, were under so strict a Government and Regulation, that, notwithstanding the Numbers of *Arabs* who are every where in the Way, intent, every one of them, upon Plunder and Rapine; yet a *Child*, (according to Their Manner of speaking) *might safely carry a Piece of Money upon his Hand from one End of the Kingdom to another*, whilst the Merchant travelled from *Salee* to *Woojeda*, and from *Tanger* to *Tafilett*, without Danger, or Molestation.

After Mawlay Ismail's death the country plunged into anarchy and brigandage under a succession of rival and ephemeral rulers. The Europeans, who had long maintained consulates in the coastal cities, became increasingly embroiled in North African affairs. The French conquered Algeria in 1832 and established it as a colony. Tunisia became a protectorate in 1883, but Morocco remained independent until 1912 when the French established a protectorate in the south and the Spanish did the same in the north. The Alawi line hung on through independence in 1956, and its members are now the kings of Morocco.

THE OTTOMANS' GREAT RIVALS TO THE EAST WERE THE SAFAVIDS (1501–1732). As with the Ottomans, the origins of the Safavid dynasty are obscure, for once they were in power, they rewrote their genealogy to suit the needs of the time. The Safavid family probably descended from one of the Turkmen tribes who had settled in Persian Kurdistan and risen to power after the Mongols. They were hereditary leaders of a Sufi order founded by the shaykh Safi al-Din (1252–1334) at Ardabil in northwestern Iran, from whom they took their name, *Safavi*. Originally orthodox Sunnis, the Safavid order switched its allegiance to Shiism in the mid-fifteenth century, and their leader at that time, Shaykh Junayd, set out to add material wealth to his spiritual power. He and his immediate successors conquered the other Turkmen confederations in western Iran and eastern Anatolia. In 1501 Junayd's grandson Ismail seized the region of Azerbaijan from the reigning Aqqoyunlu Turkmen and established the Safavid monarchy. Within a decade, the Safavids had subdued all of Iran.

Unlike the bureaucratic Ottoman state, that of the Safavids was a theocracy. Ismail and his successors traced their descent from Ali ibn Abi Talib, the son-in-law and successor to the Prophet Muhammad, through the seventh imam, Musa al-Kazim. To judge from his poetry, Ismail also claimed divine status as a reincarnation of the Shiite imam. Through this line of descent, the Safavids could claim spiritual as well as political allegiance from their Turkmen supporters, who were known as the Qizilbash, or "Red-heads," because of the distinctive color of the felt caps around which they wrapped their turbans. The Safavids imposed Shiism, which had enjoyed sporadic importance in earlier times, as the state religion of Iran, and in so doing, they distinguished the lands under their rule from those of their Sunni neighbors. In this way, Iran acquired a new sense of national identity which has survived to the present day.

The Safavids faced hostility from their Sunni neighbors on both east and west. On the northeast, the Safavids held their own against the Uzbek Turks, although such frontier towns as Herat and Mashhad frequently changed hands. On the west, the Safavids were less successful against the Ottomans, who trounced them at Chaldiran outside Tabriz in 1514. The battle was a triumph of logistics and firepower, for the Safavids, like the Mamluks of Egypt, had been slow to adopt artillery and firearms. This battle was only one in a long series of border skirmishes, and the continuous insecurity of the region induced the Safavids to move their capital from the ancient but vulnerable city of Tabriz near the northwest frontier, first to Qazvin in 1548 and then to Isfahan in 1591.

Like the great Ottoman sultan Mehmed II, Ismail's son Tahmasp was only a youth when he acceded to the throne in 1524 as a ward in the hands of feuding Qizilbash factions. Like Mehmed, Tahmasp eventually asserted his authority and regained control of the state to rule for fifty-two years, the longest reign in Persian history. By all accounts, he was a most unpleasant person: bigoted, sadistic, and debauched in his youth.

Paradoxically, many of the arts flourished under Tahmasp's patronage. Carpet-making was transformed from a cottage industry of nomads and villagers to a royal manufacture in urban factories. The arts of the book also took on extraordinary significance at this time, as the ruler commissioned splendid manuscripts to glorify his reign. For example, Tahmasp commissioned a magnificent two-volume copy of the *Shahnama* with 258 large paintings by the finest artists of the day. The pictures were supposed to illustrate the poet Firdawsi's verses, which recount the history of the pre-Islamic kings of Persia, but they also give a wonderful sense of contemporary court life in bejeweled pavilions set amidst verdant gardens.

In his twenties, Tahmasp had a change of heart and made a public act of repentance for his waywardness. He prohibited the drinking of wine and other alcoholic beverages, forbade the use of hashish, and restricted singing and playing musical instruments. He also ordered that the considerable revenues accruing to the treasury from such establishments as gambling casinos, taverns, and brothels be expunged from the official account books. In 1567–68 Tahmasp ordered the splendid copy of the *Shahnama* that he had commissioned packed up and sent off with an embassy to Istanbul to congratulate sultan Selim II on his accession to the Ottoman throne.[11]

Following the death of Tahmasp, Safavid legitimacy and power were challenged both internally and externally. Squabbles between members of the family about who was the rightful claimant to the throne eroded the theological underpinnings of their state, for the continuation of the Safavid line rested on public acceptance of the total authority of the Safavids as custodians of twelver Shiism. Already in the 1530s, the Safavids had lost control of the major Shiite shrines at Najaf and Karbala in Iraq to the Ottomans, and in 1589 the Uzbeks seized the holy shrine at Mashhad in Khurasan, burial place of the eighth imam Reza and the holiest Shiite site in Iran. Given the loss of these

---

11. The manuscript eventually passed from the Ottoman library into the hands of wealthy European and American collectors. After many of its finest paintings were sold off at auction, the remains of the manuscript, hailed as the finest copy of the *Shahnama* ever made, were returned to the Islamic Republic of Iran in exchange for a painting of a nude by the American artist Willem de Kooning, which Iranian authorities found abhorrent.

important pilgrimage centers, it was only natural that at this time the central Iranian city of Qum, burial place of Imam Reza's sister Fatima, became a focus of Safavid piety and patronage. To this day, Qum remains the most important center of theological learning in Iran.

Tahmasp's grandson Shah Abbas I (r. 1587–1629) managed to rise from these inauspicious beginnings, and his reign marked the apex of Safavid power. The near contemporary of such great rulers as Elizabeth I of England, Philip II of Spain, Ivan "the Terrible" of Russia, and Akbar the Mughal emperor of India, Abbas enjoyed major military successes on all fronts. He ejected the Ottomans from Azerbaijan and recaptured Mashhad from the Uzbeks, strengthened Persian control over the Caucasus and the Gulf, and established diplomatic contacts with Europe, thereby putting more pressure on the Ottomans. Abbas also managed to consolidate his power at home. To counteract the power of the Turkmen Qizilbash, who not only squabbled among themselves but also antagonized the indigenous Persians, the mainstay of the bureaucracy and the religious establishment, Abbas recruited more Georgians and Circassians to serve in his administration.

Shah Abbas's reign also marked the cultural apogee of Safavid rule. To bolster his line's claims to legitimacy, the shah made a penitent pilgrimage on foot to Mashhad during the winter of 1601–2 and substantially endowed the shrine there, as well as the dynastic shrine at Ardabil. A master of public relations, Abbas consciously used charitable endowments as a political instrument to shore up his two main claims to legitimacy. By restoring the shrine of Imam Reza at Mashhad, Abbas championed the Shiite cause; by restoring the shrine at Ardabil, he strengthened his family line. His bequests to these shrines included tax revenues as well as his own household estates and personal property. The shrine at Ardabil, for example, received jewelry, weapons, horses, sheep, and goats "in number beyond computation" as well as fine manuscripts and Chinese porcelains, which generations of Safavid shahs had collected. The original donation included a staggering 1,162 ceramics, many of them very large pieces, including 400-odd examples of blue-and-white porcelains, one of the largest and finest collections of such wares outside of China.

Abbas also moved the capital to Isfahan in the center of the country. This act lay at the heart of a deliberate policy to consolidate Safavid political and religious authority, develop state capitalism, and establish Safavid Iran as a world economic and diplomatic power. By the seventeenth century Europeans had established direct maritime trade links with India and the Far East, bypassing the Ottoman Levant. Abbas saw a golden opportunity in reviving Bushire and other ports along the Persian Gulf, where Safavid products, particularly silk textiles and carpets, could be exported directly and cheaply to Europe.

The urban program that Abbas carried out at Isfahan was the most visible manifestation of his cultural achievements. He relocated the commercial, religious, and political center of the city to the south, close to the Ziyanda River. The old quarter was centered on a *maidan,* or plaza, located near the old Friday Mosque. Abbas's new quarter was centered on a new square called *Naqsh-i Jahan* ("Design of the World"). An elongated rectangle, the royal maidan covered nearly twenty acres, a space far larger than contemporary European plazas such as the Piazza San Marco in Venice or St. Peter's Square in Rome. Conceived, designed, and constructed between 1590 and 1595, the new maidan was intended mainly for state ceremonies and sports, but in a second phase completed by 1602, it was redeveloped for commerce by adding two stories of shops around the perimeter. Rents were cheap to attract merchants reluctant to move their shops from the old city center.

The entrances to four buildings around the maidan symbolized the economic, social, and religious underpinnings of Abbas's new capital. On the north lies the dramatic portal to the bazaar, or covered market street, which connects the new maidan with the old one, over a mile to the north. At the other end of the square is the entrance to the monumental Shah Mosque (renamed the Imam Mosque following the Islamic Revolution in 1979), designed to replace the old Friday Mosque as the center of public worship in the city. Thus religion balanced commerce. On the east of the maidan is the Mosque of Shaykh Lutfallah, a small jewel-like building, which may have been intended for family worship or as the Shah's tomb, although he was actually buried at Kashan. Whatever its original purpose, it is covered on the interior with the finest tilework from the Safavid period. The Mosque of Shaykh Lutfallah faces the Ali Qapu (Lofty Gate). As its name suggests, it was the entrance to the palace precinct, a large garden dotted with pavilions and kiosks.

The palace precinct was bounded on the west by a long avenue known as the *Chahar Bagh,* or "Four[-part] Garden." This elegant boulevard, over two miles long, was once lined by the mansions of the nobles, who were encouraged by the Shah to construct fine residences in the new capital. Divided into two avenues by a central canal punctuated by fountains and cascades and planted with flowers and trees, the boulevard led to a magnificent bridge over the Ziyanda River. Known as the *Si-o-se Pol* ("Bridge of Thirty-three [Arches]"), it was erected in 1602 by Abbas's favorite and generalissimo, Allahvardi Khan. The bridge linked the city to New Julfa, the economically important quarter of the Armenians, who had been forced to move there from the war-torn borderlands, and to the great royal pleasure gardens on the slopes of the mountains to the south.

Safavid Isfahan was the backdrop for splendid ceremonies,

which were described by the many European travelers who visited Iran at this time. They gave vivid accounts of the parades, polo matches, and other events that took place on the maidan, day and night. Europeans also frequented the coffeehouse located at the north end of the maidan near the entrance to the bazaar. The *ulema,* or religious establishment, strongly condemned coffee drinking, but by the sixteenth century returning pilgrims had brought the practice from south Arabia to Iran. As the coffee trade came increasingly to be controlled by the Ottomans, Iranians eventually became tea drinkers. As elsewhere, coffeehouses became widespread in Iran at this time as places where well-to-do men and intellectuals could meet and talk. The one in Isfahan was no exception, and many travelers came there to gossip about commerce or the latest court intrigues.

The best-known of these travelers was Jean Chardin, son of a wealthy Huguenot jeweler in Paris, who went to Persia to make money trading precious stones. He lived in Isfahan for eighteen months in 1666–67 and again for four years in 1672–77. During this time, he learned Persian thoroughly and recorded what he saw systematically. He compiled a complete record of every quarter in Isfahan by forming a research team with the Dutch commercial agent in the city, two mullahs (who were charged with recording mosques, off limits to foreigners), and various friends. Chardin hired an artist to draw pictures, and the ten-volume account of his travels he published when he returned to Europe was illustrated by engravings made from these pictures. Initially a popular failure, his journal became the major European source for life in seventeenth-century Isfahan. He was particularly interested in local products, such as eggplant:

> Among all these sorts of *Melons*, there are *Water-Melons* or *Pateques*, that grow up and down throughout the Kingdom; but the best of these, as well as the others, come from *Bactria*.

They have *Cucumbers*, one sort whereof, have few or no Kernels, which they eat raw, and without dressing them in any manner whatsoever; and they have likewise a Fruit, which they call *Badinian*, which is the Xanthium of *Dioscorides*, and the same with what we call the *Love-Apples*. It has a Taste that comes very near that of the *Cucumber*, is as big as Apples generally are, and as long again, and when 'tis Ripe the Skin grows quite black; it grows as *Cucumbers* do, it is very good in several different Sauces, and to be dress'd up in many Things; no Body eats them till they are Roasted: They are to be met with in the Southerly Parts of *Italy.*

When Louis XIV revoked the Edict of Nantes in October, 1685, Chardin was forced to leave France for England where he became Sir John Chardin and was buried in Westminster Abbey.

Foreign travelers such as Chardin were impressed with local craftsmanship, which they compared favorably to European manufactures. They remarked on the logical layout and neatness of the bazaars where certain industries or trades were concentrated in specific areas. The area near the entrance, for example, was the royal bazaar, or *qaisariyya,* the place where fine textiles were sold. Fine silk textiles were the mainstay of the Safavid economy. Silk production was a state monopoly, and in establishing his new capital at Isfahan, Abbas used the Armenians as intermediaries to control the silk industry.

In 1603, during his campaigns against the Ottomans, Abbas had encountered the Armenian community of Julfa on the left bank of the Araxes River. He was much impressed by the merchants and their city, which had emerged in the late sixteenth century as a major commercial center, with an estimated population of ten to twelve thousand, some two thousand houses, and seven churches, as well as commercial connections stretching from Venice to India. In 1604, Abbas ordered the Armenians to move from the valley of Ararat on the war-torn borderlands of the northwestern frontier to Isfahan, where he had a small township built for them on the south bank of the river. To gain the loyalty of these industrious merchants, Abbas not only allowed the Armenians of New Julfa religious liberty under their own mayor and judges but also took the unusual step of granting them permission to build All Saviors Cathedral. (Islamic law only allowed Christians and Jews to renovate and restore existing houses of worship, not to build new ones.) The continuing prosperity of the Armenian population in Safavid Iran was reflected in the rebuilding of the cathedral, which became the center of Georgian Christianity in Persia. Between 1655 and 1664, the original small church was turned into the monumental structure that still stands.

The international connections of the Armenians facilitated the Persian silk trade. In 1602 Sigismund Wasa III, king of Poland, sent an Armenian merchant, Sefer Muratowicz, to buy silk carpets in Kashan. There he acquired six pairs of carpets, paying an extra five crowns to have the king's arms woven into the design. One of these survived, a flat-woven rug or *kilim,* now in a museum in Munich. It belongs to the group known as Polonaise or Polish carpets, because one example exhibited at the Paris exhibition of 1878 bears a coat of arms which was mistakenly believed to be that of the Polish Czartoryski family (although wrong, the name stuck). Representing the finest silk weaving produced under Shah Abbas, many of the three hundred surviving examples of Polonaise carpets were royal gifts to Europeans resident in Iran or commissions by the noble houses of Europe, showing the intimate relationships among art, commerce, and diplomacy.

The glorious reign of Shah Abbas in the early seventeenth century was followed by a century of gradual decline as Abbas's less able successors could not maintain the country's borders and encourage foreign trade. A series of Afghan invasions beginning in 1722 resulted in the collapse of Safavid rule in 1732, although members of the line continued to rule in name until 1765. The Afshars (r. 1736–96), a Turkmen tribe settled in northern Khurasan, eventually repulsed the Afghans, and the Afshar leader, Nadir Shah (r. 1736–47) was proclaimed regent for the Safavid Tahmasp II (r. 1722–40). Nadir Shah reestablished Iranian territorial integrity by driving the Ottomans out of Azerbaijan and Kurdistan, penetrating the Caucasus as far as Daghestan, and brilliantly campaigning in northern India against the Mughals. Not only did he extend Iranian power as far as the Indus, but the enormous tribute he gained from the Mughals, symbolized by his bejeweled golden throne, the Takht-i Nadiri, allowed him to cancel Persian taxes for three years.

THE SAFAVIDS' RIVALS ON THEIR NORTHEAST FRONTIER IN WESTERN Central Asia were the Uzbek Turks, who rose to power after the fall of the Timurids in the early sixteenth century and continued to rule the area until it was annexed by the Russian empire in the nineteenth century. The Uzbek capitals were the ancient Silk Road cities of Samarkand, Bukhara, and Khiva, which had glorious Islamic pasts. As before, the region derived its wealth from both agriculture and trade between Western China and the Islamic lands, but with the development of direct sea routes between Europe and Asia, this region was bypassed, and a once central region of Inner Asia came to lie on the periphery of a new world order.

In contrast to the Safavids, who maintained legitimacy through descent from the Prophet, the Uzbek rulers, although they were Muslims, derived their legitimacy through descent from the great Mongol warlord Genghis Khan. The political system was organized into khanates, or fiefdoms, headed by his descendants through his eldest son Jochi, who had died before his father. Sovereignty was corporate and embodied in the ruling clan, and succession was established by seniority. In the sixteenth century power was limited to male descendants of Jochi's youngest son Shiban (or Shayban), and the family that controlled Transoxiana from 1500 to 1598 is usually known as the Shibanids (or Shaybanids). In the seventeenth and early eighteenth centuries, legitimacy was limited to male descendants of another of Jochi's sons, Tuqay-timur, and the family that controlled most of the area is known as the Tuqay-timurids.

Although the Uzbeks and the Safavids were fierce political and religious rivals, their cultures drew from many of the same Timurid sources. The Uzbeks spoke Turki, or Chaghatay Turkish, but the court language was Persian. Just like the Ottomans and Safavids, the Uzbeks set out to leave their mark by creating a splendid new capital, and the city of Bukhara replaced Samarkand as the political and religious center of Transoxiana. In the first half of the sixteenth century, the walls around Bukhara were rebuilt, and several groups of buildings in the city were erected or restored. In the second half of the century, a branch of the Shibanid family sponsored two large-scale urban renewal projects in Bukhara: a major east-west thoroughfare and a north-south artery were cut through the old city. These streets were designed to link large madrasas which were supported by the revenues of caravansaries that catered to the many merchants who lodged in the city. The city's many madrasas coalesced into a veritable university of orthodox theological learning, attracting Sunni students from many foreign lands, particularly those who spoke Persian. Like Abbas's contemporary projects in Isfahan, these urban developments showed how Uzbek rulers used religion and commerce to bolster their waning political power.

Eastern Central Asia, also known as eastern or Chinese Turkestan, was a region of nomadic peoples and important agricultural and oasis cities such as Kashgar and Turfan. Following the collapse of the Mongol empire, the region remained under the nominal control of the Chaghatayids, descendants of Genghis Khan's second son, Chaghatay. Although they lost western Turkestan to Timur and his successors, the Chaghatayids held onto eastern Turkestan until the seventeenth century, during which time the local Mongol peoples slowly converted to Islam. Like western Central Asia, the region adopted Sunni Islam, but the Chaghatayids used Turki as their literary language.

While the descendants of Genghis Khan maintained tenuous control from the top, local Sufi leaders became increasingly important in the oasis cities surrounding the Tarim basin—Kashgar, Yarkand, Khotan, and Aqsu. Known as khojas, from the Persian word *khwaja,* or "lord," these individuals, like their counterparts at the opposite end of the Muslim world, the Sharifs of Morocco, combined Sufi qualities with legitimacy claimed through descent from the Prophet Muhammad. The most important of these khojas was the Naqshbandi shaykh, Makhdum-i Azam, who died at the Chaghatay capital of Kashgar in 1540.

In the hands of the various khoja clans, the oasis cities of the Tarim Basin became rival city-states, and the ensuing factional wars led the khojas to appeal to the nomadic peoples of the area for political support. The most important of these were the Oirats, Mongol clans who had accepted Buddhism at the end of the sixteenth century. The Buddhist Oirats took control of the oasis cities and appointed the Muslim khojas as their vassals, inaugurating nearly a century of symbiosis in the region between Oirats, Khojas, and the Chinese. The Chinese, under the guise of tributes and exchanges of gifts, imported horses, furs, metals, and jade from Inner Asia in exchange for paper, textiles, drugs, tea, and porcelain. This uneasy relationship ended abruptly in 1759 when the Manchu rulers of China, who regarded Inner Asia as part of their inherent domain, annexed the region.

BY FAR THE RICHEST RULERS OF LATER ISLAMIC TIMES WERE THE Mughal emperors of India (1526–1858). Unlike the arid regions of the Mediterranean, Near East, and Central Asia, much of the Indian subcontinent is a well-watered subtropical land where it is easy to cultivate a great many valuable crops, ranging from rice to cotton. This rich and fertile land was also blessed with great mineral resources. Although India will be the most populous country in the twenty-first century, in the past it was underpopulated and able to export many of its products, particularly textiles and spices, in return for gold.

Muslims had founded trading settlements at the mouth of the Indus River (now in Pakistan) as early as the eighth century, but large areas of the subcontinent were conquered by Muslim forces only in the late twelfth and early thirteenth centuries. A Turkish general in service to the ruler of northeast Iran established his capital at Delhi, and, until the middle of the sixteenth century, the city remained the seat of several dynasties, known collectively as the Delhi sultanates. Delhi quickly became an important center of Muslim learning and culture, as many intellectuals sought refuge there from the depredations of the Mongol conquests further west. The indefatigable Moroccan globe-trotter Ibn Battuta, for example, visited India in the 1330s. In Delhi he lodged at a Sufi hospice built by the sultan around the great reservoir known today as Haws Khass, and left a vivid account of the flourishing Sufi community there:

> Along its sides there are forty pavilions, and round about it live the musicians. Their place is called Tarababad (city of

music) and they have there a most extensive bazaar, a cathedral mosque, and many other mosques beside. I was told that the singing-girls there, of whom there are a great many, take part in a body in the *tarawih* prayers in these mosques during the month of Ramadan, and the imams lead them in these prayers. The male musicians do the same. I myself saw the male musicians on the occasion of the wedding of the amir Sayf al-Din Ghada, son of Muhanna [a Syrian nobleman], when each one of them had a prayer mat under his knees, and on hearing the call to prayer, rose, made his ablutions, and performed the prayer.

Ibn Battuta was clearly amazed by these practices, which showed that already by the fourteenth century distinctive regional forms of Islam were evolving in the various reaches of the Muslim lands.

Muslim communities also grew in other parts of India, particularly in Gujerat on the west coast, in Bengal on the east, and on the plateau of central India. Sufi orders from Iran and Afghanistan were very active throughout the subcontinent, where they won many converts to Islam among lower-caste Hindus, who, like the converts of earlier times, were quick to appreciate the equality of all believers promised by Islam. At no time, however, did more than a quarter of the subcontinent's total population ever convert.

Although Genghis Khan never conquered India, his legacy, as in Central Asia, became the foundation of Muslim legitimacy there from the sixteenth century. The founder of the Mughal dynasty, Zahir al-Din Muhammad, known as Babur, was a Chaghatay Turk descended on his father's side from Timur and on his mother's side from Genghis Khan. (The dynasty's name *Mughal* is an alternative form of the word *Mongol*.) Babur's nickname is often thought to derive from the Persian word for "tiger," but it comes, in fact, from the Indo-Persian word for "beaver." Mirza Muhammad Haydar, the historian and biographer, explained how his cousin Babur got this nickname: "At that time the Chaghatay were very rude and uncultured, not refined as they are now. Thus they found [his given name] Zahir al-Din Muhammad difficult to pronounce. For this reason, they gave him the name [of Babur]."

Unlike virtually every earlier ruler of the Islamic lands, Babur kept a diary which he began to rework as an autobiography, although it remained unfinished at his death. The book has been compared in importance to the *Confessions* of St. Augustine and other masterpieces of world literature, for Babur's memoirs were the first, and until recent times, the only true autobiography in all of Islamic literature. The biographical sketch had long been part of the literary legacy of the Islamic lands, and many biographical dictionaries compiled the lives of individuals belonging to different classes and professions, but this was something entirely new and different. Babur gave few hints about why he embarked on this unusual project, telling us only:

> I have not written all this to complain: I have simply written the truth. I do not intend by what I have written to compliment myself: I have simply set down exactly what happened. Since I have made it a point in this history to write the truth of every matter and to set down no more than the reality of every event, as a consequence I have reported every good and evil I have seen of father and brother and set down the actuality of every fault and virtue of relative and stranger. May the reader excuse me; may the listener take me not to task.

The result was an open, frank, and occasionally intimate memoir. Perhaps because he began it as his private diary, he wrote in colloquial Turki rather than in the flowery Persian used as the court language.

Babur's father had ruled a small principality in the Farghana Valley (now in Uzbekistan), but Babur was powerless in the face of the rising power of the Uzbeks. After repeated attempts to gain a foothold in Central Asia, Babur set his sights further afield, first in Afghanistan and then in India. He was invited there by a discontented faction at the court in Delhi. In 1526 Babur defeated the Muslim Lodi sultan at Panipat and in the following year the Hindu Rajput chiefs at Kanwa near Agra. He died a few years later in 1530 and was succeeded by his son Humayun.

Humayun was unable to maintain the throne his father had given him and was dislodged by insurrections of discontented nobles from the old regime. In 1540 he was forced into exile, part of which time he spent at the Safavid court in Qazwin, where he developed a taste for Persian art and culture. He re-gained his throne after fifteen years, only to die unexpectedly a year later after falling down the stairs of his library in Delhi. He was succeeded in turn by his son Akbar (r. 1556–1605). Like the Ottoman sultan Suleyman and the Safavid shah Abbas, the Mughal emperor Akbar consolidated his vast territories and embarked on an extensive program of urban development that was intended to symbolize the great power of his realm.

In 1558 Akbar moved the capital from Delhi to Agra, a hun-dred miles to the southeast, and renamed it Akbarabad in his honor. It became the greatest city in his empire, enclosed within a new wall and dominated by a fortress of sandstone, whose red color gives rise to its modern name, the Red Fort. In 1571 the emperor founded an entirely new capital at Sikri, about twenty-five miles west of Agra in the midst of a vast plain overlooking a large lake where his grandfather Babur had once constructed a pleasure garden. It was also the home of the Sufi shaykh Salim Chishti, who had presciently predicted in 1568 that Akbar would have three sons. In the following year Akbar's Rajput wife Maryam al-Zamani gave birth to Prince Salim (who later became Emperor Jahangir) at Sikri. To commemorate the joyous event, Akbar ordered the construction of the new city that came to be known as Fatehpur— "The City of Victory"— Sikri. The name became particularly apposite after Akbar's victory over the sultans of Gujerat two years later. Within a decade the red sandstone city was completed, but the emperor seldom resided there, probably because he had to deal with military and political problems elsewhere. Nor did his successors choose to live there.

Another of Akbar's major architectural projects was the construction of a mammoth tomb over the grave of his father Humayun on the banks of the Jumna River outside Delhi. From the time of the earliest Muslim conquests in India, Muslims had distinguished themselves from the indigenous Hindus by burying their dead, for Hindus believed that the dead should be cremated and the ashes scattered in the Ganges as part of the eternal cycle of rebirth. Muslims found these beliefs and practices abhorrent, as they did the idols that the Hindus worshiped. Earlier Muslim rulers in India had built great tombs to cover their graves, but Akbar's tomb for his father initiated a series of monumental buildings commemorating the Mughal emperors. The most famous is, of course, the Taj Mahal, built over the graves of Akbar's grandson Shah Jahan and his wife Mumtaz Mahal and one of the architectural wonders of the world.

These imperial tombs distinguished the Mughals from their fellow Ottoman and Safavid rulers, who made the construction of congregational mosques and charitable foundations the hallmarks of their reigns. The Mughals, in contrast, looked back to the Turco-Mongolian tradition and, like the Mongol rulers Ul-

jaytu at Sultaniyya and Timur at Samarkand, constructed great
funerary monuments to ensure the perpetuation of their names.
For these buildings, Mughal architects adopted a type of structure normally used for palaces in Persia, but replaced the Persian materials of brick and tile with the carved stone and marble
typical of India. Set in formal gardens watered by channels and
fountains, these tombs, like the palaces of Muslim rulers elsewhere, were intended as earthly representations of the buildings promised to believers in paradise.

Under Akbar, the Mughals developed unusually close relations with the Portuguese and other Europeans. The Portuguese occupied the port city of Goa in 1510, and Christian
missionaries soon followed in their wake. After Akbar besieged
the city of Surat in 1573, the inhabitants sought help from the
Portuguese in nearby Goa. When the Portuguese reinforce-
ments arrived, they took stock of Akbar's military strength and
decided to pass themselves off as ambassadors to the Mughal
court. A series of reciprocal missions ensued, and gifts were
exchanged. Several European musical instruments were
brought to Fatehpur Sikri, but none caused as much excitement
as an elaborate organ, which was exhibited to the public at the
beginning of 1581. Akbar's biographer, the orthodox Muslim
Abd al-Qadir Badawuni reported:

> It was like a great box the size of a man. A European sits in-
> side it and plays the strings thereof, and two others keep put-
> ting their fingers on five peacock-wings, and all sorts of
> sounds come forth. And because the emperor was so
> pleased, the Europeans kept coming at every moment in red
> and yellow colors, and went from one extravagance to an-
> other. The people at the meeting were astounded at this won-
> der, and indeed it is impossible for language to do justice to
> the description of it.

Jesuit missionaries accompanied these embassies, bringing religious items as gifts to the Mughal emperor. One was a multivolume copy of the Polyglot Bible, which had been prepared under the patronage of Philip II of Spain and printed in four languages (Hebrew, Chaldean, Latin, and Greek) in Antwerp between 1568 and 1572. The title page of each volume was decorated with an engraving showing complex allegorical imagery, whose arcane references would have been lost on Mughal viewers. Nevertheless these images inspired Mughal artists to concoct similar allegorical scenes in which they combined the techniques of Persian painting with European modes of representation. Other gifts from the Jesuits included painted altarpieces, crucifixes, and religious engravings, all of which Mughal artists copied without regard to the religious content of the imagery.

These frankly Christian images found a warm reception at the Mughal court, for Akbar's religious curiosity was extraordinarily catholic. Every Friday night the emperor held religious discussions in his House of Worship at Fatehpur Sikri. The participants were seated according to their affiliation on the four sides of the building, and throughout the night Akbar personally adjudicated the disputes as he moved from one group to another. During the first three years the discussions were restricted to members of the Muslim community, including orthodox mullas, Sufi mystics, jurists, and philosophers, but later a number of non-Muslims, including Hindus, Jains, Christians, Jews, and Zoroastrians, were invited to join in the discussions.

As a result of these discussions, Akbar formulated a new syncretistic religion, known as the Divine Faith, *din-i ilahi*, with himself at its center. It combined elements of many religions, including Christianity, Hinduism, and Islam. In 1579 the emperor decided to personally read the Friday sermon in the congregational mosque, following the precedent of Timur and earlier Muslim rulers. He ended the sermon with the favorite court pun, *Allahu Akbar,* which can be interpreted not only as the ubiquitous Muslim maxim, "God is great!" but also as the heretical "God is Akbar!" Akbar's Divine Faith was restricted to an elite court circle, and orthodox Muslims were, of course, bitterly opposed to it. After Akbar's death the new religion disappeared without a trace, although the Mughals were forced to be inclusive in their policies and many Hindus continued to participate in the administration and direction of the empire. Like the Ottomans and the Safavids, the Mughals had to weld together diverse ethnic elements, in this case Turks, Afghans, Persians, and Hindus, into a class capable of administering their vast domains.

Akbar had extended Mughal power over northern and central India, and his son and successor Jahangir (r. 1605–27), whose regnal name literally means "world-seizer," continued to subjugate outlying areas of the Indian subcontinent. He was also a great patron of architecture and the arts, and under his auspices artists in the Mughal ateliers continued to integrate European ideas with indigenous traditions. One allegorical painting, for example, showed the emperor Jahangir presenting a book to the aged Shaykh Husayn, superintendent of the shrine of Muin al-Din Chishti at Ajmer, where Jahangir had once lived. Below the shaykh in the lower left are small idealized representations of an Ottoman sultan, King James I of England, and a Hindu who is holding a painting of himself bowing. This last figure seems to be a self-portrait of the artist Bichitr, who was a well-known portraitist. The portrait of the Ottoman sultan is based on a generic European representation of a Turk, while the portrait of the English king is copied from a painting that the English ambassador had presented to the Mughal court. Such non-Indian, non-Islamic allegorical motifs as the cherubs, hourglass, and halo are obviously taken from European images. The painting most likely symbolizes the emperor's choice of a spiritual life over worldly power, and it alludes to the source of Mughal dynastic power by associating it with the Sufi orders.

Jahangir's son Shahjahan (r. 1628–58), as his name "World-ruler" would indicate, tried to unite Central Asia and India in a grand empire of Sunni Islam to counter the Shiite Safavids, who were at the peak of their power, ruling from their new capital at Isfahan. Shahjahan's attempt, however, ended in failure, and a conservative reaction ensued under his son Awrangzib, "Ornament of the Throne" (r. 1658–1707). Notables and provincial officials, both Muslim and non-Muslim, became increasing powerful, and by the eighteenth century the Mughal emperors in Delhi were only shadows of their former selves. Power devolved to provincial rulers and Europeans, particularly the British East India Company, which after Robert Clive's victory at the battle of Plassey in Bengal in 1757, slowly consolidated its power.

11

Expansion

I SLAM SPREAD BEYOND THE TRADITIONAL BOUNDARIES established in the eighth century to new areas, notably sub-Saharan Africa and southeast Asia. In general these areas were out of reach of the great empires, such as the Ottomans or Mughals, although occasionally an empire tried to spread its tentacles, as in the case of the Moroccan sharifs who briefly extended their power from the Maghrib southward into West Africa. In contrast to the traditional heartlands of Islam, where Muslim conquerors had brought their religion, Islam was introduced to these outlying regions by merchants and mystics. Often the local ruler and the elite were the first to convert to Islam, and the population at large would follow slowly, usually encouraged by Sufi leaders who used the tombs of saints as the foci of their devotions. In this way, rulers and elites consolidated their power through conversion to Islam, and the Islam brought by merchants and mystics was grafted onto pre-Islamic beliefs and rituals.

Muslim merchants entered the western Sudan (West Africa), the Central Sudan, the Nilotic Sudan, and the coastal regions of East Africa beginning as early as the ninth and tenth centuries, and by the eleventh to the sixteenth centuries, several successive Muslim kingdoms had become centers of trade, power, and Islamization in West Africa. The Almoravid dynasty, which came to rule Morocco and Spain in the eleventh century, arose as a group of religious reformers living at the mouth of the Senegal River on the coast of West Africa. More important centers of West African Islam, however, were further inland on the Sahel, the great grassy plains south of the Sahara. Inland port cities arose at the termini of trade routes which came across the desert from Tunisia, Algeria, and Morocco. The Moroccan traveler Ibn Battuta, who traveled from the Moroccan city of Sijilmasa south across the Sahara Desert, described how West Africans were integrated into this trading network:

On the first day of God's month of Muharram in the year [seven hundred] fifty-three (14 February 1352) I traveled in a caravan whose leader was Abu Muhammad Yandakan al-Massufi, God be merciful to him. There were a number of merchants from Sijilmasa and other places in the caravan. After twenty-five days we reached Taghaza. It is a village with no attractions. A strange thing about it is that its houses and mosque are built of blocks of salt and roofed with camel skins. There are no trees, only sand in which is a salt mine. They dig the ground and thick slabs are found in it, lying on each other as if they had been cut and stacked under the ground. A camel carries two slabs. The only people living there are the slaves of the Massufa, who dig for the salt and live on dates brought to them from the Draa and Sijilmasa, camel meat, and millet, which is imported from the country of the Blacks. The Blacks come from their country to Taghaza and take away the salt. A load of it is sold at Walata for eight to ten *mithqals*, and in the city of Mali for twenty to thirty, sometimes forty. The Blacks

trade with salt as others trade with gold and silver; they cut it
in pieces and buy and sell with these. For all its squalor *qintars*
and *qintars* of gold dust are traded there.

From the early eleventh century Muslim writers had known
of the kingdom of Takrur, located on the middle reach of the
Senegal River, to which Muslim merchants took wool, copper,
and beads and returned with gold and slaves. Although it remained an important trading center, its political power passed
first to the kingdom of Ghana and then, from the early thirteenth to the late sixteenth century, to Mali, which became the
principal center of Islam in the region. Timbuktu became an
important center of Islamic learning under the Songhay, whose
empire was destroyed by the invasion of the Moroccan sultan
Ahmad al-Mansur in 1591. By the eighteenth century, when the
growth of European shipping in the Atlantic had overwhelmed
the Saharan trade routes, the once-great kingdoms of the region had disintegrated into a profusion of small city-states.

For the Muslim world, perhaps the most colorful figure from
this region was the Keita ruler of Mali, Mansa ("king") Musa
(1307–32), who made a sensational pilgrimage to Mecca in
1324. He was accompanied by thousands of tribesmen, including his favorite wife. In Cairo he and his entourage camped
near the Pyramids, visited the Mamluk sultan, and then went
shopping, spending so much gold that it flooded the market and
its value fell throughout Egypt. Mansa Musa returned to Mali
with the Andalusian poet and architect Abu Ishaq Ibrahim al-
Sahili, who built an elaborately decorated domed building for
the king, perhaps the first of its kind in the country. The king
also brought back four descendants of the Prophet, who settled
in Mali with their families, thereby bringing prestige to his kingdom. Mansa Musa's highly Islamized state had *qadis* (judges)
and administrative departments, which used Arabic as the offi-

cial language; the state exchanged embassies with other Islamic states, including the Marinids of Morocco.

Like the western Sudan, the ruling elite of the central Sudan (present-day northern Nigeria and Chad) accepted Islam by the eleventh century, and similar types of Muslim kingdoms evolved there around the shores of Lake Chad. Although caravan routes led north from Lake Chad across the Sahara, the most important trade and pilgrimage route led directly east, crossing the Nile near Khartoum and reaching the Red Sea coast at Suakin. The oldest and most enduring Muslim states of the region were the kingdoms of Kanem and Bornu, whose first kings claimed descent—somewhat fancifully—from the pre-Islamic Himyarite princes of South Arabia. From the thirteenth century, the rulers of Kanem built mosques and madrasas, and a special madrasa in Cairo was even constructed for students from Kanem, thereby further integrating the Central Sudan into the international network of Muslim scholarship. Indeed, the earliest Arabic texts known from sub-Saharan Africa were copied in Bornu at the end of the fourteenth century. Ali ibn Dunama, founder of the Saifi line of Bornu sultans, established a new capital at Ngazargamo, just west of Lake Chad, around 1470. By the seventeenth century the city had become the foremost center of Islamic education in the region, with four congregational mosques attracting scores of religious scholars.

Unlike the western and central Sudan, where the local population followed indigenous religious practices, the Nubians in the Nilotic Sudan had been converted to Christianity before Islam. They remained predominantly Christian until the sixteenth century when Muslim Arab tribes from Upper Egypt conquered the region. The Arabs, in turn, were soon conquered by the Funj, pagan cattle-herding nomads migrating down the Nile, but this defeat was turned to victory when the Funj converted to Islam and the entire region became Muslim. The Funj sultanate flourished from the mid-sixteenth to the late eighteenth century when it was supplanted by a rival sultanate based at Dafur in the eastern province of Kordofan. The Funj monarchy was based on the concept of divine kingship, and the daily life of the Muslim ruler was circumscribed by traditional African rituals.

Islam also spread along the east coast of Africa bordering the Indian Ocean. Whereas West Africa had been Islamized from the Maghrib, and the Sudan was Islamized from Egypt, the East African coast belonged to the Indian Ocean economic system, which was governed by the regular alternation of the monsoon, so Islam came there on ships propelled by seasonal winds from South Arabia, the Persian Gulf, and India. By the thirteenth century, Muslim traders had established a string of bustling port cities along the East African coast, but this prosperous society was destroyed by the Portuguese, who reached the region in 1498 when Vasco da Gama rounded the Cape of Good Hope. By 1530 the Muslim coastal settlements were all in the hands of the Portuguese (who in turn were ejected from most areas by the Omanis in the seventeenth century). Throughout this period Islam was confined to the coastal region, and only in the nineteenth century did a handful of merchants and adventurers move into the interior in search of ivory and slaves, bringing Islam with them.

With the acceptance of Islam on the African coast, Arabic began to play a greater role in the region. Many people, especially urban folk, became more or less literate and incorporated many Arabic loanwords, particularly in matters of religion and commerce, into their indigenous Bantu language. This new language came to be known as Swahili, from the Arabic word *sawahili,* "of the coastlines." Swahili literature, known from the sixteenth century, was written in Arabic script until German colonists introduced the Latin alphabet in the

nineteenth century. Swahili poets, like their Muslim counterparts elsewhere, drew inspiration from such perennial Islamic
themes as the life of the Prophet. The earliest extant Swahili
poem is the *Hamziyya,* which was composed in 1652 by one
Idarus Othman. A verse translation of a long Arabic ode in
praise of the Prophet by al-Busiri, the noted Egyptian poet of
the Mamluk period, it testified to the important role of Islam in
bringing literacy to the region. The role of Swahili as a language of East African Islam has only grown, and throughout
East Africa preachers give the Friday sermon in Swahili, although they still use Arabic for the formulaic parts which require reading from a set text.

IN THE LATE THIRTEENTH, FOURTEENTH, AND FIFTEENTH CENTURIES,
merchants and missionaries brought Islam from India and
Arabia across the Indian Ocean to the Malay Peninsula, the In-
donesian archipelago, and the coast of China. The spread of
Islam in southeast Asia depended heavily on the peculiar geography of the region, for the Strait of Malacca served as the
funnel for all maritime movement between the Bay of Bengal
and the South China Sea. As in East Africa, Muslim settlements in southeast Asia centered on ports, which became
places for the exchange and transshipment of goods. This
east-west trade depended on the monsoon: from April to October, it came from the southwest, and from October to April,
it came from the northeast. Thus Indian ships could cross the
Bay of Bengal eastbound in summer and winter in ports along
the strait before either returning home on the winter monsoon
or waiting until April or May for the next summer one. Chinese merchants followed the same seasonal pattern of travel
and trade in reverse.

Muslim merchants from western India had been active on
Sumatra from the thirteenth century. In 1292 Marco Polo visited

the Muslim port of Pasai on the north coast of the island. According to the Venetian merchant, all the people there used to be idolators but had been converted to Islam through contact with Muslim traders, who had come there by ship. Some forty years later, the Moroccan traveler Ibn Battuta visited several ports on the island and left a flattering portrait of the local Muslim ruler of Java:

> He is Sultan al-Malik al-Zahir, one of the noblest and most generous of kings, a Shafii by practice, and a lover of jurists, who come to his audiences for the recitation of the Koran and for discussions. He often fights against and raids the infidels. He is unassuming and walks to the Friday prayer on foot. The people of his country are Shafiis who are eager to fight infidels and readily go on campaign with him. They dominate the neighboring infidels who pay the poll-tax [levied on non-Muslims] to have peace.

In many other respects, however, the Muslim court at Sumatra followed the rituals and customs practiced by Hindus and Buddhists in the archipelago. Feast days like the Prophet's birthday were celebrated with singing, dancing, and parades of elephants bedecked with silk coverings and gold ornaments.

At the beginning of the fifteenth century, a prince in the Hindu kingdom of Majapahit on Java founded the Muslim kingdom of Malacca on the southwest coast of the Malay Peninsula. The kingdom grew rapidly in importance as a trading center and a nest of corsairs, as its rulers levied transit dues on ships passing through the Strait of Malacca. The kingdom also became the main center for the diffusion of Islam to the rest of southeast Asia, as local rulers on the Malay Peninsula became vassals and converted. Similarly, the inhabitants of Brunei in northern Borneo and various ports along the north coast of Java adopted Islam through their trading connections with Malacca. By the late fifteenth century, Islam had spread inland from the port cities as well as further east to the Philippines.

By the time they conquered Malacca in 1511, the Portuguese had emerged as the major power in the Indian Ocean area. They came in search of spices, notably pepper, which had been a staple article of trade between India and Europe for centuries. Its exorbitant price was one of the inducements that had led Vasco da Gama to round Africa in 1498. A kilo of pepper, for example, worth 1–2 grams of silver at Malacca, might bring 10–14 grams in Alexandria, 14–18 grams in Venice, and 20–30 grams in the consumer countries of Europe. In 1521, the Portuguese navigator Ferdinand Magellan lost his life in the Philippines and all but one of his five ships went down, but nevertheless the surviving crew paid for the entire expedition around the world with the pepper and other spices in the hold of the last remaining ship when it returned to Spain the following year.

Paradoxically the fall of the Muslim kingdom of Malacca to the Portuguese actually contributed to the spread of Islam in the region as Muslim scholars and missionaries emigrated to northern Sumatra, Java, the Moluccas, and Borneo. Three main centers of Muslim political and cultural life emerged in the region. The first and most important was Acheh, capital of the sultanate established on the northern tip of Sumatra, which became the main rival of the Portuguese. In the late sixteenth and early seventeenth centuries the sultans of Acheh reached the height of their power by controlling much of the trade between Gujerat, on the west coast of India, and China. They even solicited and received aid from the Ottoman Turks.

The sultanate also became an important religious and cultural center. The Sufi poet Hamza Fansuri (d. ca. 1600), a native of Panurs (Barus) on the west coast of Sumatra, founded the

Qadari order in Indonesia, and wrote several mystical treatises in Malay. He perfected the *syiar,* a medium-length poem created by stringing together thirteen to fifteen quatrains, as a vehicle for propagating the teachings of the great Sufi Ibn Arabi and his doctrine of the unity of being. One of them began with a call to the community of Muslims to seek out the mystical knowledge possessed by the "friends" of God. Exemplified in the life of Muhammad, this knowledge leads to union with God. Hamza used several Koranic references as metaphors for mystical experience. One was the two "bow-lengths" Muhammad stands from God in the story of his ascension to heaven:

> The meaning of "two bow-lengths off or nearer"
> Is the meeting (of the servant) with the Lord most high.
> The words "The heart did not falsify what it saw"
> Mean, "There was nothing but what it saw."
>
> "Two bow-lengths" is an allegorical term
> Of a lofty meaning and decisive weight.
> The two seas referred to are of a supreme beauty
> Very few in number are those who are privileged to know
>> them.

The four-line form of this type of poetry was related to the classical Persian form of the lyric quatrain, but the tone and content of Hamza's Malay verses were didactic in intent.

The sultans of Acheh also came up against the second major Muslim power in the region, the local sultanates on the Malay peninsula. The most important of these was Johor (1512–1812), and a three-way struggle for control of Malacca ensued between the Portuguese, the sultans of Acheh, and the rulers of Johor. The third center of Muslim power in the region was Java, where a coalition of Muslim forces defeated the local Majapahit king in the 1510s and 1520s. Several rival Muslim states emerged, but eventually the rulers of Mataram, centered at Surakarta in the eastern part of Java, reduced the independent princes of the island to vassals.

The region-wide struggle between the Muslims and the Portuguese was complicated by the arrival of the Dutch, who took Malacca in 1641. They had also come to the region in search of pepper and other spices, and over the course of the seventeenth century became the paramount power in the East Indies, conquering first Acheh and then the rest of Sumatra. They became territorial overlords in Java, establishing forts and bases to control the spice trade and forcing local rulers to give them trading monopolies. The Portuguese and the Dutch continued to dominate economic and political life in the region over the next two centuries, while Islam became the means by which local peoples expressed their own cultural identity, political resistance, and economic competition.

Sailing on the monsoon winds, seafaring merchants had brought Islam to coastal China, reaching cities as far north as Hangzhou as early as the ninth century. Like Muslim settlements in southeast Asia, Muslim settlements in China began on the coast; unlike them, Islam never spread inland from these port cities, and the eventual penetration of Islam into the heart of China came overland from the west through Central Asia.

Maritime contacts between Chinese port cities and the rest of the Muslim world remained strong through the fourteenth and fifteenth centuries. In the mid-1340s Ibn Battuta first stepped on Chinese soil at the city of Zaytun (modern Quanzhou in Fukien province), where he had been sent by the Delhi sultan as ambassador to the Yüan (Mongol) emperor of China. Ibn Battuta noted that although the town's name meant "olive" in Arabic, there were no olives there, nor in the whole of China or India. It was a large and important city, where velvet, satin, and damask were made. Its harbor was, in his opinion, the biggest in the world, containing about one hundred large junks and innumerable smaller ones. The Muslims lived in a separate quarter with their own qadi, Taj al-Din Ardabili, and religious chief, Kamal al-Din Abdullah Isfahani. Ibn Battuta borrowed money from a rich and pious merchant, Sharaf al-Din al-Tabrizi, and visited a Sufi hospice run by Abu Ishaq al-Kazaruni. To judge from the names of these men (which all refer to towns in Iran), all of them were Persians. Ibn Battuta's report of a flourishing Muslim community is confirmed by several hundred inscriptions in Arabic and Persian that survive from mosques and cemeteries there.

The most important port of China was, however, Guangzhou (or Canton, known in Arabic as Khanfu), and Muslims had resided there from the ninth century. Its mosque, the oldest Muslim structure in China, boasted a tall cylindrical minaret in a style and form totally alien to Chinese architecture. The mosque was probably begun as early as the tenth century to serve the trading community, but local legend said that it had been founded by Saad ibn Abi Waqqas, a companion of the Prophet. Although he never actually came to China, according to this story, Saad was the Prophet's maternal uncle and was buried in Guangzhou.

With the appearance of the Portuguese in the South China Sea in the sixteenth century, the flourishing trade between China, southeast Asia, India, and the Persian Gulf waned. Cut off from the larger Muslim world, the isolated Chinese Muslim communities on the coast withered, although the Hui, the native Chinese Muslims, grew increasingly important in the cities of the interior as Islam became more widely accepted by the Turco-Mongolian peoples of Central Asia.

Epilogue

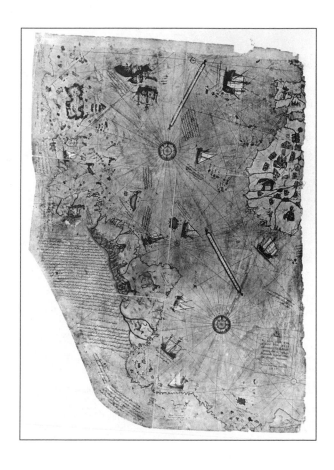

Our main story ends around 1600, about a thousand years after Muhammad had begun to receive God's revelation. Muslims themselves, who calculated with the shorter lunar calendar, celebrated their millennium in 1591. For several hundred years some believers had espoused the popular belief in the *mujaddid,* or "renewer [of the century]," whereby God sends a descendant of the Prophet's family at the beginning of each century to explain matters of religion to the people. Many theologians believed that there was no renewer for the ninth Islamic century (1398–1495), and as a result many people came to fear that Islam would not outlive a thousand years. Others, of course, felt that these were just popular rumors and that Islam would certainly outlast a thousand years. As the Egyptian theologian al-Suyuti (d. 1505) wrote, "What comes afterwards, only God knows."

In later times, the title of mujaddid was given more frequently to religious reformers, particularly in regions far from the traditional centers of Islam, such as West Africa and India. Perhaps the most famous is Shaykh Ahmad Sirhindi (1564–1624), a Sufi of the Naqshbandi order who was known as the "renovator of the second millennium." He took a strong position against the heterodox religious policies that the Mughal emperor Akbar had espoused and championed the *sharia*. His Sufi followers carried his message to the Arab lands, where they were disseminated in the writings of the prolific Damascene Sufi thinker Abd al-Ghani al-Nablusi (1641–1731).

Otherwise only a few people took special note of the Islamic millennium. The Mughal emperor Akbar, for example, commissioned a new history entitled *Tarikh-i Alfi* ("The History of a Thousand [years]"), a chronological recapitulation of the great events of the Muslim era. Elsewhere, however, matters continued much as they had before: the Saadians continued in their wars to subjugate West Africa, while the Ottomans battled the Hapsburgs and the Safavids, the Safavids battled the Ottomans and the Uzbeks, and the Mughals battled the Hindu princes of India.

In much the same way that the Syrian princes of the late eleventh century had been so busy squabbling among themselves that they did not appreciate the new Crusader enemy on the western horizon, so too Muslim rulers of the late sixteenth and early seventeenth centuries did not realize the extraordinary military and economic power western Europe had achieved with the conquest of the oceans and the discovery of the Americas. This power, fueled by the formation of nation-states and the emergence of mercantile capitalism, would make Europe the dominant force in world history for the next several centuries. In the second Islamic millennium the balance of world power thus shifted from the traditional Islamic lands.

Many of the great Muslim dynasties hung on well into the eighteenth, nineteenth, and even twentieth centuries. The Safavids faded away in 1732, although puppets and pretenders ruled for another thirty years; the Mughals continued at the sufferance of the British until 1858, but the last great emperor had been Awrangzeb (1658–1707); and the Ottomans ruled a shrinking empire until 1924, when Kemal Atatürk declared the Turkish Republic. Nevertheless these late dynasties were shadows of their former selves, and much of their power had already devolved to local potentates, such as the pashas of the Ottoman empire, or to foreign mercantile interests, such as the British East India Company. Over the course of the nineteenth century much of the Middle East came to be colonized by European powers in search of sources of raw materials, like cotton, and markets for manufactured goods.

The story of this period is not, however, all negative, and in the face of these great changes new powers and new ideas emerged in the Islamic lands, although discussion of these developments is beyond the scope of this book. Arabia reemerged as a center of a revivified Islam in the eighteenth century, and in the nineteenth century reformist movements in Turkey, Egypt, Syria, Iran, and elsewhere attempted to modernize traditional Islamic societies and institutions along Western lines. Perhaps the biggest change came in the early twentieth century with the discovery of petroleum, which reconfigured the balance of power in the region. At first this valuable resource was exploited solely to the benefit of the Europeans and Americans who controlled production, but after World War II all the countries of the region gained independence and eventually controlled their own resources. Enormous amounts of capital began to flow from the industrial nations of the West to the Near East.

Many countries in the region have tried and are trying to develop stable political systems that harmonize traditional Islamic beliefs with ideas brought from the West, and current governments range from divinely sanctioned kingship, as in Morocco, where the king is a descendant of the Prophet Muhammad, to representative democracies, as in Egypt or Turkey, to military dictatorships, theocracies, and kleptocracies. All countries in the region face vast population growth brought on by modern medicine and improved nutrition, but along with these advances have come social tensions, as large numbers of educated young people cannot find jobs, and much of the population feels that the few are thriving at the expense of the many.

Social tensions like these have often led to violence, as the disaffected seek forcibly to make themselves heard, and Islam—or a particular interpretation of it—has often become the vehicle to protest aspects of Western modernity or the inequities left unsolved by local governments. Like Christianity or Judaism, Hinduism or Buddhism, Islam has been adopted for many causes, from modernism to fundamentalism, liberalism to conservatism, which may have nothing to do with its original transcendent message of unity and equality before God.

It has often been said that if the King of the Franks, Charles Martel, had not defeated the Muslims at the Battle of Poitiers in 732, Europe would have become a Muslim continent. Although Islam made little progress in Western Europe in medieval times, it has become enormously important there in modern times, as millions of Muslims have emigrated from the traditional Islamic lands, many of them former European colonies. Even Rome, center of Catholicism, boasts a new and magnificent mosque. Many Muslims have also emigrated to North America, and Islam is the fastest-growing religion in the United States, from immigration and—particularly among African Americans—from conversion to the Nation of Islam.

In the middle of Islam's second millennium, therefore, there are, as there have always been, many Islams. To stereotype such a multifaceted and vibrant tradition in a few careless images based on the extreme positions of a few is foolish indeed. In order to understand Islam, which may well become the world's most popular religion by the end of the next millennium, one must appreciate its glorious history and achievements and not just focus on the misdeeds committed by a few supposedly in its name. In the future, the billions of believers will continue to differ, as they have in the past fourteen centuries, in their interpretations of how best to reconcile God's message as revealed to the Prophet Muhammad with the practicalities of everyday life, but they will all agree that the first thousand years of Islamic civilization was one of the most glorious in the history of mankind.

Glossary

Abd	"servant/slave of"; used in Arabic names, often in construct with one of the ninety-nine names of God
Abu	"father of"; used in Arabic names
adab	belles lettres
Ali	nephew and son-in-law of the Prophet Muhammad and one of the first converts to Islam
Allah	Arabic word for God
ayatollah	"sign of God"; title used since the twentieth century by a high-ranking Shiite leader
baraka	blessing
caliph	from Arabic *khalifa,* "successor"; supreme ruler of the early Islamic empires
caravansary	a medieval motel for caravans, either in cities or in rural areas along caravan routes
emir	from Arabic *amir,* "prince"; a prince or army commander

fatwa   non-binding legal opinion

hadith   Tradition relating to what the Prophet Muham-
                     mad said or did

hajj   pilgrimage to Mecca, one of the five pillars of
                     Islam

hegira   Muhammad's emigration with his followers
                     from Mecca to Medina in 622, which marks the
                     beginning of the Muslim calendar

houri   one of the beautiful dark-haired virgins who at-
                     tend the faithful in Paradise; mentioned in the
                     Koran

Ibn   "son of"; used in Arabic names

imam   leaders, specifically either (1) a prayer leader; or
                     (2) for Shiites, the divinely guided political and
                     religious leader of the community

Islam   from the Arabic for "submission" to the will of God

Kaaba   square building in Mecca believed by Muslims
                     to be the house Ibrahim erected for God and the
                     focus of Muslim worship

Kharijite   from the Arabic "seceder," an early political sect
                     of Islam

Koran   from the Arabic "recitation," God's word as re-
                     vealed to the Prophet Muhammad

madhhab   legal school or rite

madrasa   theological college

maghrib	from the Arabic "west," the western Islamic lands, including Tunisia, Algeria, Morocco, and sometimes Spain
mamluk	slave
mihrab	niche in the Mecca-facing wall of a mosque
minbar	pulpit
miraj	from the Arabic "ladder"; Muhammad's mystical journey to heaven
mosque	from the Arabic *masjid;* a place of Muslim worship
mufti	independent legal scholar who offers *fatwa*s, or non-binding legal opinions
mujaddid	literally, "a renewer [of the century]"; a religious reformer
mujtahid	a person who interprets the application of Islamic law
Muslim	literally, "one who submits himself [to the will of God]," a follower of the religion of Islam
qadi	judge
qibla	direction of prayer, at first toward Jerusalem and since 623 toward the Black Stone in the Kaaba at Mecca
Ramadan	ninth month of the Muslim year and the month of fasting during daylight hours
shah	Persian word for "king"
sharia	rules and regulations that govern the day-to-day lives of Muslims

Shiite   from the Arabic "party"; one who believes that authority passed from the Prophet Muhammad to his lineal descendants

Sufi   from the Arabic word for "wool"; a mystic

sultan   from the Arabic word for "power"; a title given to a powerful political leader, such as a king or sovereign of a Muslim state

sunna   customary procedure for living, specifically the ways and customs of Muhammad

Sunni   one who follows the ways and customs of Muhammad, specifically those who accept that authority was passed down through consensus of the Muslim community

ulema   religiously learned men (singular *alim*)

vizier   adviser to a ruler; government minister

Notes for Further Reading

GENERAL WORKS

Two recent, relatively readable, and well-illustrated introductions to Islamic civilization are Robinson (1996) and Esposito (2000), presenting essays by noted scholars on various aspects of the Islamic world, including history, science, knowledge, and art.

A readable and comprehensive survey of Islamic history from its origins to the present, including south Asia and Africa, is Lapidus (1988). Fully one third of this substantial book is devoted to modern times. Hourani (1991) is a sensitive and poetic elaboration of Arab history by one of the century's most distinguished historians. Hodgson (1974) is a somewhat idiosyncratic but fundamental and scholarly survey of Islamic history in three volumes. The first to write about Islam in the perspective of world history, Hodgson was also the first to make the division between the early, middle, and late periods used in almost all subsequent works.

One of the very rare examples of a medieval Muslim assessing his own civilization is Ibn Khaldun's *Muqaddima*, or "Introduction to History." It has been translated (Ibn Khaldun 1967) and abridged (Ibn Khaldun 1969). Modern Muslim writers have approached their own past in many different ways. Mernissi (1995) is an evocative memoir of the author's childhood in Fez. Naguib Mahfouz's *Cairo Trilogy* (Mahfouz 1990, 1991, 1992) consists of novels chronicling Egypt's transition to modernity through the life of a Cairene family. The *Cities of Salt Trilogy* (Munif 1987, 1991, 1993) shows the effects of oil, Americans, and local oligarchy on a fictional Persian Gulf nation. The Lebanese writer Amin Maalouf has written several evocative novels about medieval Islamic times, including *Leo Africanus* and *Samarkand* (Maalouf,1988, 1996).

There are many reference works that include information about the Islamic lands. Perhaps the most useful and comprehensive is the new edition of *The Encyclopaedia of Islam* (1960–), although most of the articles are written by one scholar for another, and it takes some skill to navigate through its idiosyncratic system of transcription and article titles. Far more accessible and sometimes surprisingly authoritative are the articles in Strayer (1982–89).

Several recent and well-illustrated books survey medieval Islamic civilization and its art. Our own glossy book (Bloom and Blair 1997) interweaves the arts of architecture, writing, textiles, ceramics, and metalwork. Irwin (1997) integrates art and literary sources, while the latest R. Hillenbrand (1999) has a provocative text and witty, urbane captions.

PART I

The quotation at the beginning of Part I is taken from Lings (1983), a chronological, but uncritical, account of Muhammad's life based on the earliest Arabic sources. The most readable introduction to the world of Late Antiquity remains Brown (1971). There is really nothing comparable covering the Sasanian empire. The *Cambridge History of Iran*, vol. 3 (Yarshater

1983) is scholarly, but not very readable. A convenient illus-trated introduction to the pre-Islamic and Islamic culture of South Arabia is Daum (1988).

Muslims believe that the Koran, as God's word, cannot be translated, but many have tried to render the original majes-tic Arabic into other tongues. Perhaps the most successful English rendition is Arberry (1973), but many others exist. Our quotations are taken mostly from Sells (1999), which includes a CD of various Koran-reciters. Western scholars often con-sider the Koran as written scripture, but the oral nature of the revelation forms a major theme in Graham (1993). A readable introduction to Muhammad's life and role in Islamic culture is Schimmel (1985). Many basic practices of Islam are discussed by von Grunebaum (1951); other useful information can be found in Endress (1988) and Esposito (1998). A wide-ranging introduction to Islamic spirituality is Renard (1996); the ac-companying volume of selected texts (Renard, 1998) inte-grates literary and visual sources. Many of the quotations in this and subsequent chapters are taken from his books. For Sufism see the classic work of Schimmel (1975) as well as the more recent Ernst (1997). The Sufi orders are reviewed by Trimingham (1971). A selection of Jalal al-Din Rumi's poetry is translated by Nicholson (1974).

For early Islamic art and architecture Bloom and Blair (1997) is a convenient introduction. More detail is provided by Ettinghausen and Grabar (1987). The poetry of al-Walid is translated in Hamilton (1988), who also discusses the ruins of Khirbat al-Mafjar.

PART II

The quotation from Ibn Khurradadhbih is translated in Goitein (1964). The relationship between the rise of Islam and the decline of Western Europe was proposed early in this century by the Belgian historian Henri Pirenne. His hypothesis has been reexamined in a readable and provocative book (Hodges and Whitehouse 1983). The most recent collection of Arab views of the Crusades is C. Hillenbrand (1999), who includes contemporary poetry such as the ode composed to celebrate Saladin's victory at Hattin. Contemporary Jewish reactions to the Crusader conquest of Jerusalem are collected in Peters (1985). For a broad and synthetic overview of the history of the Maghrib see Brett and Fentress (1996).

Recipes from medieval Baghdad are given by Arberry (1939). For the Cairo Geniza, see Goitein (1967–94 and 1973). A wonderful evocation of the life of a Geniza merchant in India is the novel by Ghosh (1993). Many details of daily life in medieval times are given by Mez (1937) and Ahsan (1979). Nasir-e Khusraw's travels have been translated by Thackston (1986). The medieval educational system has been studied by Makdisi (1981). The development of medieval Islamic cartography is discussed in Harley and Woodward (1992). Convenient introductions to Islamic science and engineering are Hill (1993) and Nasr (1976). For *convivencia* among Muslims, Jews, and Christians in medieval Spain, see Mann, Glick, and Dodds (1992).

Many contemporary literary texts, including our quotation of Ibn Hazm, were translated by Arberry (Aspects 1967). He is also responsible for the selection by al-Mutanabbi (Arberry, Poems 1967). A readable, but somewhat dated introduction to Arabic literatures is Nicholson (1907). He also translated selections from many of the most famous Arabic poets (1921). Our translation of al-Maarri is taken from this, as cited by his disciple Lichtenstadter (1976), whose anthology also contains many readable selections from Arabic literature. A more recent scholarly approach is taken in Young, Latham, and Serjeant (1990). A particularly engrossing introduction to the *Arabian Nights* is Irwin (1994). There are many introductions to Persian literature and poetry. Thackston (1994) is especially useful: although the texts are given in Persian, the pithy introductions are unparalleled.

PART III

The quotation with which the section opens is taken from Inalcik (1989). A readable history of the Mongols is Morgan (1986). There are many editions and translations of Marco Polo's travels; we have used Polo (1958). Our translation of Hafez is from Arberry (1947). Clavijo's travel account has been translated as *Embassy to Tamerlane* (Clavijo, 1928). Our quotation from Ibn Taymiyya is taken from Hourani (1991). Italian travelers to Cairo are quoted in Abu-Lughod (1971). Al-Maqrizi is quoted in Rodenbeck (1999). A convenient introduction to Mamluk art and history is given by Atil (1981). For the Alhambra and its poetry, see Grabar (1978). For the Ottomans, in addition to the general works mentioned above, see Atil (1987), the catalogue of a splendid exhibition on the art of Suleyman's time. The description of Suleyman is quoted from Fisher (1993). For the Maghrib, as well as for our quotation from Thomas Shaw, see Brett and Fentress (1996). For the Timurids and Safavids, see Jackson and Lockhart (1986); for Safavid Isfahan, see Welch (1973–4). Our quotation from Chardin is taken from Chardin (1999). For Central Asia, see McChesney (1996). Ibn Battuta's travels have been edited and translated (Ibn Battuta, 1958–94). Babur's autobiography has been edited and translated by Thackston (1996). The art and architecture of Fathepur Sikri were the focus of an exhibition, and our quotation from Badauni is taken from the accompanying book (Brand and Lowry 1985). Hamza Fansuri's poem is quoted from Renard (1996). Many of the buildings and objects discussed for this period are described and illustrated in Blair and Bloom (1994).

References

Abu-Lughod, J. L. 1971. *Cairo: 1001 Years of the City Victorious*. Princeton Studies on the Near East. Princeton: Princeton University Press.

Ahsan, M. M. 1979. *Social Life Under the Abbasids*. London and New York: Longman.

Arberry, A. J. 1939. A Baghdad Cookery-Book. *Islamic Culture* 13:21–47, 189–214.

———. 1947. *Fifty Poems of Hafiz: Texts and Translations Collected and Made, Introduced and Annotated*. Cambridge: Cambridge University Press.

———. 1967. *Aspects of Islamic Civilization as Depicted in the Original Texts*. Ann Arbor: University of Michigan Press.

———, ed. and trans. 1967. *Poems of al-Mutanabbi*. Cambridge: Cambridge University Press.

———. 1973. *The Koran Interpreted*. New York: Macmillan.

Atil, E. 1981. *Renaissance of Islam: Art of the Mamluks*. Washington, D.C.: Smithsonian Institution Press.

———. 1987. *The Age of Sultan Süleyman the Magnificent*. Washington: National Gallery of Art.

Blair, S., and J. Bloom. 1994. *The Art and Architecture of Islam: 1250–1800*. Pelican History of Art. London and New Haven: Yale University Press.

Bloom, J., and S. Blair. 1997. *Islamic Arts*. Art and Ideas. London: Phaidon.

Brand, M., and G. D. Lowry. 1985. *Akbar's India: Art from the Mughal City of Victory*. New York: Asia Society Galleries.

Brett, M., and E. Fentress. 1996. *The Berbers*. The Peoples of Africa. Oxford: Blackwell.

Brown, P. 1971. *The World of Late Antiquity AD 150–750*. History of European Civilization Library. New York: Harcourt Brace Jovanovich.

Chardin, S. J. 1999. Fruits, Ice and Coffee in 17th Century Persia. *Petit Propos Culinaires* 61 (May):19–27.

Clavijo, R. G. de 1928. *Clavijo: Embassy to Tamerlane 1403–1406*. Trans. G. Le Strange. The Broadway Travelers. New York: Harper & Brothers.

Daum, W., ed. 1988. *Yemen: 3000 Years of Art and Civilisation in Arabia Felix*. Innsbruck and Frankfurt/Main: Pinguin-Verlag and Umschau-Verlag.

The Encyclopaedia of Islam, New Edition. 1960. Eds. H. A. R. Gibb and others. Leiden: E. J. Brill.

Endress, G. 1988. *An Introduction to Islam*. Trans. C. Hillenbrand. Islamic Surveys. Edinburgh: Edinburgh University Press.

Ernst, C. W. 1997. *The Shambhala Guide to Sufism*. Boston and London: Shambhala.

Esposito, J. 1998. *Islam: The Straight Path*. 3rd ed. New York: Oxford University Press.

———, ed. 2000. *The Oxford History of Islam*. New York: Oxford University Press.

Ettinghausen, R., and O. Grabar. 1987. *The Art and Architecture of Islam: 650–1250*. Pelican History of Art. Harmondsworth: Penguin Books.

Fisher, A. 1993. The Life and Family of Süleymân I. In *Süleymân the Second and His Time*, ed. H. Inalcik and C. Kafadar, 1–19. Istanbul: Isis Press.

Ghosh, A. 1993. *In an Antique Land*. New York: Alfred A. Knopf.

Goitein, S. D. 1964. *Jews and Arabs: Their Contacts through the Ages*. New York: Schocken Books.

———. 1967–94. *A Mediterranean Society*. Berkeley and Los Angeles: University of California Press.

———. 1973. *Letters of Medieval Jewish Traders*. Princeton: Princeton University Press.

Grabar, O. 1978. *The Alhambra*. Cambridge, MA: Harvard University Press.

Graham, W. A. 1993. *Beyond the Written Word: Oral Aspects of Scripture in the History of Religion*. New York: Cambridge University Press.

Hamilton, R. 1988. *Walid and His Friends: An Umayyad Tragedy*. Oxford Studies in Islamic Art. Oxford: Oxford University Press.

Harley, J. B., and D. Woodward, eds. 1992. *Cartography in the Traditional Islamic and South Asian Societies*. The History of Cartography, vol. 2. Chicago and London: University of Chicago Press.

Hill, D. R. 1993. *Islamic Science and Engineering*. Islamic Surveys. Edinburgh: Edinburgh University Press.

Hillenbrand, C. 1999. *The Crusades: Islamic Perspectives*. Edinburgh: Edinburgh University Press.

Hillenbrand, R. 1999. *Islamic Art and Architecture*. London: Thames and Hudson.

Hodges, R., and D. Whitehouse. 1983. *Mohammed, Charlemagne and the Origins of Europe*. Ithaca, NY: Cornell University Press.

Hodgson, M. G. 1974. *The Venture of Islam*. Chicago: University of Chicago Press.

Hourani, A. 1991. *A History of the Arab Peoples*. Cambridge, Mass.: Harvard University Press.

Ibn Battuta. 1958–94. *The Travels of Ibn Battuta, A. D. 1325–1354*, 4 vols. Ed. and trans. H. A. R. Gibb and C. F. Beckingham. London: Hakluyt Society.

Ibn Khaldûn. 1967. *The Muqaddimah: An Introduction to History*. Trans. F. Rosenthal. New York: Bollingen Foundation.

———. 1969. *The Muqaddimah, an Introduction to History*. Ed. and abridged N. J. Dawood. Trans. F. Rosenthal. Bollingen Series. Princeton: Princeton University Press.

Inalcik, H. 1989. *The Ottoman Empire: The Classical Age 1300–1600*. Trans. N. Itzkowitz and C. Imber. New Rochelle, NY: Aristide Caratzas.

Irwin, R. 1994. *The Arabian Nights, A Companion*. London: Allen Lane/The Penguin Press.

———. 1997. *Islamic Art in Context: Art, Architecture, and the Literary World*. New York: Abrams.

Jackson, P., and L. Lockhart, eds. 1986. *The Timurid and Safavid Periods*. The Cambridge History of Iran. Cambridge: Cambridge University Press.

Lapidus, I. M. 1988. *A History of Islamic Societies*. Cambridge: Cambridge University Press.

Lichtenstadter, Ilse. 1976. *Introduction to Classical Arabic Literature with Selections from Representative Works in English Translation*. New York: Schocken Books.

Lings, M. 1983. *Muhammad: His Life Based on the Earliest Sources*. Rochester, VT: Inner Traditions International Ltd.

Maalouf, A. 1988. *Leo Africanus*. Trans. P. Sluglett. New York: New Amsterdam.

———. 1996. *Samarkand*. Trans. R. Harris. New York: Interlink Books.

Mahfouz, N. 1990. *Palace Walk*. W. M. Hutchins and O. E. Kenny. The Cairo Trilogy. New York: Anchor Doubleday.

————. 1991. *Palace of Desire*. Trans. W. M. Hutchins, L. M. Kenny, and O. E. Kenny. The Cairo Trilogy. New York: Anchor Doubleday.

————. 1992. *Sugar Street*. Trans. W. M. Hutchins and A. B. Samaan. The Cairo Trilogy. New York: Doubleday.

Makdisi, G. 1981. *The Rise of Colleges: Institutions of Learning in Islam and the West*. Edinburgh: Edinburgh University Press.

Mann, V. B., T. F. Glick, and J. D. Dodds. 1992. *Convivencia: Jews, Muslims, and Christians in Medieval Spain*. New York: George Braziller in association with the Jewish Museum.

McChesney, R. D. 1996. *Central Asia: Foundations of Change*. Leon B. Poullada Memorial Lecture Series. Princeton: Darwin Press.

Mernissi, F. 1995. *Dreams of Trespass: Tales of a Harem Girlhood*. Photographs by R. V. Ward. Reading, Mass.: Addison-Wesley.

Mez, A. 1937. *The Renaissance of Islam*. Trans. S. Khuda Bakhsh and D. S. Margoliouth. Patna: Jubilee Printing & Publishing House.

Morgan, D. O. 1986. *The Mongols*. Oxford: Oxford University Press.

Munif, A. 1987. *Cities of Salt*. Trans. P. Theroux. New York: Vintage.

————. 1991. *The Trench*. Trans. P. Theroux. New York: Pantheon.

————. 1993. *Variations on Night and Day*. Trans. P. Theroux. New York: Pantheon.

Nasr, S. H. 1976. *Islamic Science: An Illustrated Study*. World of Islam Festival Publishing Co. Ltd.

Nicholson, R. A. 1907; 2nd Ed. 1930. *Literary History of the Arabs*. Cambridge: Cambridge University Press.

————. 1921. *Studies in Islamic Poetry*. Cambridge: Cambridge University Press.

————. 1974. *Rumi: Poet and Mystic 1207–1273*. New York: Samuel Weiser.

Peters, F. E. 1985. *Jerusalem: The Holy City in the Eyes of Chroniclers, Visitors, Pilgrims, and Prophets from the Days of Abraham to the Beginnings of Modern Times*. Princeton: Princeton University Press.

Polo, M. 1958. *The Travels of Marco Polo*. Trans. and ed. R. Latham. London: Penguin.

Renard, J., ed. 1996. *Seven Doors to Islam: Spirituality and the Religious Life of Muslims*. Berkeley, Los Angeles, and London: University of California Press.

————, ed. 1998. *Windows on the House of Islam: Muslim Sources on Spirituality and Religious Life*. Berkeley: University of California Press.

Robinson, F., ed. 1996. *Cambridge Illustrated History of the Islamic World*. Cambridge: Cambridge University Press.

Rodenbeck, M. 1999. *Cairo: The City Victorious*. New York: Alfred A. Knopf.

Schimmel, A. 1975. *Mystical Dimensions of Islam*. Chapel Hill: University of North Carolina Press.

————. 1985. *And Muhammad Is His Messenger: The Veneration of the Prophet in Islamic Piety*. Chapel Hill: University of North Carolina Press.

Sells, M. A., ed. 1999. *Approaching the Qur'an: The Early Revelations*. Ashland, OR: White Cloud Press.

Strayer, J. R., ed. 1982–89. *Dictionary of the Middle Ages*. New York: Charles Scribner's Sons.

Thackston, W. M., Jr., trans. 1986. *Naser-e Khosraw's Book of Travels (Safarnama)*. Persian Heritage Series. New York: Bibliotheca Persica.

————. 1994. *A Millennium of Classical Persian Poetry: A Guide to the Reading & Understanding of Persian Poetry from the Tenth to the Twentieth Century*. Bethesda, MD: Iranbooks.

———, trans., ed. and annot. 1996. *The Baburnama: Memoirs of Babur, Prince and Emperor*. Washington, D.C.; New York and Oxford: Freer Gallery of Art, Arthur M. Sackler Gallery, Smithsonian Institution; Oxford University Press.

Trimingham, J. S. 1971. *The Sufi Orders in Islam*. Oxford: Oxford University Press.

von Grunebaum, G. E. 1951. *Muhammadan Festivals*. London and Dublin: Curzon.

Welch, A. 1973–74. *Shah 'Abbas and the Arts of Isfahan*. Cambridge, MA and New York: Fogg Art Museum and the Asia Society.

Yarshater, E., ed. 1983. *The Seleucid, Parthian and Sasanian Periods*. The Cambridge History of Iran. Cambridge: Cambridge University Press.

Young, M. J. L., J. D. Latham, and R. B. Serjeant. 1990. *Religion, Learning and Science in the 'Abbasid Period*. The Cambridge History of Arabic Literature. Cambridge: Cambridge University Press.

ART CREDITS
FOR ART OTHER THAN THAT IN THE COLOR INSERT

p. 9   Page from a manuscript of the Koran written in gold *(Baltimore, MD, Johns Hopkins University Library, Garrett Collection)*

p. 17 Detail of Muhammad and the Black Stone from a fourteenth-century manuscript of Rashid al-Din's universal history *(Edinburgh, Edinburgh University Library, Ar. Ms. 20)*

p. 77 Detail of a village scene from a thirteenth-century manuscript of al-Hariri's *Maqamat (Paris, Bibliothèque nationale, MS Arabe 5847, fol. 138/Bridgeman Art Library)*

p. 157 Painting showing the siege of Baghdad, detached from an unknown manuscript *(Berlin, Staatsbibliothek, Diez A. fol. 70, p.7)*

p. 233 Map by Piri Reis *(Washington, DC, Library of Congress, Collection of the Geography and Map Division)*

Index

Abbas I, 74, 202-7
Abbasid dynasty, 56, 74-75,
    171. *See also* Golden Age of
    Islam.
  Baghdad rule, 81-85
  Basasiri, revolt of, 91-92
  bloody consolidation of
    power, 74-75
  Buyids, power of, 81, 82, 89
  local dynasties, 86
  military efforts, 86
  palaces of, 85-86
  ruling style, 84-85
  Samarra, move to, 85-86
  Seljuqs, power of, 89-90
  Turkish sultanate, 89-92
Abd al-Malik, 66-68, 185
Abd al-Rahman, 74, 87
Abenhazam. *See* Ibn Hazm.
Abraham. *See* Ibrahim
Abu Bakr, 37, 49-50
Abu'l-Faraj al-Isfahani, 146-47
Abu Hanifa, 56
Abu'l-Abbas "the bloody," 74-75
Abu'l-Wafa, 126
Abu Muslim, 74
Abu Nuwas, 142-43
Abu Talib, 27, 30, 31
Acheh, sultans of, 228-29, 230
Acre, 171
adab, 145-48
Afghanistan, 167, 169, 214
Africa. *See also* specific coun-
    tries and regions
  Bornu, kingdom of, 197, 224
  eastern coast, 225-26
  Funj people, 224-25
  Maghrib, 160, 176-77,
    194-96. *See also* specific
    countries and regions

  Nubians, 224
  sailing route around, 176,
    193, 225
  Songhay empire, 223
  Sudan, 221-22, 224-26
  Swahili language, 225-26
  Takrur, kingdom of, 223
  Timbuktu, 223
  West Africa, 221, 222-24
Afshars, 208
Aga Khan, 53
Aghlabids, 86, 101, 104
Agra, 214
agriculture, 103-4
  foods and drinks, 106-9
  spread of crops, 106-7
  wine, 108
Ahmad ibn Hanbal, 133
Ahmad ibn Tulun, 86
Ahriman, 22
Ahura Mazda, 22
Akbar, 202, 214-18, 236
Alaric, 20
Alawis, 197, 199
Aleppo, 167, 172
Alexander the Great, 45, 50,
    79, 169
Alexandria, 103, 112
Alexios I Comnenos, 94
Alfonso VIII of Castile (Spain),
    177
Alfonso X, "the Wise," of
    Spain, 137
Algeria, 100, 140, 195, 198
Alhambra, 178-80
Ali ibn Abi Talib, 30, 49,
    51-52, 54, 199
Ali Qapu (Isfahan), 204
Ali Zayn al-Abidin, 52
Allah, 30

Allahvardi Khan, 204
Almohads, 101, 138, 139, 177
Almoravids, 101
American Muslims, 11
al-Amin, 83
Amu Darya River, 21
Anatolia, 90-91, 159, 182-83. *See also* Ottomans; Turks and Turkey
al-Andalus, 100
Andalusia, 100
Ankara, 167
Antioch, 21, 94
Apollonius of Perga, 125
apricot stew, 108-9
Aqqoyunlu, 169
Aqsa Mosque (Jerusalem), 97
Arabian peninsula, 23-24
Arabic language, 41-42, 66-67, 101-2, 225. *See also* literature
mathematics, in, 126-28
Arabs
  clan structure of society, 25
  culture, pre-Islamic, 25-26
  foreign powers among, 25-26
  geography, 23-24
  incense trade, 24
  naming of people, 27-28
  nomads and townspeople, 24-25
  poetry of, 25
  settlements and inhabitants, 24-25
  Spain, cultural influences on, 101-2
Arafat (hill), 26
Archimedes, 125
architecture, 223
  Akbar's projects, 214-16
  Alhambra, 178-80
  Bukhara as capital, 209
  Córdoba, 88-89

Damascus mosque, 69-71
Dome of the Rock, 67-68
Isfahan renewal, 203-6
mosque design, 69-71
Ottomans, 192
Taj Mahal, 215
arch of Khusraw, 22
Ardabil shrine, 202-3
Aristotle, 134, 139
Armenians, 206-7
Arnold, Matthew, 153
Arrivabene, Andrea, 42
arts. *See also* specific art forms
  Golden Age of Islam, 142-55
  Mughal arts, 217, 218-19
  visual imagery, 70-71
Arudi, Nizami, 151
Assassins, 53
Astrakhan, 194
astronomy, 125, 128, 139, 169-70
Atatürk, Kemal, 237
Attar, 60-61
Attila, 20
Avennasar. *See* al-Farabi
Avicenna. *See* Ibn Sina
Awrangzib, 219, 236
Axum of Ethiopia, 26
ayatollah, 53
Ayyubids, 99-100

Babur, 170, 212-14
Badawuni, Abd al-Qadir, 216
Badr, battle of, 32
Baghdad, 22, 103, 105, 107, 108, 115, 167, 172, 176, 188
  Abbasid rule and Golden Age, 80-84
  Basasiri, conquest by, 92
  "crown" of, 82
  Mongols and, 162
  Mustansiriyya in, 121-22

al-Baghdadi, Muhammad ibn al-Hasan al-Katib, 108-9
Bahai faith, 40
Bahira, 28
Baldwin of Boulogne, 95, 100
Banu Hashim, 27, 30
al-Baqir, Muhammad, 52
baraka, 61
Barlas tribe, 167
Barmakid family, 82-83
Basasiri, revolt of, 91-92
basmala, 35-36
Basra, 103, 112
baths, 113-14
Bayezid I, sultan, 167, 183
Bayezid II, 186
Baysunghur, 108
Bedouins, 24-25
Belisarius, 20
Bellini, Gentile, 192
Bengal, 212
Berbers, 100-101, 177
Bezels of Wisdom (Ibn Arabi), 187
Bilal, 37
al-Biruni, 130
Black Death, 105, 174-75
black Muslims, 37
blood feuds, 46
Bohoras, 53
Book of Healing (Ibn Sina), 135
Book of Itineraries and Kingdoms (Ibn Khurradadhbih), 78
Book of Muhammad's Ladder, 59
Book of Summary Concerning Calculation by Transposition and Reduction (al-Khwarizmi), 127
Borneo, 227, 228
Bornu, 197, 224
branches of Islam, 49-51. *See also* specific branches
  Kharijites, 51

branches of Islam, *cont.*
  schools of law,
    56-57
  Shiites, 51-54
  Sufism, 57-63
  Sunnis, 54-57
British East India Company, 219
Brunei, 227
Buddhism, 82, 210
Bukhara, 135, 208, 209
al-Bukhari, 55
Buraq, 59
Burgundians, 20
Bursa, 183
Busbecq, Ogier Ghislain de, 189, 190
Bushire, 203
al-Busiri, 226
Buyids, 81, 82, 89
al-Buzajani, 126
Byzantines, 19-21, 50, 84, 86, 91, 94, 183
  Arabia, influence in, 25, 26
  Crusades and, 94, 99-100
  Ottoman conquest of, 183-85
  Sasanians, fighting with, 21-23, 26

Cairo, 87, 103, 105, 107, 108, 138, 140-41, 171, 223
  Mamluk flourishing and decline, 171, 172-76
  medieval period, 115-17
  Ottoman conquest of, 176, 194
call to prayer, 36-37
Canon of Medicine (Ibn Sina), 135
Canton, 231
caravans and caravansaries, 112-13
Caucasus Mountains, 21
ceramics and pottery, 111, 154, 155

Chad, 224
Chaghatayids, 210-11
Chaldiran, battle of, 200
Chardin, Jean, 205-6
charity, 38, 172, 185, 202-3
Charlemagne, 83, 94
Charles V of Spain, 188
China, 162, 163-64, 168-69, 210-11, 230-31
Chishti, Salim, 215
Christianity, 35, 36, 37, 73
  Arabia, influence in, 25, 26
  Bahira's prophesy, 28
  Byzantine empire, 19-21, 22, 23, 94. *See also* Byzantines
  Crusades. *See* Crusades
  Mughals and, 217-18
  Muhammad and, 28, 29, 31
  prosperity under Islam, 79-80
  Spanish resurgence, 176-77
  toleration of, 39, 79-80
Clavijo, Ruy González de, 108, 168, 180
Clement V, Pope, 135
Clive, Robert, 219
cloak of Muhammad, 28-29
coffee, 107, 205
Coleridge, Samuel Taylor, 165
Columbus, Christopher, 161
Compendium of Chronicles (Rashid al-Din), 164-65
Constantine, 19
Constantinople, 19, 21, 100
  Ottoman conquest of, 183-85
cooking, 108-9

Córdoba, 87-89, 137-39, 177
corsairs, 195
Cosmic Tree of Existence (Ibn Arabi), 58-59
Council of Clermont, 93
Crimea, 194
Crusades, 111-12, 117
  First Crusade, 94-96
  Fourth Crusade and after, 99-100
  initiation of, 93
  Jerusalem, control of, 93-95
  Mamluk reconquest, 171
  military advantages, 96
  Muslim counterattack, 97-99
  Second Crusade, 97
  slaughters of, 95
Ctesiphon, 21, 22
Cyprus, 171, 192-93

Damascus, 97, 103, 111, 141, 167, 172, 173
  capital of Islam, 65-66, 67, 69-71
damask, 111
Dante Alighieri, 59
De Jebra et Almucabola (Gerard of Cremona, translator), 128
Delhi, 167, 211-12
Divine Comedy (Dante Alighieri), 59
divorce and remarriage, 46
Dome of the Rock (Jerusalem), 67-68, 97, 185
Doria, Andrea, 189

Écluse Charles de l', 190
Edessa, 94, 96
Edict of Milan, 19
Edict of Nantes, 206
Edirne, 183
education, 119-24
eggplant, 205-6

Egypt, 48, 87, 97, 107,
    140-41, 194
  Cairo, 115-17, 130,
    140-41. *See also*
    Cairo
  decline of, 174-76
Elizabeth I of England,
    202
engineers, 124
England, 197, 202, 219
Ethiopia, 26
Euclid, 125
Euphrates River, 21, 103

al-Farabi, Nasr Muham-
    mad, 134, 136, 153
Fatehpur Sikri, 214-15,
    216, 217
Fatima (daughter of
    Muhammad), 49,
    51-52
Fatimids, 53, 87, 91-92,
    97, 100, 116, 117
fatwas, 123
Feast of the Sacrifices,
    38-39
Ferdinand and Isabella
    of Spain, 177
Fez, 103, 110, 177-78,
    196
Fibonacci, Leonardo,
    113, 127
Firdawsi, Abu'l-Qasim,
    152-53, 201
Firuzabad, 81
FitzGerald, Edward,
    151-52
Five Pillars of Islam, 35-39
Fiver Shiites, 52
food, 102
France, 206, 207
  Chardin in Isfahan,
    205-6
  Charlemagne, 83, 84
  Francis I, 188
  Franks, 20, 83, 95, 96,
    238
  Huguenots, 205-6
  Morocco and, 197-98,
    199
  Paris, 105

frankincense and
    myrrh, 24
Franks. *See* France
Frescobaldi, Leonardo,
    174
Friday worship, 37, 109
Funj people, 224-25
al-Fustat, 115-16

Gabriel, the angel, 29,
    33, 59
Galen, 125, 132
Galland, Jean-Antoine,
    150
Gama, Vasco da, 161,
    176, 225
Genghis Khan, 160,
    162, 167, 194, 208-9,
    210, 212
Geniza documents,
    114-15
geography, 125, 128-30
Gerard of Cremona,
    128, 134, 135
Ghana, kingdom of, 223
Ghassanids, 26
ghazal, 142, 166-67
al-Ghazali, 61-62,
    119-20, 136, 138,
    139
Ghazan, 114
glassmaking, 111,
    154-55
Goa, 216
Golden Age of Islam
  Baghdad and, 80-84
  commerce and agri-
    culture in, 106-17
  ethnic spread and
    challenge, 80-81
  intellectual and artis-
    tic life, 80, 81, 84
  intellectual life. See
    intellectual life
  prosperity for many,
    79-80
  universal faith, trans-
    formation to, 80-93
Goths, 20
government, early em-
    pire, 66-67

Granada, 140, 177,
    178-80
Grand Book of Music
    (al-Farabi), 134
Great Feast, 38-39
Greaves, John, 170
Greeks, 124, 125, 128,
    129, 130-31, 132,
    134-35, 136, 139,
    183, 185, 186
Grozny, 11
Guangzhou, 231
Guide of the Perplexed
    (Maimonides), 137,
    138
Gujerat, 212, 215, 228
Gurkhanid Emphemeris,
    170

hadith, 45, 55, 119-23
Hadramawt, 24
Hafez, 160, 166-67
Hagia Sophia (Istan-
    bul), 21, 184, 185,
    192
hajj, 38-39
Hamadan, 103
al-Hamadani, Badi
    al-Zaman, 148
hammams, 113-14
Hamza Fansuri, 228-29
Hamza (uncle of
    Muhammad), 30
Hanbalis, 173
Hapsburgs, 188, 189,
    190, 193
Haram al-Sharif, 95
al-Hariri, 148-49
Harun al-Rashid, 83,
    94, 124, 143
Harvey, William, 132
Hasan "the Divorcer,"
    52
hashish, 90, 201
Hattin, battle of, 98
Haydar, Mirza Muham-
    mad, 213
Herat, 169
Hijaz, 24, 26
hijira, 31
Himyar, 24, 26

Hinduism, 212, 215, 217
Hira, 26
history, philosophy of, 141-42
Holland, 190, 230
Hospitalers, 95, 186
House of Knowledge, 84, 125, 128, 132
Hrotsvitha, 88
Hudaybiya, 32
Hugh of Lusignan, 112
Hulagu, 162
Humayun, 214
Hungary, 185, 188, 189, 190
Huns, 20, 23
Hurrem, 189
Husayn (the martyr), 52

Ibn Arabi, 58-59, 187, 229
Ibn al-Athir, 99
Ibn Battuta, 211-12, 222-23, 227, 230-31
Ibn al-Fuwati, 121-22
Ibn Hawqal, 115
Ibn al-Haytham, 131
Ibn Hazm, 137
Ibn Khaldun, 124, 139-42, 175
Ibn Khurradadhbih, 22, 78
Ibn al-Nafis, 131-32
Ibn Qutayba, 146
Ibn Rushd, 138-39
Ibn Sana al-Mulk, 98
Ibn Sina, 134-36, 138
Ibn Taymiyya, 57, 173
Ibn Zamrak, 179
Ibrahim, 18, 38-39
Id al-Fitr, 38
Ihya ulum al-din (al-Ghazali), 61-62
Iliad, 186
Ilkhanids, 162-63, 167, 182
imams, 51-54, 60
incense, 24
incest, 46

India, 22, 48, 53, 125-26, 147, 159-60, 167, 176, 202, 225, 226
Mughals, 181, 202, 208, 211-19. *See also* Mughals
See also specific cities
industries, 104, 111-12
inheritance, 46
Innocent IV, Pope, 100
intellectual life
al-Khwarizmi, work of, 125-30
education, types of, 119-24
Europe, influences on, 123, 148, 153
history, philosophy of, 141-42
literature. *See* literature
mathematics, 125-30
medicine, 131-32, 135
Mutazilite crisis, 132-33
philosophy, 124, 132-35, 136-40, 141, 142
science, 124-25, 128-32, 135, 141-42
social science, 141-42
theology, 119-20, 122-24, 132-33, 136-37
translation of foreign sources, 124-25
invoking God, 35-36
Iran, 73-74, 105, 163, 169, 176. *See also* specific cities
Mongols in, 163-67
Ottomans and, 188, 189, 193
rebels against Umayyads, 74
Safavids, 199-209. *See also* Safavids
Sasanian empire, 21-23
Shahnama, importance of, 152-53
Shiism in, 53

Iraq, 21, 73, 176, 188. *See also* specific cities
Baghdad in the Golden Age, 80-84. *See also* Baghdad
Isfahan, 103, 200, 203-6
Islam. *See also* specific subject headings
African continent, 221-26
branches of Islam. *See* branches of Islam
breadth of first empire, 50, 79
China, ports in, 230-31
cities of, 103-4, 105, 115-17. *See also* specific cities
consolidation within, 181-82. *See also* specific empires, i.e., Ottomans
first conquests, 50-51
Five Pillars of Islam, 35-39
Golden Age. *See* Golden Age of Islam
government and administration of empire, 66-67
intellectual life. *See* intellectual life
lunar year, 37-38
merchants, role of, 114-15
millennium of, 235-36
Mongols. *See* Mongols
mujaddid, 235-36
origin of terms, 33
petroleum, discovery of, 237
prayer, summoning to, 36-37
present from past, 235-39
rivers of, 103-4
southeast Asia, 226-30
trade and commerce, spread of, 106-17, 160-61, 171, 190, 193, 203

Islam, *cont.*
traditional boundaries, expansion beyond, 221-31
Umayyad dynasty, 65-74
universal faith, transformation to, 80-93
wine, consumption of, 108, 143, 152, 201
Ismail, Mawlay, 197-98
Ismail (Biblical), 39
Ismail (Safavid), 199
Ismail (son of Jafar), 52-53
Istanbul, 184. *See also* Constantinople
Ivanhoe (Scott), 99
Ivan "the Terrible" of Russia, 202
Iznik, 183

Jafar al-Sadiq, 52, 53
Jahangir, 215, 218
jahiliyya, 31
Janissary corps, 191
Java, 227-28, 229-30
Jaxartes River, 103
Jerusalem, 11, 23, 66, 103
Crusades and, 93-95, 98-99. *See also* Crusades
Dome of the Rock, 67-68, 97, 185
pilgrims to, 93-94
Jesus (Isa), 18, 44
jinn or genie, 29
Jochi Khan, 209
John of Seville, 134
Johor rulers, 229
Judaism, 26, 35, 36, 37
Crusades and, 95
Muhammad and, 31-32
prosperity under Islam, 79-80
toleration of, 39, 79-80
Junayd, Shaykh, 199
Justinian, 20-21, 184

Kaaba, 26, 28-29, 33
Kairouan, 104, 112
Kalila and Dimna (fables), 147-48
Kanem, 224
Karbala, 201
Kashgar, 210
Kashi, Ghiyath al-Din Jamshid, 169-70
Kazan, 194
Khadija (wife of Muhammad), 28, 29, 31
khalifa, 50
Khamriyyat (Abu Nuwas), 143
Kharijites, 51, 52, 54, 74, 87
Khayr al-Din (Barbarossa), 188, 195
Khayyam, Umar, 151-52
Khirbat al-Mafjar, 71
Khiva, 208
khojas, 210
Khomeini, Ruhollah, 53, 123
Khusraw Anushirwan, 147
Khusraw I, 21
khutba, 37
al-Khwarizmi, Muhammad ibn Musa, 125-30
al-Kindi, Abu Yusuf Yaqub, 133-34
Kitab al-Aghani (Abu'l-Faraj al-Isfahani), 146-47
Knights Templar, 95, 99
Koran
Arabic, primacy of, 41-42, 44
Biblical parallels, 44
early recording of, 40
Fatiha, 41
marriage and women, 45-47
Mutazilite crisis, 132-33
narrative elements in, 44-45
paradise and damnation, 43

prophets in, 44
revelations of the Prophet, 39-40
sign and say passages, 42-43, 44
slavery and slaves, 47-48
specific injunctions in, 45-48
structure of, 40-41
theological study, 119-20, 122-24, 132-33, 136-37
Throne Verse, 43
translations of, 42
Kritovulos of Imbros, 186
Kublai Khan, 163
Kurds, 96
Kushyar ibn Labban, 126

La Fontaine, 148
Lakhmids, 26
Leo, 84
Liber abaci (Fibonacci), 127
Libya, 100, 195
literature, 164-65. *See also* Arabic language
Abu'l-Faraj's anthology, 146-47
Babur's memoirs, 213-14
belles lettres, 145-48
fables, 147-48
instructional books, 147
Maqamat stories, 148-49
mirrors for princes, 147-48
Ottomans, 186
Persian language, 150-53
poetry. *See* poetry
popular literature, 149-50
Tarikh-i Alfi (history), 236
London, 105
Louis IX of France, 100

Louis XIV of France, 197, 206
Love's Awakening (Hafez), 166

al-Maarri, 145
madhhabs. See schools of law
madrasas, 121-23
Magellan, Ferdinand, 228
Maghrib, 100, 160, 176-77, 194-96. *See also* specific countries
Mahmud of Ghazna, 135
Maimonides, Moses, 137-38
Makhdum-i Azam, 210
Makran Desert, 21-22
Malacca, 227-28, 229-30
Malay sultanates, 229
Mali, 197, 223-24
Malik ibn Anas, 56
Malikshah, 121
Malta, 171
Mamluks, 48, 107, 170-72, 186, 191
Cairo and 172-76
decline of, 174-76
reconquest from Crusaders, 171
trade, 171
al-Mamun, 83-84, 124-25, 128, 129, 132, 133
Manchu rulers (China), 211
Mansa Musa, 223
al-Mansur, Ahmad, 81-83, 196-97, 223
Manzikert, battle of, 91, 159
Maqamat stories, 148-49
al-Maqqari, 88
al-Maqrizi, 28, 175-76
Marinids, 177
markets, 109-10
Marrakesh, 139, 196, 197
marriage, 45-47
Martel, Charles, 238
Marwan II, 74
Maryam al-Zamani, 215

Mashhad, 201, 202
Mataram rulers, 230
mathematics, 125-30
Mecca, 24, 109
Arafat, 26
Black Stone and Kaaba, 26, 28-29, 33
cults of, 26
Muhammad and, 28-29, 30-33
pilgrimage to, 38-39
Quraysh, rise of, 26
medicine, 131-32, 135
Medina, 24, 109
Muhammad and, 31-32, 33
Mehmed II, 192
Mehmed "the Conqueror," 183-86
Meknès, 196, 197
merchants, 114-15
Merv, 103, 112
metalworking, 111, 112, 155
Mevlevi, 62-63
Mishna Torah (Maimonides), 137
mohair, 111
Moluccas, 228
Mongke, 162
Mongols, 100, 105, 108, 114, 141
Ilkhanids, 162-63, 167
invasions of thirteenth century, 160-61, 176
Oirats, 210
origins of, 161-62
Pax Mongolica, 163, 175
Timur and Timurids, 108, 141, 167-70, 180, 183, 209, 217
Morocco, 100, 101, 177-78, 195-99, 223, 224. *See also* specific cities
Moscow, 167
Mosque of al-Azhar (Cairo), 116
Mosque of Ibn Tulun (Cairo), 116

Mosque of Shaykh Lutfallah (Isfahan), 204
Mosul, 111
Mount Hira, 29
Muawiya, 54, 65
muezzins, 36-37
mufti, 123
Mughals, 181, 202, 208, 211-19, 236
Akbar's reign, 214-18, 236
arts, 215, 218-19
Awrangzib, 219, 236
Babur, 170, 212-14
Delhi under, 211-12
European relations, 216-19
Humayun, 214
Jahangir, 215, 218-19
Plassey, battle of, 219
Shahjahan, 219
Taj Mahal, 215
Muhammad
ascension of, 58-59
Christians and Jews, attempts to convert, 31-32
cloak of, 28-29
conversions and spreading of message, 30-33
death of, 33, 49
early life of, 27-29
hijira of, 31
idols and icons, destruction of, 18, 33
Islam, origin of, 33
marriage and family, 28-29, 31
Mecca and Meccans, 28-29, 30-33
Medina and, 31-32, 33
miraj of, 58-59, 98
revelations of, 29-30, 33, 39-40. *See also* Koran, the
succession of and successors to, 33, 49-52. *See also* branches of Islam

mujaddid, 235-36
mujtahid, 53
Muqaddima (Ibn Khal-
dun), 140, 141-42
al-Muqtadir, 85
Musa al-Kazim, 53
music, 101-2, 134,
153-54, 216
Muslims. *See also* Islam;
specific headings
conquests of, 50-51
disunity among, 49,
51-52. *See also*
branches of Islam
guidance for living,
45-48
Koranic injunctions,
45-48. *See also*
Koran
other faiths, attitudes
toward, 39-40
muslin, 111
al-Mustansir, 121
Mustansiriyya (Bagh-
dad), 121-22
al-Mutanabbi, 143-45
al-Mutasim, 84-85, 133
al-Mutawakkil, 133
Mutazilite crisis, 132-33

al-Nablusi, Abd
al-Ghani, 236
Nadir Shah, 208
Najaf, 201
al-Nasir Muhammad (Al-
mohad caliph), 177
al-Nasir Muhammad
ibn Qalawun, 171
Nasir-e Khusraw, 116-17
Nasrids, 177, 178,
179-80
Ngazargamo, 224
Nicaea, 94, 183
Nicholson, R.A., 143
Nigeria, 224
Nile River, 103, 104
Nishapur, 103
Nizam al-Mulk, 121,
136
Nubians, 224
Nur-al-Din, 97

Oirats, 210
*On Calculation with Hindu
Numerals* (al-Khwariz-
mi), 125-27
organ, 216
Orontes River, 104
Ottomans, 181, 182,
200, 236-37
cultural life, 191-92
decline of, 193-94
devshirme system, 191
Europe, proximity to,
191-94
expansion under
Bayezid and Selim,
186-87
Lepanto, battle of, 193
Maghrib expanse,
194-95
Mehmed "the Con-
queror," 183-86
origins and rise of,
182-83
Preveza, battle of,
188-89
Russia and, 194
state control, 190-91
Suleyman "the Mag-
nificent," 158,
187-90, 192-93
trade, 190, 193
Vienna, siege of, 188,
192-93
Oxus River, 103

paper, use of, 82-83,
120, 154
Paris, 105
Pashazada, Kamal, 187
Pax Mongolica, 163, 175
People of the Book, 39
Persian Gulf, 22, 193,
203, 225
Persians, 21, 23, 50,
147-48. *See also*
Iran; Sasanians
poetry. *See* poetry
Safavids. *See* Safavids
Peter the Venerable, 42
petroleum, discovery
of, 237

Philip II of Spain, 202
philosophy, 124, 132-35,
136-40, 141-42
Mutazilite crisis, 132-33
pilgrimage to Mecca,
38-39
piracy, 195
Plassey, battle of, 219
poetry, 25, 71-72, 98,
115, 120, 122, 160,
179, 186, 201, 223
Golden Age, 142-47,
150-53
Hafez's ghazals, 166-67
Hamza's Malay
verses, 229
Persian poetry, 62-63,
150-53, 160,
166-67
Rumi, 62-63
Suleyman, of, 189
Swahili poetry, 226
wine and, 108, 143, 152
Poitiers, battle of, 238
Poland, 207
Polo, Marco, 161,
163-64, 226-27
Polonaise carpets, 207
polygamy, 45-47
Portugal, 216, 225, 228,
230, 231
Africa, around, 176,
193, 225
prayer, summoning to,
36-37
Prester John, 163
Preveza, battle of, 188-89
printing press, 192
Profession of Faith, 35
prostitution, 46
Ptolemy, 125, 128, 129,
131
punishments of Han-
balis, 57

Qadari order, 229
qadis, 123
Qalawun, sultan, 171
qanats, 104-5
Qaraqoyunlu, 169
qasida, 25, 142

Qazvin, 200
Qizilbash, 202
Quanzhou, 230-31
Qum, 202
Quraysh tribe, 26, 27,
  28-29, 31, 32

Rabia, 60-61
Ramadan, 29, 37-38, 39
Rashid al-Din, 164-65
rashidun, 65
Reconquista, 101
*Revivification of the Reli-
  gious Sciences*
  (al-Ghazali), 136
Rhodes, 171, 186
Richard the Lionheart, 99
Robert of Ketton, 42, 128
Romanos I, 91
Romans, 19-20, 50, 79
  sack of Rome (410), 20
*Rubá'iyyát of Umar
  Khayyam* (FitzGer-
  ald, translator),
  151-52
Rub al-Khali desert, 23-24
Rumi, Jalal al-Din,
  62-63, 160
Rushdie, Salman, 123
Russia, 194, 202
Rustamids, 87
Rustem Pasha, 191

Saad ibn Abi Waqqas,
  231
Saba, 24
sabil, 38
Safa al-Din, 199
Safavids, 199-200, 236
  Abbas I, reign of, 202-7
  Afghan invasions, 208
  Armenians of New
    Julfa, 206-7
  Isfahan as capital,
    200, 203-6
  Nadir Shah, 208
  origins of, 199
  Persian Gulf trade, 203
  silk trade, 207
  Tahmasp I, reign of,
    200-201

Tahmasp II, 208
Uzbeks contrasted to,
  208-9
Saffarids, 86
saffron, 111
Sahih (al-Bukhari), 55
al-Sahili, Abu Ishaq
  Ibrahim, 223
Saladin, 97-99, 117
Sale, George, 42
Samanids, 86, 135
Samarkand, 103,
  167-70, 208, 209
Samarra, 85-86, 108
Saracens, 93
Sasanians, 19, 21-23
  Arabia, influence in,
    25, 26
  Byzantines, fighting
    with, 21-23, 26
  destruction by Mus-
    lims, 50
schools of law, 55-56
  Hanafi school, 56
  Hanbali school, 56-57
  Maliki school, 56
  Shafii school, 56
Scott, Walter, 99
Seleucia, 22
Selim I, 186
Selim II, 190, 201
Seljuqs, 89-90, 121
Senegal, 101, 197, 222,
  223
Sevener Shiites, 52-53
Seville, 112, 177
al-Shafii, 45, 56
Shahjahan, 219
Shahnama (Firdawsi),
  152 53, 200-201
Shahr-i Sabz palace, 180
Shams al-Din Muham-
  mad Shirazi. See
  Hafez
sharia, 45-47
Sharia Muizz li-Din
  Allah (Cairo), 116
Shaw, Thomas, 198
Sheba, Queen of, 24
sherbet, 107
Shibanids, 209

Shiites, 51-54, 60, 74,
  75, 90, 116
  Fatimids. *See* Fatimids
Shiraz, 166, 167
Shirkuh, 97
shops, 110
Sicily, 101
Sigismund Wasa III of
  Poland, 207
Sijilmasa, 115
silk trade
  Persian (Safavid), 207
  Silk Route, 169, 208
Sinan, 191
Sirhindi, Shaykh
  Ahmad, 235-36
slavery and slaves, 47-48
social science, 141-42
Sohrab and Rustum
  (Arnold), 153
Songhay empire, 223
Spain, 100, 137-39,
  188-89, 193, 202
  Alhambra, 178-80
  Granada, fall of, 177
  Muslim influence on,
    101-2, 126
  New World discover-
    ies, 176
  resurgent Christianity
    in, 176-77
  Toledo translations,
    126, 128, 137-39
  Umayyad Muslims in,
    74, 87-89, 137
spice trade, 228
stereotypes, 11-13
Sudan, 115, 221-22,
  224-26
Sufism, 57-58, 108, 136,
  152, 187, 199, 228-29,
  235-36
  chains *(silsila)* or or-
    ders of, 62-63
  classical Sufism, 61-62
  fundamentalists' atti-
    tudes to, 58
  Mevlevi or Whirling
    Dervishes, 62-63
  miraj of the Prophet,
    58-59

Sufism, *cont.*
  saints or God's
    friends, 59-61
  spread of, 63
sugar, 106-7
Suleyman "the Magnifi-
  cent," 158, 187-90,
  191
sultanate, 90
Sultaniyya, 165-66
Sumatra, 226-27, 228
sunna, 45
Sunnis, 54-57, 101, 200
  Abbasid dynasty. *See*
    Abbasid dynasty
  schools of law, 56-57
Surat, 216
Survey of the Sciences
  (al-Farabi), 134
al-Suyuti, 235
Swahili language, 225-26
Syria, 21, 23, 73, 95-98,
  104, 111, 167. *See
  also* Damascus
  Umayyad capital,
    65-66, 67, 69-71

Tabriz, 163, 164, 165,
  200
taffeta, 111
Taghaza salt mines, 197
Tahmasp, 200-201
Tahmasp II, 208
Taj Mahal, 215
Takht-i Nadiri throne, 208
Takrur, kingdom of, 223
Tamerlane. *See* Timur
Tancred, 94-95
Taq-i Kisra arch, 22
Tarikh-i Alfi (history), 236
textiles, 110-11
al-Thaalibi, 142
Theophilos, 84
*Thousand and One
  Nights,* 149-50
Tigris River, 22, 81, 103
Timbuktu, 223
time measurement, 37-39

Timur and Timurids,
  108, 141, 167-70,
  180, 183, 209, 217
Tlemcen, 177
Toledo, 126, 177
Traditions. See Hadith
Transoxiana, 104, 105
Trench, battle of the, 32
Tripoli, 95
Troy, 186
True Cross, fragments
  of, 23
Tughril, 89-90, 91-92
tulips, 190
Tunisia, 100, 104, 195,
  198
  Tunis, 103, 112, 139,
    140, 177
Tuqay-Timurids, 209
Turks and Turkey,
  159-60, 169, 176, 181.
  See also Anatolia
  Atatürk, 237
  Mongol invasion. *See*
    Mongols
  Ottomans. *See* Otto-
    mans
  Seljuqs, power of, 89-91
  Uzbeks, 200, 201,
    202, 208-9, 214
Twelver Shiites, 53

Uhud, battle of, 32
ulema, 55
Uljaytu, 165-66, 169
Ulughbeg, 169-70
Umar ibn al-Khattab,
  30, 49
Umayyad dynasty, 65-74
  buildings and public
    works, 67-72
  new government of ad-
    minstration, 66-67
  Spanish branch,
    87-89
al-Uqlidisi, 126
Urban II, Pope, 93, 94
Urgench, 111

Uthman, 51, 65
Uzbeks, 200, 201, 202,
  208-9, 214

Vandals, 20
Venice and Venetians,
  99-100, 105, 161,
  163-64, 185, 188-89,
  191, 193, 226-27
Vienna, 188, 192-93
Virgin Mary, 18
Visigoths, 20

Wahhabi movement, 57
al-Walid, 67, 69
al-Walid II, 71-72
al-Waqidi, 18
al-Wasiti, Yahya, 149
water and irrigation,
  103-5
West Africa, 221, 222-24
wheat, 106
Whirling Dervishes, 62-63
William of Tyre, 88
wine, 108, 143, 152, 201
women
  Friday worship and, 37
  infant females, 30, 46
  Koranic injunctions
    regarding, 45-47
  veiling of, 47

Xanadu, 163, 165

Yathrib, 31. *See also*
  Medina
year, measurement of,
  37-38
Yemen, 24, 26

Zaganos Pasha, 183
Zahir al-Din Muham-
  mad. *See* Babur
Zangi, 96
Zaydis, 52
Zerafshan River, 169
Zoroastrianism, 22-23,
  73-74

About
the Authors

JONATHAN BLOOM and **SHEILA BLAIR**, the Norma Jean Calderwood Professors of Islamic and Asian Art at Boston College, are a husband-and-wife team of historians and award-winning authorities on Islamic culture. Co-authors of *Islamic Arts* and *The Art and Architecture of Islam: 1250-1800* as well as individual authors of many other books and articles on Islamic art and civilization, they have taught widely both in the United States and abroad. They live in New Hampshire with their two children.